BOOK OF RACING CAR
TRACK TESTS

BOOK OF RACING CAR TRACK TESTS

Willie Green

Edited by Mark Hughes

Patrick Stephens Limited

This edition first published in 1989

British Library Cataloguing in Publication Data

Green, Willie
'Classic and sportscar' book of racing car track tests.
1. Racing cars. Track tests
I. Title II. Hughes, Mark
629.28'24

ISBN 1-85260-123-X

Patrick Stephens Limited is part of the Thorsons Publishing Group, Wellingborough, Northamptonshire, NN8 2RQ, England.

Printed in Italy by G. Canale and Co SpA, Turin

10   9   8   7   6   5   4   3   2   1

CONTENTS

ACKNOWLEDGEMENTS

Our appreciation is due to all the owners of the cars featured in this book for allowing their cars to be track tested, and for providing the information required to update the older track tests.

In alphabetical order, these owners are Alfa Romeo SpA, Anthony Bamford, David Black, British Motor Heritage, Martin Colvill, the late John Foulston, Bill Friend, John Godfrey, John Harper, Mike Harrison, Peter Kaus, the late Hon Patrick Lindsay, Peter Mann, Nick Mason, Anthony Mayman, Bob Roberts, Ernst Schuster, Cedric Selzer, Bill Symons, Tom Wheatcroft, Mike Wheatley and Jost Wildbolz.

Many talented photographers have attended track test sessions, often having to work quickly and in bad weather. The man responsible for more than half of the photographs in this book, John Colley, must be singled out for special mention, especially in view of his cheerful willingness to rearrange his busy schedule when notice has been short. The other track test photographs have been taken by Mick Walsh (now *Classic and Sportscar*'s Editor), Paul Debois, Andrew Yeadon, Jeff Bloxham, Mike Valente and Mel Dew. Archive photographs have been provided by the Haymarket Publishing Motoring Archive, Geoff Goddard, LAT and Cyril Posthumus.

A great deal of effort behind the scenes has been put in over the years by Mike McCarthy, now Editor-in-Chief of *Classic and Sportscar*. His tenacious work at race meetings and over the telephone produced many of these track tests (including the Alfa Romeo 159), and he was the ghost-writer of most of the original texts.

In the editing process required to give this book continuity, some of the research of several historians, who contributed background stories to supplement Willie Green's driving impressions, has been incorporated in condensed form in these track tests. The work of Doug Nye, Cyril Posthumus, Peter Hull, Mike McCarthy, Mark Gillies and Mark Hughes is acknowledged.

INTRODUCTION

Several years have passed since the conversation which laid the foundations for this book. Our best ideas at *Classic and Sportscar* invariably come over a drink after work, and during one of these sessions someone suggested that Willie Green's track tests would make a fine book. The trouble was that there always seemed to be a couple of irresistible track tests on the horizon to prevent us doing today what could be left until tomorrow. This is still the case, but our alternative would be to wait until Willie finally hangs up his helmet forever, a day which could be years away.

Willie's relationship with the magazine goes back to 1981, when it was called *Old Motor*. He came down for lunch in London one day to discuss with myself (then a staffman on *Autosport*) and Simon Taylor (*Autosport*'s publisher) a feature about all the cars he had raced. We soon decided that *Old Motor* was the right home for such a story, but by the time the third bottle of wine was open the idea had evolved into something else. Why not try the occasional track test, so that readers could taste what it's really like to drive great historic racing cars?

Eight years and nearly 90 track tests later, he is still going strong, finding exciting new cars to drive,

pulling off the occasional coup. It is beyond doubt that Willie has now driven a wider variety *and* a greater number of racing cars than anyone else in Britain, and probably the world. There have been some amazing highlights, like the Alfa Romeo 159 and BRM V16. There have been oddballs, like the Turtle Drilling Special Indy roadster or wooden-chassis Formula 2 Protos. There have been mighty powerhouses, like

Willie Green in his workshop with a Maserati 250F which he has recently restored. Few British racing drivers, if any, have driven so many cars of such varied character.

the CanAm Lola T260 or Napier-Railton. There have been humble racers too, like the Cooper 500 or the Cognac Special. Think of your all-time great racing cars, and the chances are that Willie has track tested them.

A great debt, of course, is owed to all the owners who have agreed over the years to let Willie loose in their cherished possessions. Without their generosity, and willingness to stay in the pits biting their fingernails, none of this would have been possible. It says a great deal for Willie's reputation that so few people decline the magazine's requests for track tests, and the knowledge that Willie has never damaged a car, bodily or mechanically, during a test has sometimes swung the issue. Indeed, many people have valued his thoughts about how their cars might be improved, although Willie has been known to be embarrassed about setting quicker times after a few laps than an owner has managed in years...

When Darryl Reach of Patrick Stephens Ltd picked up the baton which we on the magazine held out to him, the idea for this book moved quickly to reality. Knowing that it would be impossible to include every car which Willie has ever track tested, we eventually settled on a total of 30, debating endlessly which cars should reach our final list. We apologise if you are sad that cars such as the Maserati 6C–34, Lotus 16, Lister-Jaguar and BRM P154 have been omitted, but the agonising over our eventual selection was considerable. There are a very few choice track tests — such as an example of one of the Mercedes-Benz or Auto Union pre-war 'Silver Arrows' — which have yet to happen, but we had to take the bull by the horns at some point.

Throughout this book, Willie has called upon his immense racing experience, spanning 25 years, in commenting about the cars he has track tested. Coming from a car-minded family — his father, Wilfred Green, drove for works Lea-Francis and Austin teams before the war, and played an important part in bringing Grand Prix racing to Donington — set him on the right road, and he always had an ambition to race. That moment came in 1963, when he made his debut in a Triumph Spitfire, finishing last!

He then campaigned a Turner-Climax in 1964, followed over the next two years by an ex-Team Elite Lotus Elite and a Ginetta G12. It was with the Ginetta that he began to make his name, winning 21 races out of 23 through 1967. For the next two years he shared Peter Sadler's Ford GT40 in a number of European endurance events and even raced his own road-going GT40 occasionally. A Chevron B5 and a B8 followed, but by the end of 1969

there was no money left to take his career further.

Willie's long and fruitful association with JCB began in 1971 with his first drive in Anthony Bamford's Maserati Birdcage. Apart from a brief spell in 1973 racing a Trojan Formula 5000 car for Hexagon of Highgate, almost all of Willie's exploits until the early 'eighties came at the wheel of JCB cars. There were two Maserati 250Fs (a *Piccolo* car and the offset 2525), Jaguar D-type, Ferrari Daytona (entered for Le Mans in 1973), Ferrari 512, Lister-Corvette, Ferrari Testa Rossa and, of course, the Ferrari Dino 246 pictured on the cover of this book. Willie established himself as the fastest and most spectacular driver in historic racing, and over 10 years he won four prestigious championships — the JCB in 1972 and 1975, and the Lloyds & Scottish in 1979 and 1980. No top flight historic event was complete without him on the grid, his presence invariably guaranteeing an exciting race.

Since JCB pulled out of historic racing at the end of 1981, Willie has enjoyed numerous guest outings in other cars, many of which have been subjects for track tests. He even did a three-year spell on the Truck Grand Prix circuit around Europe at the wheel of an ERF. These days he can devote more time to his motor business near Derby, but he is far from retired.

Throughout these track testing years, the highlight for Willie was one glorious week in the summer of

1985 when he drove an Alfa Romeo 159 and a BRM V16 within days of each other. While he found the 159 satisfying and the V16 quite mind-boggling, neither of these rates as the *most* exciting car he has experienced — that accolade belongs to Nick Mason's 1978 Ferrari 312T3 which he drove in 1988. He enjoyed that for the fact that its sophistication does not obscure its excess of power over grip (a character shared by all his favourite racing cars), making it a great challenge to drive quickly.

Although Britain is still the best country in the world in which to see historic cars being raced hard, fewer of the truly great machines are exercised regularly these days. In many cases their value is so high, and still on the increase, that owners understandably are reluctant to put them at risk. It is sad, but a fact. It is unlikely that any driver in the future will be able to create all the opportunities which Willie has enjoyed simply because access to the cars becomes more and more difficult. Embracing as it does most of the great classics of motor racing history, this book hopefully will stand as a lasting record of what they are like to drive, of their weaknesses as well as their qualities.

We hope you gain as much pleasure in reading it as Willie and I have in putting it together.

Mark Hughes

1924
BUGATTI
TYPE 35B

Any top ten list of Grand Prix greats has to include the Bugatti Type 35. Everybody recognizes it instantly, it has pedigree, and character, and performance, and a remarkable racing history. It is almost the ultimate racing cliché.

And deservedly so. For years it was – and still is, for all I know – the most successful racer ever made, with literally thousands of wins to its credit, including just about every major race in its heyday. It has led to more purple prose than any other car (remember 'tearing calico'?). It is regarded as highly collectable today, but has never really fallen out

Among the most famous of the Type 35B's many successes was that of 'Williams', the Francophile Englishman, in the first ever Monaco Grand Prix, in 1929. This is a rare picture of him on the startline for that race.

of grace, become merely second-hand. It was part of the reason for the formation of one of the first one-make car clubs, the Bugatti Owners Club which owns Prescott, the international hill climb venue in Gloucestershire. It is the front view of a Type 35, wheels akimbo, which adorns the BRDC badge. I think I've made my point.

It has also come in for criticism in recent years. Some of the engineer-

ing is looked on askance, and even mocked. It is said that, when it was current, it used to win races through sheer force of numbers and a rather dramatic lack of opposition. It has been called idiosyncratic (which is true), and all sorts of other things. All of which may be so, but the fact remains that it did all that was expected of it — it won races, and that's all that really counts in the final analysis.

It was, of course, the product of that arrogant, eccentric, flawed genius — Ettore Arco Isidoro Bugatti. Its predecessors were the straight-eight Type 30 tourer (and its single-seater derivative, sometimes

called the Type 29) and the abortive Type 32, the hideous and totally unsuccessful 'Tank'. That engine suffered two fairly major faults: there was only a three-bearing crankshaft, and lubrication was pathetic, being kind. After the débâcle suffered by the 'Tanks' in the 1923 Grand Prix de l'ACF at Tours, Ettore sat back for a radical re-think. The result was inspired — it was, of course, the famous Type 35.

All Type 35s were powered by variants of the Type 30's straight-eight engine but with a significant difference: five main bearings and a somewhat better lubrication system. The engine came in a variety of sizes,

from 1,100 cc through 1,500 cc and 2,000 cc to 2.3 litres, with and without blowers. There were two blocks of four cylinders mounted on a single crankcase, and topped by a single casting in which ran the camshaft, operating the three valves — two inlet, one exhaust — per cylinder. The Type 35B featured here is a 2.3 litre, with cylinder dimensions of 60 mm bore and 100 mm stroke. The engine is a monoblock in that cylinders and combustion chambers are cast in one, which makes machining of the valve seats something not to be undertaken lightly! Fortunately the valves are arranged in line, and operated via rockers. The eight plugs are in a row down the side of the engine. Lubrication is by a gear-type pump and from there the oil travels by a tortuous route to the bearings. If this was Ettore's 'improvement', I wonder what the earlier car must have been like?

On the 35B, the supercharger sits low down on the offside of the crankcase, driven by a train of gears and a shaft from the front of the engine. It sucks through an up-draught carb, compresses the mixture, passes it to a T-branch manifold which in turn divides it into two, one for each block of four cylinders. In all, the mixture has to work its way past six right angles between carb and valve, and this is where Ettore is most often criticized. It's easy to see why the Type 35's engine took to supercharging like a duck to water ... In this form, the 2.3 litre gives 140 bhp at 4500 rpm as recorded on a dynamometer: in case you're wondering, the Audi 200 Turbo (2,144 cc) gives 182 bhp, the Lotus Esprit Turbo (2,172 cc) 210 bhp, and the Citroën CX 25 GTi Turbo (2,473 cc) 168 bhp, at considerably higher revs, so the output of the Type 35 50 and more years on is no disgrace. Helping out, though, is an exhaust system that is visually as clean as the intake system is convoluted.

The whole thing, of course, looks like a highly polished, rectangular box with only the essentials protruding — it has to be one of the cleanest engines ever made, and always brings forth comments about Ettore's eye for design. They say it was made this way because the artisans at Molsheim could only make straight lines, but I suspect that is one story that needs no investigation. It should be dismissed out of hand!

Power is fed to the separate gearbox through a small diameter, multi-plate clutch that is pure Bugatti. It is operated via a toggle-switch arrangement, and centrifugal force comes into play at higher revs. It's light, with very little flywheel effect and low pedal pressures. The gearbox is a straightforward, non-synchromesh four-speed unit.

The chassis is another work of art. It tapers in height from less than an inch at the front to a maximum of nearly 7 in at its deepest, and is gracefully swept out around the cockpit. Cross-bracing consists of the engine, mounted rigidly to it at four points, the gearbox and a couple of cross-members.

Suspension is by beam axles at either end, but to call them simply 'beam axles' is a bit like saying that the Pope is a priest. That at the front can only be called a piece of sculpture, and gives the lie to the Molsheim workers' abilities! It is hollow, tapering cow-horn-like at each end to take the hubs, and the springs actually pass through forged slots in it — you just have to take one look at it, all highly polished and pure smooth curves, to believe that Ettore was, indeed, an artist and an engineer.

Steering is by worm and wheel, and the brakes are operated by cables with a unique chain and bevel gear mechanism to give side-to-side

compensation. Springs all round are leaves, semi-elliptic at the front, quarter elliptic at the rear. Those at the back, in fact, are mounted behind the axle, splaying forwards and outwards, thus giving a modicum of sideways location but also allowing them to be hidden in that shapely tail. Trailing arms give fore-and-aft location, and there is a torque arm fitted 'twixt diff and cross member.

Then, of course, there are those wheels. At a time when wires were *de rigueur*, Ettore designed himself as neat a set of cast alloys as you'll find today. The spokes are angled, in theory to act as vanes and thus pass air over the drums, but the aerodynamics of this theory are highly dubious. Still, they look lovely. Cast into them are the brake drums, which led to easy brake checks, lighter weight, yet quick wheel changes. Wonder why it took everyone else so long to latch on to some of these features?

The Type 35 first appeared on 3 August 1924, at Lyons for the

The 2,262 cc engine, which develops around 140 bhp, could be hewn from solid aluminium. The intake system is convoluted: below the T-branch manifold, which feeds mixture to each block of four cylinders, can be seen the supercharger's ribbed casing.

French Grand Prix, and it would be nice to record that it won first time out. It didn't, mainly due to some faulty tyres which let the cars down. From then on, though, they were seldom out of the winners' circle until the appearance of the Type 51, the twin-cam version of the Type 35 — but that's another story. However, it must be admitted that these were lean years on the racing scene: from 1925 the limit for engines was reduced to 1,500 cc and almost all other manufacturers dropped out of the scene. The only cars really to give the Bugs a run for their money were the gorgeous straight-eight 1½ litre Delages, one of which I have track tested. When they survived they knocked the Bugs into a cocked hat.

It is true that Bugattis usually won because they were the most numerous on the circuit, but that is not to decry them: you could say the same about sports car racing in recent years, with the Porsches dominating everywhere, yet still providing some superb scraps. Strangely enough, like Bugatti, Porsche also have a policy of selling competitive cars to customers, and it works — in 1984 and '85 at Le Mans a privateer was first past the chequered flag ...

There was both triumph and tragedy — and high farce — in the Type 35's career. There were wins in the Targa Florio five years on the trot, from 1925 to 1929, and the first Monaco Grand Prix by the Francophile Englishman 'Williams'. The farce came in 1926 at the French Grand Prix, when only three cars, all Bugattis, started, and only one finished in anything like running condition! Some of the greats of the day appeared behind the wheels of Type 35s: apart from the aforementioned 'Williams', Louis

Chiron, 'Phi-Phi' Etancelin, George Eyston, Malcolm Campbell, Madame Elisabeth Junek (a lady of formidable talent who nearly won the Targa!), Jules Goux, René Dreyfus and the great Tazio Nuvolari all starred in Type 35s.

The car I drove for my track test is one of the best-known Bugs around, Nick Mason's Type 35B. It says much for Nick's faith, and the reliability of the car, that when I arrived at an exceedingly cold and damp Silverstone to track test it Nick wasn't there, but John Dabbs had it started instantly and warming up after something like a five-month lay off!

The cockpit is nicely spacious one-up, which is understandable since the car was designed to be raced two-up, under which conditions I reckon it would be a mite cramped. In front of you is that big steering wheel with those exquisitely carved spokes, another lovely Bugatti touch. There's a smallish but readable tacho just above the steering column, and an equal-sized clock in front of the 'passenger', with smaller fuel tank and oil pressure gauges beneath it, the latter nearly off the clock because of the cold! There's no temperature gauge, just a Motometer on the radiator cap, but somehow I didn't reckon overheating would be a problem at freezing point temperatures! Also protruding through the engine-turned dashboard is the magneto with the advance and retard lever on its left. The pedals are arranged in the conventional manner and there's no problem heel-and-toeing, though there's not much room so it's more a case of side-to-side of foot. The gear-lever and handbrake poke out of the bodywork on the right.

The clutch, a little inaccessible down in the footwell, feels curiously light at first, as if there's no grip, but once you're on the move that centrifugal assistance comes into play and there's plenty of bite. Engaging first is a pig of an operation, but I was told just to chonk it in. You do so and there's a rather unprofessional graunch, but everybody does

it, so I was told.

The gear-lever gate is a mirror image of normal, in that first is towards you and down, second straight forward, third across and down (where fourth normally is) and top straight forward again (where third usually finds itself). As I'm lucky enough to drive a broad spectrum of cars, with all sorts of odd gate patterns, I didn't find the lever positions difficult: most newcomers, it seems, do. What I can say is that the change is a delight. It's a sliding pinion type, wherein the gears themselves slide on the shafts, not any dog-clutches or synchro cones, and the startling thing about it is that you can literally feel the gears feeding into each other: it's quite unlike any other 'box I've known. And the upward changes take place as quickly as you can move your hand – superb. Coming down requires double-declutching, of course, but with the light clutch and that superb change it's almost as quick as going up.

Then there's the engine. Even after all these years of hearing that proverbial 'tearing calico' sound, it *still* makes noises that tingle the spine. Words cannot really describe just how evocative and glorious it is, but once heard, never forgotten. Useful power comes in around the 2,000 rpm mark, and then just flows on up to the (self-imposed) 4,800 rpm red line — the roller-bearing crank is said to be safe up to 5,500 rpm and I can well believe it. The lasting impression of this astonishing unit is the torque — it almost makes the gear-lever redundant! I did notice, though, a flat spot at about 2,800 rpm on part throttle in third — but only because it occurred half-way through Becketts. I must say it ran faultlessly for more laps than I usually cover in a track test, and is obviously beautifully prepared. You don't know just how much confidence you gain when you know a car has been properly set up ...

Obviously the damp, cold conditions of the test weren't the best in which to explore the handling, but it

did mean that things happened at a somewhat lower speed! The fact is, though, that narrow tyres, a lot of torque and a damp surface don't add up to a whole lot of grip, which meant I was having great fun! It doesn't take long to see why the Type 35 became renowned for its handling — you really can throw it around and play with it to your heart's content.

The steering is proverbially light and accurate, if a bit low-geared compared to more modern cars, which means quite a lot of wheel twirling, which in turn gives the impression to on-lookers that you're sawing away frantically — in fact there's so much feel to the system, through the steering and the seat of your pants, that you're doing it all automatically without a great deal of thought. I suppose you could say it oversteers, but I prefer to say you can slide it controllably: it's not only more in keeping with the character of the car, it's actually more accurate. Wonderful! The brakes require quite a lot of pedal pressure but work well with no darting or pulling, even on the odd bump or two.

It seems that, after the gear–change, the impression left in most drivers' minds is the rock-hard ride. Even Silverstone doesn't feel all that smooth in a Type 35. It's an odd sensation to be belting along full-bore on the pit straight and hear the engine note sounding like a machine-gun, staccato burps, as the back wheels bite and slip, bite and slip, over the damp bumps!

I didn't find it uncomfortable: I reckon I could drive the car quite happily in a 24-hour race at somewhere like Silverstone or Le Mans. On the other hand, something like the Targa back in the 'twenties must have been brutally pummelling — drivers then must have been real heroes with the strength of cart-horses.

The Type 35 is a splendid example of a beautiful piece of vintage engineering. The Delage I've driven feels immeasurably more advanced, as indeed it was in almost all

Right *The steering is light and accurate, but its low gearing means quite a lot of wheel twirling. The magneto, with advance and retard lever to its left, protrudes through the centre of the dashboard.*

Below *A Motometer on the radiator cap, not a gauge in the cockpit, registers water temperature; overheating did not seem a possibility at a freezing Silverstone.*

respects, but by the same token was just that little bit more tricky to drive. The Bugatti is the sort of car that most people can drive quickly quite easily, and the real hot-shots, like Chiron and Nuvolari, could drive very, *very* quickly. Quick, rugged, reliable, with superb handling, it is the epitome of all a great racing car should be. My thanks to Nick and the folks at Ten Tenths for a chance to try an all-time great.

And it is at this point that I must point out that I started my racing career in a Bugatti. It was a Type 52, and I was about four years old, and I had this circuit that went down the drive at my parents' home, turned round in the road and came back up again!

1925
SUNBEAM TIGER V12

It could be argued that Brooklands actually put the cause of British motor racing back instead of advancing it. During the inter-war years we tended to build cars which were superb for our own adventure playground, but which were usually blown off by Bugattis, Alfas *et al* when it came to road circuits. Happily there was at least one exception to this rather vague generalization, and that was Sunbeam — or, to be more accurate, Louis Coatalen. This French mastermind had been with Sunbeam since 1909, and among his achievements were the twin overhead camshaft, four valves per cylinder 1914 Tourist Trophy and Grand Prix cars, of which more anon. In 1920 Sunbeam became Sunbeam-Talbot-Darracq, an Anglo-French group which began to suffer economic difficulties during the 'twenties. Coatalen often had to improvise using existing resources, and in 1926 he managed to persuade his bosses that he could cheaply build an all-round car capable of breaking the World Land Speed Record (which was then held by Malcolm Campbell in his 18.3 litre 'Bluebird' at 150.76 mph), as well as being successful in racing and hillclimbing.

Coatalen suggested a supercharged 4 litre V12 constructed from two 2 litre GP type cylinder blocks,

heads and valve gear, since this unit was rendered obsolete by the new 1½ litre Formula of 1926. Working away in Wolverhampton, he arranged these blocks in a 60° vee on a common crankcase, employing dry sump lubrication, a large Roots-type supercharger with a Solex carburettor, and Bosch twin magneto ignition. Bore and stroke of 67 mm × 94 mm gave a capacity of 3,976 cc, and the initial power output was 291 bhp at 5,000 rpm on pump petrol or 306 bhp at 5,500 rpm on a 60/40 petrol-benzole mixture.

The chassis was a stronger version of the 2 litre design, with the wheelbase stretched by 3½ in to 8 ft 10 in, but with the track of 4 ft 3 in front and 3 ft 11 in rear remaining. A multi-plate clutch transmitted power to a four-speed gearbox and torque tube final drive.

After a trial run in late 1925 at Brooklands, where Henry Segrave reached 145 mph in the new V12, Sunbeam went to Southport sands in March 1926 for an attempt on the World Land Speed Record. The supercharger proved very fragile, with five casings failing, but a sixth held together long enough for Segrave to take the record by a whisker, setting a new mark of 152.33 mph.

Through the rest of 1926 the V12 proved its versatility by dominating every road race, speed trial and hillclimb for which it was entered. Segrave retired while leading the Spanish GP at San Sebastian and the GP of Milan at Monza, but he won the international speed trial at Boulogne, and Albert Divo set a new record at the Gaïllon hillclimb (where the car was painted blue and named a 'Talbot'). A second car was built that winter, and both V12s were fitted with smaller twin superchargers.

There were fewer outings in 1927 as STD's financial difficulties deepened, but the sale of several other racing cars enabled the factory to retain the two V12s for Kaye Don to race at Brooklands. Naming his cars 'Tiger' and 'Tigress', Don raced with great success for the next three seasons, his achievements including 24 new world or class records, three race victories (including the 1928 Gold Star handicap) and three new lap records, the final 137.58 mph one standing for two years.

Most racing cars would be nearing pensionable age by this stage, five years after being built, but Tiger and Tigress are remarkable machines, having raced since 1926 to this day almost without a break, the Second

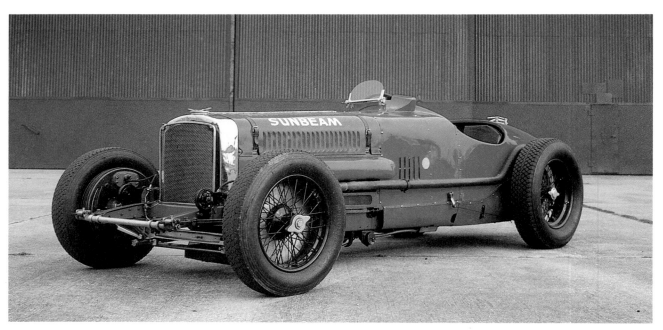

Above *Although it has been successful in races, speed trials and hillclimbs, the Sunbeam Tiger was built to take the World Land Speed Record; Sir Henry Segrave did just that with a speed of 152.33 mph at Southport sands in 1926.*

Left *The Tiger is faster than a Maserati 250F in a straight line: the power starts to come in at 2,500 rpm, by 3,000 rpm it is really beginning to go, and towards 5,000 rpm the output is something prodigious — probably well over 350 bhp.*

World War marking the transition from 'modern' to 'vintage' competition.

Malcolm Campbell bought the cars in 1932 and had Reid Railton devise modernizing modifications, the work being carried out by Thomson and Taylor at Brooklands. Each car was stripped down and given a new chassis frame with an underslung rear, a new axle, new Lockheed hydraulic front brakes, a new radiator, an overhauled engine and a Wilson four-speed preselector gearbox. In this form the

two cars were raced by Campbell until 1935, at which point John Cobb bought the Tiger. Successes diminished over the years, but there were occasional wins at Brooklands, including a Mountain Championship race win for Campbell in 1932 and another first for Cobb in 1936 in a match race against Oliver Bertram's Bentley.

Post-war, after two other changes of ownership, both cars passed to J. M. James, who gave the Tiger a busy couple of seasons in races, sprints and hillclimbs. Among his

successes were two second places in the very first VSCC Silverstone meeting in 1949. Sir Ralph Millais then acquired the Tiger in 1952 and gave it a complete rebuild. Although there were a few outings in succeeding years, it wasn't until 1965 — and the conversion of the V12's troublesome roller bottom end bearings for plain ones — that the car enjoyed real success in vintage races. That year George Burton won both the Itala and Seaman Trophies, and Ronnie Symondson completed a hat-trick by winning the Boulogne

The 4 litre V12 is constructed from two 2 litre Grand Prix type cylinder blocks, heads and valve gear. It has dry sump lubrication, a large Roots-type supercharger (just visible on the left) and Bosch twin magneto ignition.

The driver's seat is mounted low, alongside the propshaft and the exquisitely made linkage from gear lever to four-speed preselector 'box. Instruments include a boost gauge which registers 11 to 12 psi at full power.

Trophy too. Further victories for the Hon Patrick Lindsay and Neil Corner (who bought the car from Millais in 1969) brought the Tiger's final tally of VSCC successes by 1970 to three in the Itala Trophy, three in the Boulogne and two in the Seaman.

Thereafter, Corner sold the car to Bob Roberts, who allowed the Tiger to retire gently to the Midland Motor Museum at Bridgnorth. After breaking its gearbox at the 1982 Brooklands Reunion it had yet another rebuild, carried out by John

Merrifield and John Baker-Courtenay ('A matched pair,' says Bob), but subsequently showed its old mettle by leading the 1985 Itala Trophy until suffering a puncture. I was immensely pleased when soon afterwards Bob Roberts agreed to this track test, as I had been wanting to drive the Tiger for a long, long time. The trouble with Bob is that he is an arch-enthusiast, and he talks a blue streak, so much so that you're almost loath to interrupt and drive the car. However, I did manage to steer the conversation around to the Sunbeam by asking him how he acquired it, and back came the classic reply, 'Well, I think it was in a pub, over a pint or so ...'

The Tiger is still astonishingly original considering the intensity of its racing history, although some changes have been made in the interests of reliability or because parts simply have not been available. For example, Cosworth pistons are now fitted, and there are two instead of three valve springs to reduce valve inertia. There used to be a dog-

Anthony Powys-Lybbe in John Cobb's Sunbeam, which he shared with Charles Brackenbury to fourth place in the 1937 Brooklands 500 km race despite lubrication and tyre trouble.

clutch between engine and gearbox ('Talk about agricultural!' – Bob) but there's a rubber doughnut there now. Large scoops in the brake plates give vastly better cooling to the linings so that they last somewhat longer, while considerable time was spent getting the mixture spot-on. I must not cast aspersions on the intake system, via two long pipes from each of the superchargers, for the previous system was even odder. Sunbeam also tried this twin inlet system during the development period. Even more time, apparently, was spent on curing oil leaks ...

During the rebuild all sorts of oddities cropped up, like the fact that the gearbox weighs some 3 cwt ('It's about the size of three Mini engines' – Bob), and the fact that the crankshaft is almost identical to that

of a Ferrari Daytona, in spite of being originally designed for roller bearings.

Climbing into the Tiger, you notice a number of things. First, after a little adjustment to the seat, you're immediately comfortable. You sit low, alongside the propshaft, the other side of which is the complicated but exquisitely made linkage from gear-lever to 'box (there's a system to prevent moving the lever more than one notch at a time). Ahead of you is an enormous steering wheel which dominates everything, and in front of that a large aeroscreen. Naturally all the instrument dials are beautiful to look at, pure 'thirties, and — like a modern turbo tin box — there's a boost gauge which, at full power, registers something like 11 to 12 psi.

Starting is dead easy — a touch of retard and then, when it's caught, a touch of advance. Once on the move, the engine is so untemperamental that you could drive the Tiger on the road, which, I believe, is how they used to get it to

Brooklands — no transporters.

Ah, but this is not a car for shopping in. There is only one word, and a very over-worked word at that, to describe the engine, but it's absolutely accurate: sensational. The red line is at 5,500 rpm, but for this test I kept it to 5,000 rpm. No matter: the power starts to come in at 2,500 rpm, and when it does it's something else again. By 3,000 rpm it's really starting to go, and towards 5,000 rpm the output is something prodigious — well over 350 bhp, I reckon. From his experience with the Tiger, Neil Corner reckons that it's faster than a Maserati 250F in a straight line, and I'm prepared to believe him. This must be the most gutsy, most torquey, and simply powerful pre-war engine I've ever sat behind, and I'm not forgetting the Alfa Romeo P3. With big superchargers you can sometimes get surge in a corner, but the Tiger's throttle response is unimpeachable in this respect. There is just instant, solid, *vast* power on tap. Interestingly, Bob noted his times in

The Tiger's VSCC successes include three wins in the Itala Trophy, three in the Boulogne and two in the Seaman. This is Bob Roberts leading the 1985 Itala after the car's most recent mechanical rebuild.

the VSCC's 1985 Colerne Speed Trials shortly after I drove the car. The standing kilometre took 23.47 sec with a terminal speed of 140 mph (an outright course record), while the standing $\frac{1}{4}$ mile took just 13.38 sec (compare this figure with the 13.0 sec obtained by *Autocar* for a Lamborghini Countach 5000S quattrovalvole, the fastest road car ever tested by the magazine). Innes Ireland also took some fifth wheel acceleration times (in thick fog!) when he tested the Tiger in the 25 December 1969 issue of *Autocar*. Then owned by Corner, it achieved 0–60 mph in 6.4 sec, 0–100 mph in 14.5 sec and 0–120 mph in 23.6 sec.

What is just as surprising is the quietness of the Tiger's engine. I don't mean from the exhausts,

which bellow beautifully and deeply and very basso profundo behind you, overlaid with that hair-raising scream from the blowers as they come on song. I mean mechanically: there are no rattles or clanks or squeaks. You know it has been put together like a Swiss watch.

And you might expect, with all that power and a car weighing $27\frac{1}{2}$ cwt without driver ready to race, that there might be handling problems. Not a bit of it. It feels a much smaller, lighter car than it is. You can throw it into a corner, then power through in one great, glorious power slide, just like in days of old. There's no limited slip differential, but the rigidity at the front means that the car doesn't heel over in corners and lift the inside rear wheel — but you can still spin the wheel on full throttle. This doesn't affect the handling, and the Tiger can only be described as totally predictable.

The steering, too, is surprisingly light considering the weight of the car, near perfect in gearing and lack of free play which, with all the power available, means you can steer it beautifully on the throttle. Matching the rest of the mechanicals, the brakes are superb, pulling you up most reassuringly. All in all, the Sunbeam has to be one of the greatest racers I've ever driven, and that's really saying something. And I haven't even mentioned those perfectly proportioned looks, have I?

As it happened, soon after this track test I had a run in one of the Tiger's most distinguished predecessors, a 1914 TT Sunbeam owned by Neil Corner. I haven't the space to cover it in depth, but I think that some words are called for as it

has a place in the Tiger's bloodline, and is significant in its own right.

The most remarkable thing about this older Sunbeam is its engine, with a specification which would sound good in a road car today: twin overhead camshafts, four valves for each of its four cylinders, and hemispherical heads. This 3,255 cc unit (together with a 4,441 cc engine used in Sunbeam's GP cars) was Coatalen's work, although the great engineer was guilty of the most blatant plagiarism from Peugeot, who pioneered the twin overhead camshaft layout. Coatalen secretly bought one of the racing Peugeots — which had shown their effec-

tiveness by winning the 1912 and 1913 French GPs — and dismantled it in his Wolverhampton workshops, producing near copies of its engine to power his TT and GP cars.

Coatalen's TT was every bit as successful as he hoped, performing faultlessly as Kenelm Lee Guinness led the 1914 Tourist Trophy on the Isle of Man from start to finish, averaging 56.44 mph in the two-day 16-lap race. Whether this is the car now owned by Corner is hard to say, for the three TT Sunbeams which survive cannot be positively identified.

Neil allowed me a few laps at Silverstone, and my main impres-

Right *Paired André Hartford dampers and conventional semi-elliptic springs provide the front suspension; the quality of engineering is superb.*

Below Left *One of the Tiger's most distinguished predecessors is this 1914 TT Sunbeam owned by Neil Corner. It has twin overhead camshafts and four valves per cylinder, and handles beautifully, like an early Maserati 250F.*

sion was of the engine's remarkable liveliness for its era. Its output of 90 bhp at 3,000 rpm was amazing for the time, and at peak revs of 3,200 rpm it will bowl along at 96 mph. Not that everything comes at the top end: the engine's long stroke (156 mm against an 81 mm bore) means that it has loads of torque low down, giving a good steady push, with surprising smoothness, at all revs. And all the time you are accompanied by a lovely, jolly burble from the exhaust.

The rest of the TT Sunbeam's design was conventional: it's suspended on leaf springs all round, there are live axles fore and aft, and braking is by drums at the rear wheels and a lever-operated transmission brake. Nevertheless, it all comes together remarkably pleasantly. The steering is decently weighted and direct once you're moving, and the big wheel gives plenty of leverage if you need it.

The handling is sensational, and best described as like an early Maserati 250F. Beaded-edge tyres don't give much grip, and there isn't enough power to hang the tail out under full throttle, but I could still chuck it around to my heart's content. You drive in broad sweeps and slides which require just slight steering corrections to keep the car on course — I'm told that it's even more like a 250F in the wet, when power matches grip more evenly.

Braking is untemperamental, but you have to remember that only the skinny back wheels are stopping you. It's best to use the foot brake and lever together on the track, but don't try outbraking something equipped with discs! Possibly the least pleasant aspect of the car is its transmission: changes with the big lever outside the cockpit tend to be ponderous, and there's an enormous gap between third and fourth. It's also incredibly noisy in the indirect gears, sounding like the proverbial bag of heavy nails being rattled furiously!

I can see why Neil is so fond of the Sunbeam. Like all good racing cars — or road cars, for that matter — it responds well to the helm, and is a beautifully balanced design. It's a lot quicker than you would expect from a 75-year-old, and behaves impeccably on the move. You have to be careful about the brakes, and the gearbox isn't its best feature, but I wish now that I'd driven it on the road, just as Neil and his son, Nigel, do around their home in the Yorkshire Dales. Modern saloon car drivers would get the shock of their lives. Not only would this apparently ancient vehicle give them a run for their money in a straight line, but also it would leave them cross-eyed and cross-handed — or just plain cross — in corners.

Interesting, isn't it, that these two great Sunbeams are so versatile, and still going strong after all these years? The Tiger is one of motor racing's great all-rounders, and the 1914 TT is equally at home on road and track. With this pair, you wouldn't need anything else ...

1930
BLOWER BENTLEY

Blower Bentley. Was there ever a more famous name in British motor racing history? You immediately conjure up a vision of a hugely majestic dark green machine, thunder personified, pounding down the dusty, tree-lined Mulsanne Straight at Le Mans, or around the rough, lumpy, precipitous banking at Brooklands, driven by a small, dapper man, a spotted scarf flying out behind him.

The Blower Bentley is probably the most instantly recognizable of the breed, the epitome of the vintage sports car. Even those with only a hazy knowledge of pre-war cars can tell one at 50 paces, if for no other reason than that it has to be one of the most modelled cars ever. Remember that huge Airfix kit? It is also the most glamorous of a truly glamorous range, yet its reputation comes more from image than results. In pre-merger terms it was not one of the company's successes. It did *not* win Le Mans, yet those with little interest in pre-war racing always assume it did. But that is to belittle it: it *is* a truly magnificent machine, and it is as much through bad luck as anything else that it wasn't more successful. When it was on the full song, literally nothing could touch it.

It was, also, obsolete from the moment it hit the road or track. As Bunty Scott-Moncrieff once put it, 'It is a great advance on the big engined racing cars, Panhard and Mors for example, with which men wrestled along the dusty roads of pre-1914 Europe — but it is definitely a car of this character, not the character of the 1750 Alfas, Bugattis and Delages that were its contemporaries and handled like polo ponies.' It was, if you like, the last of the Leviathans, and like the last of many breeds, perhaps the finest.

And the subject of this test is one of a unique foursome, the *crème de la crème*, a legend within a legend, for it is one of the Birkin/Paget Blower Bentleys.

The name of Bentley had burst into prominence in 1924 when a 3 litre won Le Mans, the first of five Bentley wins. Success evaded the company in 1925 and 1926, and by the latter year it was obvious that more power was needed. There was a two-fold choice: turn the new 6½ litre into a racer, or enlarge the 3 litre. Owing to lack of time, the latter course was chosen. The chassis, transmission, brakes and some other items were retained from the 3 litre, while the bottom end of the new engine was basically 3 litre but with four of the six cylinders from the 6½ litre grafted on top.

With a bore of 100 mm, and a stroke of 140 mm, the capacity was 4,398 cc. The cylinder head was non-detachable, and there was a single overhead camshaft operating four valves per cylinder. The power output varied from about 105 bhp for saloons to 130 bhp or more for the works racers. The second great Bentley model had been born: the 4½ litre.

The prototype was entered for Le Mans in 1927, along with two 3 litres. It raised the lap record while leading the race, but was involved in the famous 'White House crash' which involved all three of the Bentleys — but one of the 3 litres survived and went on to win. A couple of months later the same car scored a 4½ litre's first victory by taking the 24-hour GP de Paris at Montlhéry.

By 1928 the 4½ litre was well on its way to fame, driven by 'the Bentley Boys', and that year a 4½ litre was sold to a gentleman who was to become legendary, and synonymous with Bentleys — Sir Henry Ralph Stanley Birkin, usually known as 'Tim'. His racing career started in 1921 and continued sporadically until he bought the 4½ in 1928 and went racing seriously. His father was Sir Thomas Stanley Birkin, who headed a successful lace business in

Nottingham, so 'Tim' was 'not short of a bob or two'. He was also a crack shot and keen sailor. He was the very epitome of the English gentleman, and was every schoolboy's hero back in the early 1930s, helped by the publication of his book *Full Throttle*. By the end of 1928 he was most definitely one of 'The Bentley Boys', his record that year including a fifth overall at Le Mans, partnered by Jean Chassagne, an eighth in the German GP at the Nürburgring, a fifth in the Ulster TT, and a fifth again in the Boillot Cup at Boulogne.

By the end of that year too, Birkin and W.O. Bentley were agreed upon one thing: more power was going to be needed if Bentleys were to continue winning. And there the agreement stopped. W.O. believed firmly that the best course was to fettle the Speed Six: Birkin reckoned that a supercharged 4½ litre was the way to go. W.O. was subsequently proved right, but both courses were eventually adopted, Birkin in effect taking over the supercharged 4½ litre and W.O. taking over the six-cylinder model.

Since W.O. was so set against the blower, Birkin hired one Charles Amherst Villiers to adapted the 4½ litre. Amherst Villiers is a man of extraordinary talent. Quite apart from his work on superchargers, he

is a professional portrait painter — he painted the official portrait of Ian Fleming which appeared on the dust jacket of the *James Bond* books, and another, with papal blessing, of Pope John Paul II — and an expert on space travel, becoming President of the American Rocket Society in 1948 and even designing a rocket to reach Mars. He had made his reputation working with Raymond Mays, first on his Brescia Bugatti and later the famous Vauxhall Villiers.

'Tim Birkin had seen the results we'd obtained with the Vauxhall,' explained Amherst Villiers in a *Classic and Sportscar* interview of 1983, 'and he came and asked me to design a blower for the 4½ litre. He told me that "they" wouldn't like it very much, but that it didn't matter, that it had all been arranged. I had an appointment with W.O. and he showed me the car, saying, "You can't put the blower inside the engine compartment — it might make it look untidy." He was, it must be said, straight and to the point, because he told me he wasn't going to pay me because the publicity from having my name on the blower would be enough.

'So far we were in agreement, but then I said I must have the right to alter the engine in any way I pleased. W.O. said I may have to lower the

compression ratio a bit, but that should be all. I asked to have a look at the blueprints and I took one look at them and could see that he had a very spidery crankshaft with no balance weights. I told him we'd have to have balance weights and he replied that they were the last thing he wanted. However, we eventually signed an agreement, and I only insisted on one other thing — that my name appear on the blower and in all publicity pamplets. W.O. never really liked the idea of an outside engineer coming in, of course, but it was more or less thrust down his throat and he had to accept it because of financial pressure.

'I did, in fact, redesign the engine with balance weights and a dry sump lubrication system. I licensed David Brown to make the rotors on the Maag principle [Maag was a firm which made gear teeth grinders with an involute form which was ideal for the rotors as well since it cut down any backlash], and we made the first three blowers ourselves.

'But Tim Birkin had taken on a fellow called Clive Gallop. He was a very tiresome man because he was one of those people who knew everything and wouldn't listen to anyone else. To me, you're learning all the time, and you have to keep a very open mind. Anyway, Gallop became the "expert", and Tim

'Tim' Birkin in a Blower Bentley at Phoenix Park in 1928 for the Irish Grand Prix, in which he finished third.

swallowed all his guff, but I'd had enough and after delivering those three blowers had no more to do with the Blower Bentley. The dry sump system went out of the window, of course, and instead of the cars being designed and built properly from the beginning it all went off half-cocked. It's amazing to me how much the cars did achieve in fact.'

The first blower was fitted in 1929 to Bernard Rubin's personal $4\frac{1}{2}$ litre, registered YU3250, a standard 10 ft 10 in 1928 Le Mans type raced by Rubin and Benjafield in the 1928 Six Hour race. This, originally with the chassis number HF3187 which was later changed to a 'Birkin' number, HB340/R, would eventually become known as the No 3 car.

At about the same time, Birkin took delivery of two more chassis, HB3402 and HB3404 (to be registered UU5871 and UU5872 respectively), again both standard 10 ft 10 in chassis.

The first of these, UU5871, was to

become very famous indeed as the 'single-seater'. Among its memorable achievements in 1928 was a third in the Irish GP at Phoenix Park, a handicap event, where Birkin had a monumental dice with 'Scrap' Thistlethwayte's blown Mercedes, and an eleventh on handicap (but second on speed) at the Ards TT — W.O. himself acted as riding mechanic. During the 1928–29 winter it was kitted out with the single-seater body, designed by Reid Railton, in which guise it is most famous — at one time it held the Brooklands lap record at 137.96 mph for two years, being eventually overtaken by John Cobb in the mighty Napier Railton. This car is very well known in VSCC circles, and used to be driven with considerable verve by the late 'Rusty' Russ-Turner.

The second car, registered UU5872, wasn't finished in time for the 1929 Le Mans race, so it was debuted in the Irish GP driven by Rubin, who was plagued with a misfire, eventually finishing eighth

— behind three unblown $4\frac{1}{2}$s and a Speed Six. Shortly afterwards Rubin took it to the Ards for the TT, where he managed to roll it! By May 1930 it had been rebuilt on to a short (9 ft $9\frac{1}{2}$ in) chassis and ran in the Double Twelve Hour race at Brooklands where it retired with a cracked chassis frame.

At Le Mans in 1930 No 2 was driven by Birkin and Chassagne, and Tim pulled off one of his heroic drives by taking the mighty Mercedes-Benz of Caracciola on the Mulsanne Straight at over 120 mph — with the nearside wheels on the grass verge! The Blower Bentleys suffered severely from thrown treads in this race, but it was an engine blow-up that eventually brought about the retirement of this car at noon on Sunday. In the Irish GP the Birkin/Caracciola duel was renewed, victory going this time to the German, and in the TT which followed it Birkin clobbered a telegraph pole and a brick wall, forcing retirement. At the BRDC race at Brooklands in October 1930

Left *The car on test, No 4 in the series of Blower Bentleys, was built in 1930 for the Hon Dorothy Paget. Its greatest moment came at Pau in the French Grand Prix of 1930, when 'Tim' Birkin finished second against intense Bugatti opposition.*

Right *The driving position is fine, although the big steering wheel is so close to the cockpit lip that you skin your knuckles. You cannot drive with your arms outstretched, but this is no bad thing considering the muscle needed.*

For such a big, heavy car, the handling is excellent. You do not really talk of understeer and oversteer with a car like this; you skid it round corners.

Ettore Bugatti referred to the Bentleys as trucks, but a better comparison would be with one of those glorious steam locomotives of the inter-war years; massive, but immensely fast and beautifully built.

UU5872 was driven to a fighting second place — with a fastest lap at 122.97 mph! — by Dr J.D. Benjafield and Eddie Hall, behind Sammy Davis and the Earl of March in an Austin Seven. Of course, it was a handicap race! That was the last appearance of the car in Birkin/Paget colours, and subsequent owners include M.N. Mavrogordato and Stanley Sears.

And so to the car I tested, No 4 in the series. It was built in 1930 on the short chassis, at the same time as No 2 was converted, for the Hon Dorothy Paget, and indeed bears her crest on a small badge above the winged 'B' on the radiator.

The Hon Dorothy came into the picture in late 1929. She was, according to Bunty Scott-Moncrieff, 'about the richest woman in Europe, one of the fattest, and certainly the most difficult to deal with'. He also 'doubts if she ever actually drove the car, as there is just not enough room between the seat and the steering wheel for anyone of her considerable proportions'!

Birkin appears to have been something of a charmer as far as the ladies were concerned, and this certainly must have been the case with the Hon Dorothy. By the end of 1929 Birkin was literally broke, so to continue racing he persuaded this 'most difficult' lady to sponsor him for 1930. He had personally financed the building of the first three cars, so the cash injection from the Hon Dorothy was most timely.

One of the first actions of the joint venture was to rebuild No 2 on to the shorter chassis, and the second was to commission the building of No 4, chassis number HR3976, registered UR6571.

Its debut race was, as ever, at Brooklands, in the Double Twelve Hour race in May. Driven by the Baron d'Erlanger and Dr Benjafield, it caught fire on the first day (no night racing was allowed at Brooklands, so any 24-hour race had to be split into two 12-hour stints during daylight) and broke a back axle on the second, Benjafield pushing it a mile to the pits for a new

one to be fitted, but to no avail.

At Le Mans the engine had to be hurriedly modified in practice so that the car could run on benzole instead of the witches' brew supplied by the organizers. It ran quite well initially, but behind the flying Caracciola Mercedes and the two works Speed Sixes. Around midnight the second driver, Giulio Ramponi, fell ill, and 'Benjy' was forced to continue single-handed, which he did for 10 hours. Like its sister, this hefty — 40 cwt, remember — car suffered continuous tyre problems, and almost all the pictures you see of it in the race show buckled wings where treads went flying. It was, though, a broken piston which forced its eventual retirement just after midday on Sunday.

This was followed by the Irish GP and the TT, in neither of which did the car distinguish itself. But, in September 1930, No 4 covered itself in glory and put the Blower Bentley firmly into the annals of motor racing history. It finished second in the French GP.

Now, to be honest, GP racing was at the time in the doldrums. Grids tended to be sparse, thanks to the depression, and were invariably filled with Bugattis — in fact the entry list for the French GP consisted of 25 cars, of which 18 were Bugattis. The circuit was a new one at Pau: roughly triangular in shape, it was 15 km (9½ miles) in length. Much to the amusement of the French, Birkin entered No 4, stripped of lights and wings (and probably anything else he could safely ditch). The equivalent today would be the entry of the Group C Jaguars in a current GP. Not a hope, you would have thought.

It was an eventful race, attrition being the operative word. As expected, the Bugattis disappeared off into middle distance from the start, while Birkin found that the big Bentley was as fast, if not faster, on the straights, but lost out on the wiggly bits where the car was a real handful. The first lap, though, saw at least two of the favourites,

Wimille and Lehoux (both Bugatti-mounted) blow up, followed on the sixth lap by another Bugatti hotshot, Williams. Chiron took over at the front, but, soon ran into trouble. That left 'Phi-Phi' Etancelin in the lead from Zanelli — with Birkin, plugging on, third. Zanelli fell back with problems which seemed to cure themselves after a while for he repassed Birkin, having dropped to third for a while. While all the fun and games were going on Birkin showed just how brilliant a driver he was, for a gent named Charavel (who raced under the pseudonym 'Sabipa') crashed his Bugatti, and was thrown out right in the path of the thundering Bentley. It was only with remarkable skill and sheer good luck that Birkin avoided him.

By the 18th lap (out of 25) Birkin was slowly catching Zanelli, and passed him when the Bugatti had to stop for fuel. Etancelin eventually finished up as the winner, allegedly with but a half-gallon of fuel in the tank! Birkin finished second, 2 min 33 sec behind, having averaged 88.5 mph — a race of a lifetime for him, and some say his finest. The French weren't smiling at the finish.

No 4's last race under the Birkin/Paget colours — the team was disbanded in late 1930 — was the 500-mile race at Brooklands, where it retired with magneto problems.

The car was sold to France, and appeared twice more at Le Mans. In 1932 it was entered by J. Trevoux and 'Mary', but the former rolled it at White House Corner before the latter had a chance, and in 1933, again entered by Trevoux but with a certain M. Gas as co-driver, it was put out when Gas shoved it into the sandbank at Mulsanne. It returned to England, being owned by Robert Murton-Neale for a while before passing on to Peter Robertson-Rober, who blew it up comprehensively in 1939. He brought No 1, the single seater, from the Welwyn establishment, and this was cannibalized to rebuild the engine. Among subsequent owners we find Neil Corner and it was he who discovered that bits and pieces were swopped around between the cars with considerable abandon during their early days, and in fact the registrations of No 2 and No 4 had been exchanged somewhere along the way! Both cars now wear the appropriate numbers.

The Birkin Blower Bentleys were, of course, built with one purpose in mind, to win Le Mans, and as you stroll around No 4 you cannot but be impressed with some of the detailing involved for this event. One example: press a toggle and the glass and gauze wire covering the headlamp swivels aside so that changing a bulb is a matter of seconds. In fact, W.O. served an apprenticeship with the railways, and there is much in common between a Bentley and those magnificent old steam engines — beautiful polished forgings and castings, for example, not to mention the sheer solidity of the car.

You climb into it from the passenger's side, as there is no driver's door (or you could be very athletic and vault over the side!) since the gear-lever is right where any door would be, to your right and down by your shins. The pedals, too, are massive affairs, none of your bits of bent tin, with a central accelerator, which I prefer, since it makes heel-and-toeing much easier.

The steering wheel is of very large diameter, and — something I hate — flexible. It's not too close to the driver, but it *is* close to the cockpit lip and the windscreen, so that when you apply effort, which is every time you go round a bend, you find your knuckles minus a little skin... The driving position is fine, and the little bucket seat quite comfortable. You can't drive with your arms stretched out in front of you, but considering the amount of muscle required, this is no bad thing.

In front of you there is a very busy facia. There are two common-or-garden round household light switches for the magnetos, and another for the headlights. Plus a great big brown knob for the starter, and the oil feed drips. Instrumentation is comprehensive with a huge clock (24 hours of racing, remember), two air pressure gauges, an oil pressure gauge, a vast tachometer, a supercharger vacuum/pressure gauge, an ammeter, a water temperature gauge and another oil pressure gauge. No speedo — who needs one?

You start on retard, then advance for action. The engine starts on the first touch of the button, and from the exhaust comes that deep burble that is so characteristic of a big four-cylinder Bentley — and of the Edwardian machines Bunty Scott-Moncrieff mentions. No mega-revs, tearing calico here, but a purposeful deep-chested growl. The clutch is smooth and untemperamental, so pulling away is no problem.

But then you have to change gear, and I must say that, at low speeds, this is quite the most difficult gearbox I have ever encountered. If you don't get into second in one go you have to stop and start again; you have to gauge the revs exactly. Mind you, when you do — and it's relatively easy at higher revs — then it's as sweet as could be, slipping from one notch to the other like the traditional knife through butter. More of W.O.'s railway background coming through? Fortunately, with a big, long-stroke engine, there's so much torque available that, when you do reach top, you seldom have to change down again. I quite see what Bunty meant when he commented that 'The gearbox is a joy in itself, but oh so difficult to master...'

The engine is, of course, the heart of the car, and a truly magnificent piece of engineering. The acceleration isn't of the neck-snapping variety, but it just keeps going on, and on, and on. It's rather like a V-twin Vincent motor bike: you don't get an impression of the engine revs rising through the exhaust note — it just gets louder. This is very deceptive, because you don't realize just how fast the car has accelerated — no speedo, remember — until you're travelling very, very fast indeed. I suppose top speed is only (nowadays) in the 105 to 110 mph region, but cruising at 100 mph, given the right road conditions, is not only feasible but a natural gait. I've driven this car on a number of occasions to Silverstone and back, and put up very respectable average speeds in the process. On one occasion Charlie Lucas in a Porsche was touching 125 mph at times trying to keep up when Neil Corner was driving it. Again there's that impression of a steam train, an inexorable gathering of speed and weight and momentum, as if nothing could stop you.

And here the brakes don't really help! Remember that the car is coming up for 60 years old, it weighs 40 cwt and it's fitted with drums, so you have to allow yourself plenty of room to slow down. Drivers in modern tin boxes don't help either, as, when you do leave yourself room, you often find someone slotting into your gap. Mind you, the sight of that massive radiator looming in the rear view mirror soon gets them out of the way...

The steering is heavy, but acceptably so, becoming heavier as you apply lock into a corner, and you definitely need to use your shoulders. And, for such a big heavy car, the handling is excellent. You can really hang the tail out, the only proviso being that flexible steering wheel and the likelihood of skinned knuckles as mentioned earlier. Of course you don't really talk of understeer and oversteer with a car like this: you *skid* it around a corner, and the Blower Bentley skids beautifully. Mind you, I wouldn't have liked to have been Tim Birkin at Pau, sliding it constantly through the twisty bits. I would have been exhausted after the first lap...

Talking of Birkin, I reckon those Bentley Boys really were the heroes the schoolboys loved. The sheer effort required to drive this machine quickly is enormous: it's as big and hefty a car to drive as it looks, make no mistake, and the controls reflect this. There's that gearbox which is definitely of the crash variety and more crash than most, that weighty

The engine is a magnificent piece of engineering; the 4½ litre four-cylinder (with Amherst Villiers' supercharger mounted at the front, out of sight here) produces so much torque that you seldom have to use the difficult gearbox.

There is a clock, but no speedometer, on the busy facia. Household light switches (visible through the steering wheel) control the magnetos and headlights.

steering, and those incredibly heavy brakes. It's built to argue with things — and *win*.

Against that, due to its length and weight, it's very comfortable and rides well, and it has the torque to eliminate much of the gear-changing, so in that respect it's not tiring. Then again, there's that feeling of sheer solidity, of strength, of purpose.

Ettore Bugatti, in one of the most quoted quotes of all time, referred to Bentleys as trucks. I reckon the true comparison should be with one of those glorious steam locomotives of the inter-war years: massive, agreed, but immensely fast and beautifully built, purposeful and potent. But then that would be no insult, would it?

1932
NAPIER-RAILTON

There is a particular word which exactly describes the Napier-Railton, but for the life of me I cannot recall just what it is. Gargantuan? That misses some of the incredible finesse in it. Massive? That makes it sound crude. Charismatic? That's a word you can use about a flamboyant Ferrari but not really about a machine as dignified as this. Dignified then? It's too fleet for that.

Unique, of course, is a good word, but even surrounded by other unique machines it is special. Gorgeous too is accurate, but that suggests it's just a pretty face. Powerful is another word that goes without saying — anything weighing two tons which could lap Brooklands at 143.44 mph had to be ultra-powerful (*that's enough words— Ed*).

The Napier-Railton hits the senses from the moment you first see it. It is *huge*, but the proportions of the Gurney Nutting bodywork, from that curious peaked prow — a masterpiece of the panelbeater's art if ever there was one — to the shapely tail, are perfect, and emphasized by the gleaming, polished alloy bodywork. But look more closely. Look at the workmanship that went into it. Look at the suspension components, at the castings and the finish: each is polished and gleaming

like the bodywork, many items carved from solid, shaped and machined and smoothed as if produced from a tool-room rather than just a machine shop. Important bolts, for example, have a tab washer, a locknut *and* a split pin in addition to the standard nut. Scuttle and tail, split to cater for flexing, are held together with myriad small clips, each perfectly formed.

Bob Roberts, who owns the car and keeps it in the Midland Motor Museum at Bridgnorth, told me that it cost £20,000 to build back in 1932 when the pound was worth a great deal more than today, and it shows. The Napier-Railton is, without question, the most beautifully-constructed car I have ever driven.

John Cobb conceived this behemoth as his ultimate weapon for Brooklands and long-distance record breaking. He was a big man who liked big cars, such as a pre-1914 10 litre Fiat, Parry Thomas's 27 litre 'Babs', the 7.2 litre Leyland-Thomas and the 10½ litre 12-cylinder Delage, all of which he raced with success on the Brooklands Outer Circuit. For his new project he commissioned Reid Railton to design a powerful, strong and reliable car which would be built by Thomson & Taylor, the famous Brooklands-based engineering and

tuning specialist.

Railton drew up a sturdy chassis with massive side members and underslung front and rear axles. Conventional semi-elliptics at the front and long twin cantilever leaf springs at the rear looked after the suspension, providing the good bump absorption and low unsprung weight which were essential to cope with the rough surface of Brooklands — tyre wear was Railton's greatest worry with this fearsome car. There were double Hartford friction dampers all round with André Telecontrol action.

Everything about the car was enormous. Its wheelbase was 10 ft 10 in, and both tracks measured 5 ft. Its unique Rudge wire wheels carried massive 35 × 6 in tyres. Weight was given as about 30 cwt dry, but with the 65 gallon fuel tank filled it came close to two tons.

Mounted in a subframe at the front was a 12 cylinder water-cooled Napier 'Lion' engine displacing 23,970 cc (with cylinder dimensions of 139 × 130.2 mm). The Lion's successful aviation background guaranteed the reliable power which Cobb was seeking, delivering 450 bhp at a mere 2,000 rpm with more further up the scale, and it had proved itself in Land Speed Record cars driven by Campbell and Se-

Left *The Napier-Railton's 24 litre 'Lion' engine, designed as a single-speed unit for use in an aircraft, comes on song above 1,500 rpm, and will go to 2,700 rpm. I saw 2,200 rpm (over 130 mph) on Silverstone's Hangar Straight.*

Left *Look at that massive exhaust system and those twin cantilever rear springs, essential for the rough surface of Brooklands. Flexing is allowed by the split scuttle and tail, fastened by a row of small clips.*

Right *A massive car weighing two tons, the Napier-Railton has a big wheel at each corner. It handles rather like a king-size go-kart which you can balance beautifully on the throttle, sliding the tail out just so.*

grave. Railton reckoned that the car would achieve 170 mph. Its 12 cylinders lay in 'broad arrow' formation, forming three banks of four 60° apart (the central bank was vertical) with each bank having a single overhead camshaft actuating overhead valves. Needless to say, it's a very unstressed, amiable giant of an engine.

The Napier-Railton proved to be all that Cobb had hoped, and he described it as 'the finest, most comfortable racing car I ever drove'. Perhaps its greatest epitaph was its 1935 143.44 mph lap of Brooklands, an outright record which remained intact at the outbreak of war and the end of the circuit's active life.

Among the Napier-Railton's greatest races was the 1937 10-lap Broadcast Trophy at Brooklands which Cobb won at an average of

136.03 mph, the fastest winning average ever achieved at the circuit. In 1935 it also won a dramatic 500 Miles race at 121.28 mph average (that compares with 106.24 mph for the same year's Indianapolis 500!). The pace was so fast that part of the Members' Banking started to break up, and when Cobb pulled in to hand over to 'Tim' Rose-Richards he had blood running down his face from a wound inflicted by a lump of concrete.

There were successful record breaking attempts too, culminating in an expedition to Bonneville salt flats in 1936 to regain the Napier-Railton's 24-hour record which had just been broken by George Eyston. With Rose-Richards, J. S. Hindmarsh and C. Brackenbury sharing the driving, Cobb raised the 24-hour average to 150.6 mph, added nine other world records in the process

and set an astonishing one hour average of 167.69 mph.

It was with these awesome achievements in mind that I arrived at Silverstone for this track test. I wasn't going to break any records, but at least I had the Grand Prix circuit to play on. Starting couldn't be easier. All you need is a couple of strongish men to give you a push after you've given the Ki-gas pump a few squirts and switched on the magnetos — via an incongruous 'twenties brass household light switch! It catches instantly and you can then burble away as cleanly and flexibly as you wish — in fact, when I arrived at Silverstone, Bob's right-hand man Mike Barker was warming it up by idling gently around the paddock.

Cobb was a very big man, a gentle giant like his car, so there's plenty of room in the cockpit. In true 'thirties

fashion, the big steering wheel is quite close to you, and the right-hand seating position upright. The bucket seat is made for one of ample proportions, but fits beautifully. To the driver's left is a 15-gallon oil tank for the dry sump engine, and behind is the fuel tank.

Coincidentally, just before I drove the Napier-Railton, the film in which she was the star, *Pandora and the Flying Dutchman,* had been shown on television. It starred Ava Gardner and James Mason, and featured world speed record breaking. Romulus Films had hired the car from Cobb in 1949 to make the film, and to modernize it an unsightly new nose was fitted over the old one, together with a long faired central tail which looked incongruous with the driver still sitting on the right-hand side. The film wasn't very good, but at least you could

hear the growl of the Lion engine as the car got up to 150 mph. Some of the sequences were pretty way out: not only was the car described as being capable of 400 mph, but it was also driven up what appeared to be Alpine passes — quite how, with a turning circle close to that of *Queen Mary*, I don't know! All credibility was blown when we were told that Miss Gardner sat next to the driver. If that is the case it would have explained the look on her face, for she would have been perched on a vast oil tank, and the gear lever...

In spite of being a single-speed engine designed for use in an aircraft, the Lion is astonishingly flexible, but with the Claudel Hobson carb fitted it isn't really interested at speeds much below about 1,500 rpm. It'll pull cleanly enough, but above that speed it really comes on song. Bob Roberts showed me

the original power curve for this particular engine, dated 24-2-33, and at 2,100 rpm it's giving 511 bhp, rising to 602 bhp at 2,700 rpm. And, if my calculations are to be believed, peak torque is no less than 1,280 lb ft at 2,100 rpm! With that sort of tractability you can see why only a three-speed gearbox is needed. In fact, three speeds seem one too many.

I saw 2,200 rpm down Hangar Straight at Silverstone, which, at roughly 60 mph/1,000 rpm, means about 130-plus mph, all achieved quite effortlessly. However, you really do need to use second on a couple of corners — Copse and Becketts, for example. This is rather a pity since the gear-change is... well, let's just say ponderous. It's a good thing the engine makes so much noise on overrun — it quite drowned out the sound of graunched changes! The term 'rock-crusher' was never

Left *John Cobb, a big man who liked big cars, with the Napier-Railton at Brooklands. The car holds the lap record in perpetuity at 143.44 mph.*

Below left *The 12-cylinder, 23,970 cc Napier 'Lion' water-cooled engine provided the reliable power which Cobb was seeking for his ultimate Brooklands weapon, delivering 602 bhp at its 2,700 rpm peak.*

Right *Although the right-hand cockpit looks tight here, there is plenty of room in the upright bucket seat behind that huge steering wheel and tidy instrument panel.*

more appropriate than for this specially made Moss 'box. There's also a biggish gap between second and third, but with all this you have to remember that the car was originally designed for Brooklands, which meant basically get into top and leave it there.

The exposed single-plate Borg & Beck clutch is designed to take 2,800 rpm, but the way the engine revs so easily gives the impression that it would just keep going until it blew... So strong is this impression, in fact, that I had visions of enlarging the circuit at the end of Hangar Straight via a new, and as yet unheard-of, run-off area at Stowe.

It's very good in the corners, fortunately. It's a big, heavy machine, with a big wheel at each corner, and the result is rather like a king-size go-kart which you can balance beautifully on the throttle, sliding the tail out just so. The steering is quite heavy and — strangely — tightens up on opposite lock, a factor I can only put down to the steering damper, which is otherwise very effective since there's no kickback or fight.

Because of its weight and the steering, you really have to keep hold of it, take it by the scruff of the neck, not let it get too far out of line, but get it sliding just right and it's enormous fun. The ride, too, is excellent — deliberately so since Brooklands was notoriously bumpy. Most of the classic shots of the car on the banking either have it with all four wheels in the air or right down on the bump stops.

Then there are the brakes — or lack of them. Since the car was designed for going, not stopping, Cobb and Railton deemed a set of internal expanding brakes at the back to be all that was necessary. When, in another reincarnation, Sir Geoffrey Quilter's GQ Parachute company turned it into a mobile test bed — you can't say the car has led an uneventful life — a set of aircraft disc brakes replaced the drums, again only working on the rears. Quilter wanted a fast, powerful machine to test braking parachutes at speeds up to 150 mph, and the veteran track car (bought by Quilter after Cobb's death on Loch Ness in

1952) apparently did the job well.

The result of this minimal braking is slightly hilarious — with only a light dab on the appropriate pedal the rear wheels stop rotating instantly, but the car doesn't slow down an awful lot. Going into a corner is quite an experience: there are those typical pops and bangs and splutters from the exhaust which is the sign of a healthy Lion on the overrun, the crunches from the gearbox as you change down, and little chirps as the rear wheels lock each time you touch the brake pedal.

To be honest, Peter Morley's Napier-Bentley is a much better *circuit* racer than the Napier-Railton, for two obvious reasons — brakes on all four wheels and triple SUs for greater tractability. But circuits with corners are not what the Napier-Railton is all about, in spite of the exploits of the late Hon Patrick Lindsay. His efforts in the car, in the rain, during a *Formule Libre* race at Silverstone in 1964 will be remembered forever by those who were there. Patrick was a great connoisseur of historic racing cars, and

bought the Napier-Railton after Sir Geoffrey Quilter died. He twice had it rebodied to the original shape, because he wasn't entirely satisfied with the result first time! The Lion engine, incidentally, developed serious water leaks over the years, but these were cured and the whole engine rebuilt by Dick Crosthwaite and John Gardner.

I suppose I didn't really test the

Remarkable workmanship went into the Napier-Railton, which cost £20,000 to build in 1932. Notice how important bolts carry a lock-nut, tab washer and split pin on top of the standard nut.

Napier-Railton in the right circumstances. It was designed and built for one purpose: to go as fast as possible in a straight line or on bank-

ing (or a long, open salt-flat circle). The fact that it's as good as it is on a twisty race track speaks volumes for its design and construction.

The Napier-Railton is a very, *very* special machine both in lore and in practice. Its reputation is awesome, and by Heavens, it is awesome to drive. Not difficult or beastly, but thunderous — mighty.

There. That's the word. Mighty.

1934
ALFA ROMEO P3

The Alfa Romeo P3 is an absolutely sensational car, and after driving it in 1983 I had to put it near the top of my list of all-time favourites. I suppose I had better explain why. Even before I drove it I was well disposed towards the car because it is one of the most beautiful machines ever made. Apart from that, however, the driver who was most closely associated with the P3, Tazio Nuvolari, was one of my childhood heroes — I always think of him in a P3 because of that amazing win over Mercedes-Benz and Auto Union in the 1935 German Grand Prix at the Nürburgring. But these factors are intangible: the real reason I love the P3 is because of the way it does things...

This Alfa Romeo was never officially known as the P3, the colloquial designation having been created by Italian journalists looking for a shorter way of describing the *Tipo B* Monoposto, the successor to Vittorio Jano's P2. The car arrived in 1932 when the rule requiring GP cars to have two-seater bodywork (even though riding mechanics had not been carried in GP cars since 1925) was eventually abolished. Jano, who had joined Alfa Romeo back in 1923, took full advantage of the rule change to produce the *Tipo B* Monoposto —

meaning single-seater — as a follow-on from his bizarre but successful twin-engined *Tipo A*.

The P3's engine was an extensively modified version of the Alfa Monza's glorious 2,336 cc straight-eight supercharged unit. The stroke was increased to give cylinder dimensions of 65 mm × 100 mm, creating a capacity of 2,654 cc. Like the Monza's engine, drive for the two overhead camshafts was central, between the two four-cylinder alloy blocks. Although the Monza's engine had used two separate cylinder heads, the *Tipo B*'s used an integral head which allowed the blower pressure and compression ratio to be increased. Two superchargers, each with its own carburettor, were fitted in place of the single blower and carburettor of the Monza. More powerful supercharging and the extra capacity took power up from the Monza's 165 bhp at 5,400 rpm to 215 bhp at 5,600 rpm, but the *Tipo B* engine remained an unstressed unit capable of lasting for the five hour minimum duration then specified for GPs.

With the freedom to design a car for the first time for just one occupant, Jano made the chassis and body just 26 in wide, and engineered the transmission so that the driver didn't have to sit on top of it. The

differential was integral with the rear of the gearbox casing, from which two propshafts emerged at an angle to form a triangle where they joined the back axle. Each propshaft met the rear axle at a bevel gear mounted not far inboard of the rear wheel. In the end, the driver's seat was placed above these propshafts rather than between them, because drivers of the time were supposed to like a high, commanding driving position. With its two bevel gears, the rear axle was no lighter than a conventional one, but the lay-out at least allowed easy changing of the final drive ratio for different circuits.

The P3's maximum speed was around 145 mph, and a particular advantage against Bugatti, Delage and ERA opposition was its light weight of only 700 kg, thanks to extensive use of aluminium, elektron and duralumin in its construction.

Jano's Monoposto was instantly a success, winning its first race, the Italian GP at Monza, in Nuvolari's hands at an average speed of 104.13 mph for the five hour duration, a speed which was just 1 mph short of the lap record established by a Monza the year before. The Alfas went on to take 1-2-3 placings in the French and German GPs, Nuvolari winning the former and

Left *The P3 is one of the finest cars I have ever driven. Quite apart from all the torque produced by its straight-eight engine, it handles with wonderful precision, totally predictably and controllably.*

Right *I drove this P3 straight after it emerged from restoration during 1983, but over the following five seasons David Black, driving here, has taken it to 17 wins from 27 starts, including two Seaman Trophy successes.*

Below *The P3 is forever associated with Tazio Nuvolari, one of my childhood heroes. Here he pulls away from the Mercedes-Benz and Auto Union cars at Montlhéry in the 1935 French Grand Prix, but the season's great highlight came when he won at the Nürburgring.*

Rudi Caracciola the latter.

Economic reasons dictated Alfa's announcement that it would retire from GP racing in 1933, the company putting its six Monoposto cars (and enough spares to build up another three) in storage. Enzo Ferrari, who was contracted to run Alfa's racing activities, continued with Monzas which he enlarged to 2.6 litres, emblazoning them with his 'Prancing Horse' badge. The cars were quick enough, but the extra power showed up a rear axle weakness, causing many retirements. Nuvolari then transferred his allegiance to Maserati, and enjoyed sufficient success to cause Alfa to release its Monoposto cars again, resulting in wins at Pescara and in the Italian and Spanish GPs.

New GP rules for 1934, requiring a maximum weight of 750 kg, a race distance of at least 500 km and a minimum cockpit width of 33.5 in, brought changes for the P3. The body had to be widened, and bored-out 68 mm × 100 mm engines took capacity to 2,905 cc and power to 255 bhp, giving a maximum speed of 170 mph. This was the year when the 'Silver Arrows', in the shape of the Mercedes-Benz and Auto Union teams, arrived, but Alfa had its successes nonetheless. The cars were supreme in races where the German teams were absent, but a significant success against this new opposition came in the French GP at Montlhéry, where Louis Chiron led home an Alfa 1-2-3.

The German tide was more formidable in 1935, and Alfa was fighting a losing battle despite further P3 developments. New suspension and hydraulic brakes were fitted, and the gearboxes were reduced to three speeds in the interests of strength (the straight-eight's torque was strong enough to cope with the loss of a ratio), but these changes weren't enough to thwart the German threat, despite some cars being fitted with 3.2 litre engines. Nuvolari and Chiron raced at Montlhéry with 3.8 litre engines, Nuvolari setting a new lap record before both cars succumbed to back axle trouble, but the season's great highlight came at the Nürburgring when Nuvolari vanquished the German teams.

Today, David Black's P3 is one of several seen regularly at historic race meetings, and it has a relatively unbroken racing history since the day it was built, like so many ERAs. Having chassis number 50003, it is the third of a batch produced in 1934 and modified with reversed quarter elliptic rear suspension in 1935. Records are too sketchy to allow its works racing history to be deduced, but in 1936 it was bought for £1900 by Charles Martin through Thomson & Taylor. Martin had campaigned a Type 59 Bugatti (Ettore's reply to the Monoposto) in 1935 in which he was second in the Mannin Moar in the Isle of Man, and third in the Donington GP. Of that Type 59 he wrote: 'She was a magnificent car to handle and a joy to drive when she was running properly, but she gave me endless trouble and cost me a small fortune in repairs...'

The Alfa Romeo proved to be a bit more reliable and less expensive to repair in 1936, when Martin scored second places at Pau, Deauville and in the Donington GP, using a 3.2 litre engine in the last two events. In the British Empire Trophy race at Donington and the Cork GP he retired with scavenge pump failure, and he overturned the car in the rain in the *Eifelrennen* at the Nürburgring, without hurting himself.

In his disarming way, Martin described this incident in two letters to David Black: 'June 14, 1936, Nürburgring, on honeymoon, turned it over for the first and only time. Waving to some supporters and

completely lost it. Walked back to the pits, where, being on honeymoon, I was not popular.'

The following weekend he packed up with back axle trouble in the Hungarian GP after 35 laps of the 50 lap race. In 1937, with a 2.9 litre engine, he was third in the 220 miles handicap at Cork, and the fastest car in a field of Alfas, ERAs, Bugattis, Altas and MGs.

At some time before the war the car was fitted with a 2.9 litre meehanite iron block produced by Frank Ashby who, after much Riley racing, considerably modified his own Monoposto in a similar way, but on his personal engine he also altered the manifolding. No doubt the change in material was intended to eliminate the tendency of the alloy blocks to crack in their cylinder heads.

After the war the ex-Martin car appeared in Australia, having been purchased, it is said, from Georges Raph in Paris by Lex Davison. After proving it was one of Australia's fastest racing cars, Davison sold it in 1955 to Steve Ames in Queensland, who won the Southport GP with it. It was sold again in 1956, and then had an ignominious career deteriorating in yards in the Brisbane area, until it was found in a sad state beneath a pile of furniture under a house in Toowoomba by Lawrence G. Rofe of Mitcham North, Victoria! Rofe made a huge effort and rebuilt the car in eight weeks, raced it for a period and then sold it to Doug Jarvis, who in turn sold it to Sir Ralph Millais back in England. He raced it in VSCC events with Patrick Wicks, who maintained it. Despite the meehanite, a crack in the fixed head led to a difficult repair requiring all the expertise of the London welding experts, Angell & Williams.

The next owner was Robert Cooper who raced it with Gary Woodhead, the latter doing the maintenance. The car finally passed to its present owner, Alfa enthusiast David Black, in 1978, and David undertook an extensive rebuild including the fitting of an alloy 3.2 litre block, specially made to pattern, and an increase in blower pressure obtained by using the larger blower designed for the 3.8 litre engine. Alfa Romeo in Italy, particularly Luigi Fusi, provided considerable assistance by lending factory drawings which simplified the task of returning the car to original specification, not that it had been messed around too much.

Over a period of some 40 years, as many as four or five 2.9 litre P3s have competed in VSCC events at irregular intervals, and until recent years they had always been over-shadowed by ERAs and the odd Maserati. David Black changed all that, however, after his first post-rebuild race at the VSCC Silverstone meeting in 1983. Up to the end of 1987, his record comprised 17 wins, two second places, four thirds and nine retirements from 27 starts.

Perhaps the highlights have been David's pair of wins in the Seaman Trophy at Oulton Park, but he has also held lap records at Silverstone (Club and GP circuits), Ingliston, Oulton Park and the Nürburgring. He even raced the car in 1985 at Laguna Seca when the Monterey Historic Meeting honoured Alfa Romeo's 75th anniversary. He has held a 35.44 sec record at Shelsley Walsh (pre-war the target was 40 sec) and 41.85 sec at Prescott (for pre-war and post-war historic racing cars).

I drove the P3 in 1983 before David accumulated all these results, and on the same day that I had a run in Albert Obrist's Maserati 6C–34, which — visually at least — is a very similar car. Both are big, brawny GP racers, not *voiturettes*. As it turned out, the Maserati lived up to its image, feeling a heavy handful of a car, but the P3 belies its looks. Its size may make it off-putting, but once you drive it you find that appearances are deceptive. It starts instantly, with a quarter turn of the handle (always a good sign, but, as David said, this was the result of a lot of hard work!). The cockpit is very spacious — the body width rules when it was built ensured that — and all the controls well spaced. The gear lever sprouts out of the centre of the floor, but is then cranked over to the left beside the steering wheel, highly convenient if you want to change gear.

If you want to change gear? Yes — if! What surprises many people is that the P3 is fitted with a three-speed gearbox, which at first sight appears to be one cog too few. In fact the gutsy straight-eight engine has so much punch that, at Donington where I drove it, you could

put up quite respectable lap times using top gear only. Mind you, it's a lot more fun using second as well. The ratios are really like those of a normal four-speed without an off-the-grid first gear. There is no need for four gears, and David later confirmed my view of what you can do with top alone by finishing seventh in the 1987 Seaman Trophy after losing first and second for all bar the last lap. On the other hand, he set his Prescott record without changing out of first...

Power comes in as low as 1,200–1,500 rpm, and from 2,000 rpm on it pulls like the proverbial steam train. Allied to that is the unique, indefinable but ex-hilarating noise that only a straight-eight gives, a cross between the deep, uneven beat of a V8 and the growl of a straight-six. It has such amazing torque that you

could pull away from virtually anything. David has seen 235 bhp on a rolling road at the 5,400 rpm peak, and that translates to around 300 bhp at the flywheel. As an indication of the sort of performance this produces, David clocked a standing kilometre time of 23.98 sec (with a terminal speed of 134.2 mph) at a VSCC Colerne Sprint. Simply changing from petrol to methanol produced 50 bhp, yet David said he always found the P3 a very docile car over the 500 miles he covered running on petrol on the road.

But where the P3 most belies its bulk is in its handling. Where with some cars you have to set up for a corner a long way beforehand, with the P3 you simply arrive at the corner, steer into it and go exactly where you want. Depending on how clever you want to look, you simply give it more

The rule requiring a body width of 33.5 in gave the P3 a spacious cockpit, and the combination of accurate handling and perfectly weighted steering makes the car far easier to drive than its size would suggest.

The throttle is in the centre and the gearbox has only three speeds. Power is fed through a differential, integral with the gearbox casing, to a pair of propshafts emerging at an angle just below the seat.

or less right foot. You can drive it with the tail hanging way out (which is, like the gear change, great fun) or take a tidier, cleaner (and perhaps quicker) line — the car responds exactly as you want it to do. *That* is why I like the P3 so much — it is so totally predictable and controllable that it is a real joy to drive.

On the day I drove the P3 there were some wet patches on the track: you would have needed to tread warily in something like a Maserati 250F or, to an even greater extent, the 6C–34, but the P3 inspired so much

confidence that it was probably quicker than the Maseratis on those slippery bits. David's car runs on 16 in wheels instead of the original 18 in — unfortunate though this is from the originality and visual points of view, it does make the car much more competitive. Allied with the handling is steering that I reckon to be just right (David was finding some problems in going from lock to lock, but I found no sign of anything wrong). About the only slight quibble I would have is that the brake pedal pressure is incredibly high, but

there was no sign of fade. David tells me that a great deal of work has been put into the brakes since I drove the P3, and that the pedal pressure is acceptable now.

Finally, one other feature which must be mentioned is the car's immaculate preparation. As anyone who has inspected it will confirm, the P3 is a credit to David and his mechanic, Len Harper. I am grateful for the opportunity to drive a dream — and not have any myths shattered. The Alfa P3 is indeed a beautifully engineered car.

1934
ERA

If you follow historic racing, it's easy to acquire a somewhat distorted view of the cars which are winning today, because they were not always as significant as they might seem. Take the ERA as an example: seeing a host of them still racing — and winning — can lead you to imagine that they were very important cars.

The truth is not quite so simple. In fact, in their day they were competing at the equivalent level of present day Formula 2 and 3, and were totally outclassed by machines from Germany and Italy. Although they did a great deal to boost British morale during the 1930s in *voiturette* racing, that doesn't make them anything more than beautiful-ly–built second division cars. That said, I have always loved driving them, and they have a special place in British motor racing history.

Indeed, the ERA record must be unique. A total of 17 A, B, C and D-types were built, and all 17 survive despite Marcel Lehoux writing off R3B (and, sadly, himself) in an accident at Deauville in 1936. Today they still beat potentially faster, more modern cars in historic racing, although this might have something to do with the fact that eight of them now have 2 litre power units (instead of 1.5 litre) compared with

the three that had larger engines pre-war. Three E-types were built, of which two survive, and the G-type apparently became the basis for the Bristol Le Mans coupés. The glory, however, belonged to the conventional cars. I have been lucky enough to drive examples of A, B, C and D-types, so ERAs have a special place in my heart.

Until the ERA's arrival in 1934, British motor racing had been characterized by its insularity and an inability to meet foreign competition on equal terms, except in sports car races with minimal opposition. Brooklands may have been the home of racing, but it did little but breed track cars with virtually no application elsewhere. Hillclimbs were the only place in Britain where the importance of good handling, braking and throttle response came to the fore, so it's no surprise that the ERA developed from this branch of motor sport.

It all began with the 'White Riley'; a project developed by Raymond Mays, with design help from Peter Berthon and Murray Jamieson, as well as material support from Riley. The car used a supercharged version of Riley's 1,486 cc six-cylinder engine fitted into a TT racing chassis, and with it Mays broke the Shelsley Walsh

record in September 1933. Finance to take the project further came from Humphrey Cook, a wealthy amateur driver, and the *voiturette* based on the 'White Riley' was to be called the English Racing Automobile.

The first ERA was a conventional design, priced to sell in reasonable numbers. Reid Railton designed its chassis, overslung at both ends, giving it beam axles and semi-elliptic springs all round. The seating position was quite high, making the car seem outmoded compared with the new Auto Union and Mercedes cars. The engine was loosely based on the Riley 'six', retaining the twin high-mounted camshafts (operating overhead valves by pushrods) and the three bearing crankshaft. With dry sump lubrication and a Jamieson supercharger driven off the crankshaft nose, it was effective-ly a new engine. Three capacities were planned: 1,100 cc, 1,500 cc and 2,000 cc. Among the ERA's un-usual features was its Armstrong preselector gearbox, which allowed simple and quick gearchanging, these assets being thought to out-weigh the system's weight and power absorption. There was no clutch or flywheel.

The 1934 season brought the in-evitable teething problems before

the first victory came late in the year. For the following season the B-type ERA was introduced, with a stiffer frame and different spring rates. Although opposition was limited, the ERA was incredibly successful in 1935. The Bugatti Type 51As and Maserati 4CS/4CMs which competed against them had respectively around 20 and 45 bhp less than the ERA's 170 bhp, so the English marque swept the board — they won the Dieppe Grand Prix, 1,500 cc *Eifelrennen,* Coppa Acerbo, Prix de Berne and numerous lesser events.

More serious opposition arrived in the following couple of years. For 1936, Maserati produced the 6CM, which had the same sort of horsepower but a better chassis with independent front suspension. And Dick Seaman, fed up with ERA factory service, commissioned Giulio Ramponi to modify a 1927 GP Delage with which he went on to embarrass the ERA team.

In this barren 1936 season, Bira won the Coupe Prince Rainier at Monaco, but the works team, ex-

R4D gave Raymond Mays many sprint and hillclimb successes up to 1950, and still wins races today in Anthony Mayman's hands. This photograph shows how dramatic roll oversteer makes it such a handful, but it is very rewarding to drive.

perimenting with Zoller blowers, had a dire time. Not only was reliability poor, but the blower's position over the gearbox (and between the driver's legs, heaven forbid!) upset the handling to the extent that ballast had to be tried under the dumb-irons to balance out the understeer.

The C-type was born from the rethink necessary for 1937. This car featured a modified engine giving about 220 bhp, and a new chassis with Porsche trailing link and torsion bar independent front suspension, as well as hydraulic brakes. At least the works cars could now stay with the Maseratis, driven by names such as Trossi, Villoresi and Dreyfus. Mays won at Picardy and d'Albigeois, Arthur Dobson was first at Berne, and Charles Martin

won the *Avusrennen* and came second at Brno.

Thereafter, only the occasional victory came ERA's way on the continent, Mays' win at Picardy in 1938 standing out. By now the car was long in the tooth, a stillborn GP car was taking too much money and time, and the latest cars from Alfa Romeo (the sensational *Tipo* 158 or 'Alfetta') and Maserati were much faster. The elegant E-type ERA, with svelte lines reminiscent of the Mercedes W154, proved fast but fragile, and was destined never to win a race. By this stage, Mays had departed from ERA, and Cook was prepared to support the cars only for the 1939 season.

There is a school of thought which rates the years immediately post-war as the ERA's best, simply because the cars became eligible for the 1½ litre blown/4½ litre unblown GP formula. When the Alfettas were absent, the ERAs often did well against Talbot Lago and Maserati opposition. Bob Gerard was the most notable exponent, taking third place in the 1948 British GP

and second a year later.

Sometimes 'Mr Bob' even humbled the BRM V16s, an irony in view of Mays' and Berthon's involvement in that unhappy project. The motoring press loved to see the pre-war *voiturette* beat the complex and expensive BRM, but this mocking is unfair in hindsight. Between them ERA and BRM laid the foundations for a British racing industry which now leads the world.

As I said, I have been fortunate to drive many ERAs over the years, so the most obvious way to discuss them is to analyse, with the help of others who have driven them, the four conventional types in chronological order.

R1A (the final letter refers to the type) is the very first ERA and must be accorded the status of one of the most historic of the 17 A, B, C and D-types built. It made its bow during a testing session at Brooklands in May 1934, and its racing debut came later that month during the Mannin Moar races. However, the handling was appalling, and the car was withdrawn after practice.

Three ERAs driven by (left to right) Raymond Mays, Dick Seaman and Pat Fairfield line up on the front row for the 1935 Dieppe Grand Prix. Fairfield won from Bira on his first outing in R2B.

Before its next appearance, revised rear springs were fabricated, and the original steering arrangement was changed, with the drop arm moved from outside to inside the chassis frame.

At this stage, the car had the old ERA rising sun badge, a design changed for the now familiar three ringed affair by the Dieppe GP at the end of July. By that time, the original bucket seat had also been replaced by the more usual armchair version. The first victory for R1 (as it was known before the 1935 introduction of the B-type) came in the Nuffield Trophy at Donington with Mays driving.

The car was used by the works throughout the 1935 season, driven by Cook and Mays mainly, as well as Prinz Zu Leiningen, Tim Rose-Richards and Seaman. Major race success eluded the car (third in the 1,500 cc *Eifelrennen* was its best result), but Mays became the first man to break the 40 sec barrier at Shelsley. The original small tail had been changed to a larger 28 gallon B-type tank-cum-tail unit but such features as the A-type steering box (with its two retaining bolts) were kept.

In 1936, the car appeared twice, driven by Kay Petre and the Hon Brian Lewis, before being acquired by Norwegian driver Eugen Bjornstad, who was apparently the all time 'rock-ape' of a driver. He is reputed to have said that 'I always have 7,000 revolutions, no more, no less' and 'Every race I run off the road, once, no more', but despite this he was quick, winning the '37 Turin *voiturette* race, among other events.

The car then went through a succession of owners, including the Ashmore brothers (Fred and Joe), Reg Parnell, Ron Flockhart and A. Birrell, Bill Moss and Sandy Murray, before ending up in the hands of Swiss enthusiast Jost Wildbolz.

Left *I drove Jost Wildbolz's R1A at Cadwell Park, and found it very predictable, like all beam axle ERAs. You need to be confident to extract the best from it, for it needs to be picked up by the scruff of the neck.*

Below right *An outing at Donington in Peter Mann's R9B, once owned by Charles Martin and Brian Shawe-Taylor. It is similar to the A-type, and I remember it particularly for the unsettled braking which seems to be a feature of all ERAs.*

The car was a very familiar sight to historic race fans through the 'sixties and 'seventies, mainly in the hands of Tony Merrick, who tended the car for owner Sandy Murray.

Tony's view of R1A is very straightforward: 'I suppose that R1A must be my favourite racing car. It's exceedingly well balanced, but quite difficult to learn to drive. It really is a sideways machine, and once you get to grips with it, it's absolutely fabulous. We always used to have great fun going to Silverstone in the middle of the week and getting up the noses of Formula Ford drivers by being so quick in a straight line!'

My drive in R1A came at Cadwell Park, where I found it unfortunately down on power, but, like all the beam axle ERAs, it is such a predictable car to drive. If you are nervous of an ERA, then it becomes tricky to go quickly, but if you are confident, it's magnificent. To drive one fast you must pick it up by the scruff of the neck and throw it around — it lacks the fingertip precision of something like a Lotus 16. Like all the ERAs, R1A is fitted with a preselector 'box which is superb — you preselect the gear you want, dip the 'clutch' pedal when you want to change ratio, and you've got the quickest gearchange imaginable.

In 1935, ERA introduced the B-type chassis, with lowered rear spring mountings, a more rigid frame thanks to diagonal cross bracing under the seat, a lowered seat position, 10 leaf springs, a new steering box with four securing bolts and a 28 gallon fuel tank which meant a different shaped tail. As the A-type engine had been prone to overheating its big ends and cracking its centre main bearing, the B-type had strengthening fins along the lower part of the crankcase, and an improved oil feed system. Visually, there were new rounded rocker covers, but A-types were all subsequently fitted with these.

The first B-type, R1B, was delivered to Seaman in April 1935, and the majority of the rest of the B-types were also customer cars. R9B, the car which I drove, was bought by Denis Scribbans, a Birmingham businessman, in the spring of 1936. It was a relatively successful national racing car in his hands, although its best victory came when driven by Charles Martin in the 1936 Nuffield Trophy at Donington.

It then went to brewer Bob Ansell, his brother Geoff, Brian Shawe-Taylor, J. Lewis, Terry Car-

son, Douglas Hull and Peter Waller before Peter Mann acquired it in 1976.

Charles Martin drove R9B only in that one race, although he was very successful with another ERA, R3A, as well. He also drove P3 Alfa and Type 59 Bugatti GP cars pre-war, and is able to put the ERA in true perspective. 'For what they were, they were very good indeed. They were very tough cars, and you were able to really boot an ERA off the line, unlike the P3 which has a very delicate rear end. It was very comfortable to drive, and that gearbox was foolproof. Handling was very straightforward — you just belted it into a corner, kicked the back end out and it went round. It was a different ball game from the GP cars though — not terribly quick. That Nuffield Trophy win was interesting — the car missed and farted all the way round Donington for 200 miles. God knows how it won!'

Brian Shawe-Taylor drove R9B before and after the war. It was actually his first racing car, and he came fourth in the 1939 Nuffield Trophy with Bob Ansell. 'The difference was extraordinary compared to the sports cars that I'd driven before — it was incredibly fast and powerful. The steering was quite low geared, and as you were sitting so close to a massive 18 in steering wheel you felt that you could never catch a slide, unless you spun the wheel through your hands. Fitting a 16 in Bluemels wheel transformed the car, so that suddenly you felt safe. My final memory of the ERA is how the front wheels pattered under braking. When I first drove the car, Bob Ansell was paying the bills, so I only moaned a bit. Thomson & Taylor said that patter was normal, and that all I had to do was let off the brakes and re-apply them!'

After those memories, I find it very difficult to add anything on the B-type compared to R1A — they are very similar, as you would expect. Like all ERA engines, R9B's does

not really need to be revved unduly — 6,000 rpm is about all you need. It's interesting that Brian Shawe-Taylor thought the brakes unnerving at first — all ERAs seem to do it, and yet the actual stopping power is first class!

Of all the ERAs built, the most evocative must be the ex-Bira cars, especially if finished in the blue and yellow racing colours of Siam. Bira used four cars: R2B 'Romulus', R5B 'Remus', R12C 'Hanuman' and R12B/C 'Hanuman II'. R12C was a works car initially, before Bira bought it for the 1938 season to replace 'Remus', although he retained 'Romulus'.

On the C-type, the front half of the frame was cut off, and replaced with a new box section carrying the Porsche-designed independent front

suspension, while there were softer rear springs. The whole steering geometry was changed, and the steering arm operated in the reverse direction of the B-type. The brakes came in for attention, too, with the A and B-type rod/cable Girling system dropped in favour of Lockheed hydraulic actuation. The brake drums were also new. Before the C-type appeared in 1937, ERA brakes used steel liners shrunk onto the drums, but C-type versions had a cast iron finned ring attached to an aluminium backplate by 24 2BA bolts. They work so well that all the earlier cars racing today have them.

There was a new ribbed 38 gallon fuel tank, a new 'box with ratios in between the wide ratio A-type and close ratio B-type, while the engine was quite highly modified. New,

Left *Tony Stephens at the wheel of R12C, a car which he and Bill Morris restored from little more than a chassis frame. My chief impression of the car was of its engine's immense power, perhaps 220 bhp.*

Below left *Aboard R4D for an Oulton Park start: its 2 litre engine gives what feels like a disproportionate amount of extra power compared with a 1½ litre, and it is the trickiest of all ERAs to drive.*

Right *ERA cockpits are cramped — although there is plenty of elbow room — and the supercharger is mounted, worryingly, between the driver's legs. This is R4D, which was successfully fitted with an experimental Shorrock vane blower.*

strengthened four-bolt con-rods were fitted to obviate the previous season's distressing spate of broken rods and ventilated crankcases, Bosch magnetos were used instead of Scintillas, and there was a Zoller blower running at round 26 psi. With something like 220 bhp on tap, the C-types were extremely fast cars.

Initially, R12C was driven by Dobson, Mays, Pat Fairfield and Cook, and its victories included the 1937 Nuffield Trophy, the Albi GP that year and the Prix de Berne. It was one of only three ERAs to use a 2 litre engine pre-war.

Bira won the 1938 Cork Light Car race and the Nuffield Trophy in 1938 and 1939 before crashing R12C badly at Reims in July 1939. Most parts were stripped out and placed in a B-type frame known as 'Hanuman II', but the chassis was kept, and when Bill Morris bought 'Hanuman II' from Rhodesia, R12C's frame came with it.

Since then owner Bill Morris and

Tony Stephens have completed a monumental reconstruction of a car that can claim justifiably to be R12C. It doesn't have the long arm C-type suspension, though, as the one good side left after Bira's accident was used when R8C was rebuilt after Brian Shawe-Taylor had crashed it. Instead it has the spare set of short arm independent front suspension from R4D. The engine is all ERA, to C-type spec (except that it has a Godfrey instead of a Zoller blower), and the tail and cowl are genuine R12C.

Some parts are new, like the rear axle tubes, differential case and steering arm. A new steering box had to be made, as a B-type box would have caused the wheel to act in the reverse way to normal with the independent front suspension — you would have turned the steering wheel to the left, and the car would have gone right! Tony Stephens has been racing the car for several years, and when I drove it in 1985 it had a

demon tweak added — a front anti-roll bar.

My first impression behind the wheel was that the engine is magnificent — I reckon it must be capable of beating all the other 1½ litre cars with around 220 bhp. Without the anti-roll bar, it suffered from a lack of traction, probably roll oversteer, but with Tony's modification I reckon it must be 10 mph faster through the corners. The car actually feels super — that anti-roll bar is as good as a limited slip diff. One problem about the car is that I reckon it has ruined my back (Tony's bigger than the average ERA driver, so doesn't use an air cushion in the seat), while another is that blower between your legs — if that goes, then it'll take your manhood with it...

R4D is a classic case of racing car development. It started life as a works 2 litre B-type car in 1935. During that season it was driven mainly in sprints and hillclimbs by Mays, although it did compete in the

1935 German GP at the Nürburgring. After the 1936 season it was converted to C-type spec, and Mays won the British Empire Trophy, the Picardy GP, and the JCC International Trophy.

The car became the only D-type in the winter of 1937-38. Rubery Owen produced a new one-piece, fully boxed frame with drilled side members, which was some 70 lb lighter than the C-type version. The front suspension was modified, as the long radius arms on the C-types had caused excessive wear to their bushes and tended to 'give' *in extremis*, so for the D-type there were shorter arms and larger flanges on the bushes. Luvax hydraulic dampers were new, as were twin leading shoe brakes.

Another feature that made R4D stand out was the nearside mounted bell crank, which angled the steering column to that side. The reason for this difference was that Mays could not fully extend his left arm after a childhood accident.

Mays drove R4D in 1938, and in between the mechanical failures he managed to win the Picardy GP again and make BTD at both Shelsley meetings. For 1939, he purchased the car after parting company with ERA and began an incredible run of sprint and hillclimb successes which lasted until he sold it in 1950. By this time it had apparently been fitted with a spare frame, rear radius arms, softened torsion bars and compression springs instead of the standard front suspension stops. It then continued its successful career, driven in the 1950s by Ron Flockhart and Ken Wharton, and more recently by Neil Corner and myself.

Writing in *Autosport*, Flockhart said that, '...although the driving position is high it has its advantages, giving a "sense of approach" into corners, and this, coupled with plenty of warning of breakaway at the rear, makes for a feeling of being in command on corners. Steering and braking were in keeping with the rest of the car...the D-type is well balanced in all senses.'

Neil Corner, who used to own R4D, doesn't agree with that judgement: 'It was not a well-balanced car — in fact it was the most difficult car I've driven. It was a bit exciting in corners, especially as the throttle linkage for the Shorrock blower was all or nothing and there was no room for your right foot in the cockpit. The independent front suspension does nothing for the handling and the beam axle cars are far more fun. Mind you, R4D gave me my most exciting season's racing bar none. Off the start line nothing would live with it, but that throttle linkage and the car's roll-oversteer made it an absolute handful. I remember it with a lot of affection, though, and it was a tremendous "grunt and squirt" machine for hillclimbs.'

I think Neil is almost being generous about R4D, for it has a mind of its own. With the roll oversteer the inside rear wheel would lift, causing the limited slip diff pawls to lock then unlock when they shouldn't have, which was exciting. That engine is tremendous, although I think that 'Remus' is giving a little bit more power — which explains why I was trying so hard when I beat the late Patrick Lindsay at Silverstone in 1984, although, to be fair, the engine in 'Remus' was having an off day. With R4D you've got the blower between your legs again, and it's definitely a very powerful motor car which repays smooth power application.

Neil Corner reckons that the 2 litre engine has a disproportionate amount of extra power compared to the 1½ (nearly twice as much as the small unit), and I'd agree with him there. Overall it's a great car to drive, but very tricky too.

Each ERA has a distinct character of its own, and all of them have *lots* of character. How else can you explain why their owners love to race them so often and so hard? ERAs are tremendously enjoyable, if not great, racing cars with a special place in patriotic hearts.

1950
ALFA ROMEO 159

Where do I start? With the telephone call telling me that a track test of the 159 was a possibility? No. Perhaps the call telling me that it was definitely on? Perhaps not. Maybe when I had to jump out of the cockpit of an ERA on the start line at Silverstone to catch a plane to Italy — but maybe not. Let's start as we nosed into Balocco, Alfa's beautiful test track set in the plains of the Po valley, on a glorious, sunny, still, Sunday morning. In particular, as we walked into the courtyard, surrounded by the old stables that are now workshops, and saw it for the first time. Quite literally, a tingle ran down my spine.

Was there ever a car quite so beautiful? Others may match it — none is superior. From that distinctive nose to the perfect curves of the tail, there isn't a line wrong. A pause, to take it all in. Walk round it: from *any* angle it is so right. And I'm going to drive it.

The two technicians who look after it, Bruno Bonnini and Antonio Deledorne, give me a very level look. This is their car. It is brought out only very, very occasionally. I am the first journalist to drive it: more than that, apart from World Champion Phil Hill, I'm the first non-works driver to drive it. I'm as much under trial as I've ever been in my

life. Dear Lord, let it all go right ...

Bruno leans down, gives the starting handle a quick half-turn, and the engine burps into life. The 159 just sits there, idling easily and untemperamentally with that characteristic 'vroom, vroom, vroom' of a highly supercharged engine. That tingle in the spine appears again.

The Alfa Romeo 158/159 is possibly the most successful racing car ever made. Out of 54 races (some of which were heats) it finished first 45 times. Apart from its first season in 1938, when teething troubles could be expected, it was only ever beaten by two cars: the incredible Mercedes-Benz W165 at Tripoli in 1939, and the $4\frac{1}{2}$ litre Ferrari. It started life as a *voiturette* and finished up as the best Formula 1 car of its day. Its domination in 1950 was total — 11 firsts out of 11 starts. It gave the world its first World Champion, Nino Farina, and Juan Manuel Fangio his first world title. It raced for eight years over a 13-year period, won its first race and last race, began by developing 195 bhp at 7,000 rpm and finished up pushing out no less than 420 bhp at 9,600 rpm. It *was* Grand Prix racing in the immediate post-war years.

You can imagine, then, the thrill of that day at Balocco. As I change

into my overalls, one of the mechanics rumbles the beast out onto the track. Apart from an apparent sharpness from the clutch, he could be driving any car, anywhere — it is totally untemperamental. His first blip on the throttle is an indication of what is to come, an ear-shattering 'whoop, whoop'. No way does the sound give any indication that this is a $1\frac{1}{2}$ litre. It has a deep, heavy bark overlaid with supercharger scream.

Climb into it. There's a broad, comfortable, corduroy-covered seat, and a spacious cockpit. The propshaft runs down the centre, with the brake and central throttle on the right (Bruno is a little concerned about that central throttle, then relaxes when I tell him that I'm used to them) and then the clutch pedal and a foot rest on the left. The gear change, too, is on the left, and has a reverse-pattern change (first and second are towards you, third and fourth away from you).

In front of you are the instruments, a vast tacho on the right, and an equally large dial on the left containing the water temperature, oil temperature and oil pressure gauges. Between the two big dials is a fuel pressure gauge, and down on the bottom left of the dashboard is a St Christopher badge. All 158s and

Left Gingerly getting the feel of the Alfa Romeo 159. By the end of its life the car was producing 420 bhp at 9,600 rpm, sufficient to induce wheelspin like no other car, with the exception of the BRM V16.

Below left The handling is very predictable until traction breaks at the back: this is easy to provoke with all the power, the lack of weight at the tail and the narrow tyres.

Below From the distinctive nose to the perfect curves of the tail, there isn't a line wrong. The tail would sit lower if there was a full load of fuel, weighing 5 cwt, on board.

Above right One of several 158/159s which have never left Alfa's hands, this car is in highly original condition. Notice the crooked lines of the front grille and the massive 15 in finned brake drums.

Right The 159 with its custodians, Bruno Bonnini (wearing cap) and Antonio Deledorne, before my outing. They were concerned about how I would manage with the centre throttle, a feature that I have always liked.

159s apparently had them. Very Catholic, Italy! The scuttle sweeps round and back, and in its curves are the rear view mirrors.

The clutch is a bit sharp, an in-and-out affair, and you have to time a throttle blip and clutch release just right, but once it's gripping you're away. I'm on tyres that look original, and are certainly very hard, while there is hardly any fuel in the 66 gallon tank, so the car sits nose-down, tail-up. This means, too, that there is very little load on the back (in a race there would be another 5 cwt of fuel there), so there is nothing to keep the rear wheels on the road. The result, with *any* sort of throttle, is instant wheelspin. At any revs. In any gear.

The power, and its delivery, are gorgeous. There are no flat spots or anything like that, and from 3,500 rpm on there's more than 200 bhp, at 4,000 rpm there's 220 bhp, at 5,000 rpm 266 bhp, and at 5,500 rpm — the rev limit I was set — near enough 300 bhp. And these are real horses, not ponies. The instant power is fantastic. You feel that this *cannot* be a 1½ litre, it's beyond credibility. At one point, 4,000 rpm in third, I thought for a horrid moment that I was experiencing clutch slip — but it was wheelspin! Talk about an excess of power over grip — this must be the ultimate example, apart, perhaps, from the BRM V16. I believe that towards the end of the 159's life the drivers were limited to 8,500–9,000 rpm in the interests of survival: it was exciting enough at 5,500 rpm, so it must have been incredible on full song, particularly with the sensation that power was doubling with every 1,000 rpm. Nerve-shattering, I should think.

The non-synchromesh gearchange works better the higher the revs, simply because at low revs matching engine and gears is a little tricky. At high revs, though, it can only be called fabulous.

With all that power available, the lack of weight on the tail, and the narrow, hard tyres, cornering is purely a matter of how hard you

One of Geoff Goddard's greatest photographs, of the first World Champion, Giuseppe Farina, hustling a 158 on its way to victory in the European Grand Prix at Silverstone in 1950. The 158/159 cars won all 11 races they entered that year.

For a fraction of a second at Balocco, I was Farina or Fangio in the immortal 159 — photographer Mick Walsh skilfully duplicated Goddard's picture of 35 years before! The excess of power over grip makes it easy to balance the car on the throttle.

tramp on the accelerator pedal. The steering is superbly responsive, and you can balance the 159 through a corner with the greatest of ease. I must admit the 159 was a bit of a handful through Balocco's twisty infield — the car's so long that you almost have to take two bites at a corner! — but on the fast open bends of the outer circuit (one is called after the Curvone at Monza, the other after the first Lesmo bend) it comes into its own. You can sweep through, balancing grip against throttle, in one great, glorious, old-fashioned drift. For a fraction of a second I *was* Fangio or Farina at Monza.

And all the time there's that uncanny howl from the engine. Yet another lasting impression was blasting up the main straight, using full throttle in each of the gears, and just listening to the rise and rise of the exhaust note.

There's only time left now for a couple more laps, and I notice other things. Like how far you are from the wheel compared to other contemporary machines: was this because Farina liked it that way, started the long-arm driving position? Or did he adopt it when he drove the 158? I haven't mentioned the brakes, either, but then I haven't used them in anger, and as far as I

can tell they work beautifully. And how predictable the handling is — it's only when you break traction at the back that it becomes even slightly twitchy. And the wheelspin seems to be almost as much a product of axle tramp — at 4,000 rpm, remember — as of excess power. And I remember one of the mechanics telling me that he rated Jean-Pierre Wimille and Fangio as equally great, but that Farina only rated one of those most telling shrugs that mean so much, and that Fangio always seemed to be using one gear higher than anyone else — he was that much faster.

The track test finished when I ran

out of fuel, would you believe! I had to push the 159 back to the workshops, but you've never seen such a smile on my face as I rolled it to a stop. Even Bruno and Antonio burst out laughing when they heard what happened. An inglorious end to a far too brief half hour aboard one of the greatest machines ever.

The 158 had been born almost in a fit of pique. The return of the Germans in the mid-'thirties had seen the classic Alfas, the P3s, humbled in a very big way, only the great Tazio Nuvolari managing to challenge the silver hordes before he, too, changed allegiances. With their massive government backing, the Germans were unbeatable — Alfa couldn't find the cash to take them on at their own game. There was an alternative game, though, in which the Germans weren't taking part: *voiturette* racing, for cars with engine capacities up to $1\frac{1}{2}$ litres supercharged. It was the preserve of Maserati and ERA, and the budgets were much smaller.

Enzo Ferrari, then head of the Alfa racing effort, asked for, and was given, a new car to campaign from 1938 onwards — the 158. The designer was Gioachino Colombo, working in the Ferrari plant at Modena where the first four cars were assembled. Then Alfa started its own racing team, Alfa Corse, with Enzo Ferrari as manager, and in 1939 the company opened its racing department in Milan.

Colombo's design was an all-time classic. From its basics — 1.5 litres, eight cylinders — came the car's name. There were two four-cylinder head-cum-block units, bolted in line together and to the two-piece cast Elektron crankcase: steel liners, screwed into the heads, bridged the joint. There were gear-driven twin overhead camshafts operating two valves per cylinder in a hemispherical head, with a centrally mounted spark plug. The crankshaft, machined from a solid billet, ran in nine main bearings. A slender shaft from the camshaft gear train drove a Roots supercharger on the nearside of the engine. When

first tested on the bench at Modena it gave 180 bhp at 6,500 rpm, but by the time of its first race this had been increased to 195 bhp at 7,000 rpm.

The clutch was in unit with the engine, connected to the four-speed and reverse transaxle by a one-piece propshaft. The chassis consisted basically of two oval tubes, 4.8 in deep and 1.4 in wide, running fore and aft. Four cross-members, the engine and the transaxle joined the two main tubes together to give a rigid structure. Suspension at the front was by trailing arms and transverse leaf springs, and at the rear by swing axles and transverse leafs again. Brakes were massive drum affairs, 15 in diameter at the front and 14 in at the back.

The first appearance of the 158 was at the Coppa Ciano at Livorno in July 1938. The slim cars, with their abbreviated tails and tall, slender grilles, walked away with the race, Emilio Villoresi (brother of Luigi) finishing first and Clemente Biondetti second. It wasn't long before these pretty machines were dubbed 'Alfetta' (little Alfa) by the *tifosi* . . .

Modifications came pretty thick and fast in the first couple of years of the 158's life. One of the most significant was the adoption of needle roller big end bearings, so revs were no longer a problem, and an alteration to the bolt pattern which held blocks to crankcase, and bearing caps to crankcase, which prevented major cracks appearing. By the end of 1939 power was up to 225 bhp at 7,500 rpm.

Mind you, the year started badly. At the Tripoli GP, the Italians' showcase race, the *verdammt* Germans showed up with the V8 Mercedes-Benz W165s and won the only race these cars ever took part in. Alfa's problem was simple: overheating. Three of the four cars finished their races in the pits in clouds of steam, and only Villoresi finished behind the Mercs, simply by keeping his revs down. Alfa immediately modified the cooling system, and it never gave trouble again, though in cold races it was

necessary to blank off part of the grille, giving another characteristic Alfetta look to the nose. That year, 1939, the 158s cleaned up the Coppa Ciano (giving Nino Farina his first win in the model), the Coppa Acerbo and the Prix de Berne (Farina again), while the cool Doctor of Law finished a splendid sixth in the Swiss GP against the might of Mercedes-Benz and Auto Union. They only raced once in 1940, not really surprisingly, at Tripoli: again, not surprisingly, the Alfettas romped home first, second and third — at a new record pace.

Believe it or not, Alfa continued working on the 158s in the early years of the war, with seven more cars laid up in 1942, including a 158D with a de Dion rear axle. When the Germans took control in 1943, the 158s plus spares were hidden away at Monza, safe from bombs and looters.

Alfa entered the post-war years in a position of considerable strength. The Germans, even had they had the money, time or political inclination, weren't allowed to race, which removed any possible major opposition to the Alfettas. All that was left was a clutch of ERAs, Talbot-Lagos and assorted Maseratis. Alfa, on the other hand, had a full set of ready-to-race machines. The Ferraris, BRMs and other potential rivals were but a gleam in their respective designers' eyes when a pair of 158s lined up for the St Cloud GP in Paris in June 1946. Both Farina and Wimille retired after one of the Alfetta's rare lapses (seized clutch shaft splines were the cause).

There were four Alfettas entered for the GP des Nations at Geneva the following month, of which two featured two-stage supercharging. This raised the power yet again, to 254 bhp at 7,500 rpm, and Farina and Varzi finished first and seventh with these 158/46Bs. This became standard wear for the rest of the season, which consisted of two races, the Turin and Milan GPs: Varzi, the dour, drug-addicted Italian, won the former and the aristocratic, pipe-smoking Count

Trossi the latter. Wimille didn't take part in the Milan race, apparently miffed at being ordered to let Varzi win at Turin, while a relative newcomer to the team, Alfa test driver Alfredo Sanesi, finished third.

In 1947 there was a new GP formula — 1½ litres blown, 4½ litres unblown. Alfa entered four races — the Swiss, Belgian, Bari and Italian GPs — and won them all, Wimille taking the first two, Varzi the Bari, and Trossi the Italian, without any real opposition. For this season the engines developed 275 bhp, but in the wings was the 158/47, with a bigger low-pressure blower boosting power up to 310 bhp, still at 7,500

rpm. But it wasn't needed . . .

The Alfettas were entered in only four GPs in 1948, the Swiss, French, Italian and Monza events. The first was tragic for, though Trossi won with Wimille second, the veteran Varzi was killed in practice in the pouring rain. Wimille proved his mettle by taking the other three races — had there been a World Championship that year, he would have won it.

Alfa withdrew from racing in 1949. There were a number of reasons: effort was being concentrated on getting the 1900 road car into production; government funds were curtailed; and, in short succession, Alfa lost three drivers — Varzi

at Berne, Wimille in a piffling little race in South America in a Gordini, and Count Trossi from cancer. Work continued on the 158/47, however, and power was increased yet again to 350 bhp — but at 8,600 rpm...

Whatever the reasons for the sabbatical in 1949, Alfa were back with a vengeance in 1950. What's more, there actually seemed to be some opposition. Ferraris were getting faster with every race, and the threat from BRM seemed at the time quite strong. Maserati, the perpetual second-stringers, could not be ignored either. Alfa's driver line-up comprised the famous 'Three Fs': Dr Giuseppe Farina, 44 years old,

Left *Instrumentation includes a massive rev counter (I was limited to 5,500 rpm), another large dial containing water temperature, oil temperature and oil pressure gauges, and a small fuel pressure gauge between them. A St Christopher badge is partially obscured by the wheel's bottom left spoke.*

Above right *Being allowed to drive one of the 158/159s from the Alfa Romeo Museum was the greatest honour of my track testing career; apart from 1961 World Champion Phil Hill, I am the only non-works driver to have driven it.*

cool to the point of being cold, un-communicative, and proud; Juan Manuel Fangio, the bow-legged, squeaky-voiced, 38-year-old Argentinian whose genius was just coming to a peak, and whose presence in the team annoyed Farina and many Italians; and the veteran Luigi Fagioli. This was the year of the perfect score: 11 races and 11 wins.

Not that they had it all their own way. At Monaco Farina skidded on spray blown over the wall at the Tabac corner and the ensuing mêlée took out nine of the 19 cars entered. Fangio showed his genius by threading his way through the drama, and carried on to win, although Alberto Ascari's second place showed the looming threat of Ferrari. At the GP des Nations at Geneva, Ascari in a 4.1 litre Ferrari ran second to Fangio for most of the race, too. Towards the end of the year further changes were made, power increased yet again, and the name was changed to 159 in time for the final race, the Italian GP at Monza. Ascari's Ferrari actually led for a couple of laps, Fangio's gearbox failed, Farina won and became the World Champion.

By 1951 the 158/159 basic design was 13 years old. It was now giving 420 bhp at 9,600 rpm, a vast increase in both power and revs (the superchargers alone were absorbing some 135 bhp, and consumption of the 98 per cent methanol fuel was less than 2 mpg, leading to fuel tanks being slotted in wherever there was room). The extra weight did nothing for the handling either, although changing to a de Dion rear axle helped. No result was a foregone conclusion . . .

The first defeat came at Silverstone, at the International Trophy meeting. Fangio won Heat 1, Farina Heat 2, but the heavens opened for the final, and Reg Parnell in the Thin Wall Special, basically a $4\frac{1}{2}$ litre Ferrari, won when the race was stopped after six laps.

The next three GPs, the Swiss, Belgian and French, saw Alfa win — but in each case a Ferrari was second. Then came the amazing British GP at Silverstone on July 14. Froilan Gonzalez, the 'Pampas Bull' and friend of Fangio, took his $4\frac{1}{2}$ litre Ferrari by the scruff of its neck and in a display of controlled fury brought it home first. It was the first major defeat of the Alfetta since 1939. It was followed up by yet another defeat, at the Nürburgring, and a third in the Italian GP. So to the final race of the year, the Spanish GP, held on the Pedralbes Circuit in Barcelona.

Either Fangio or Ascari could win the championship. The critical factor was the long straight, and Ferrari made the wrong choice of tyres: Ascari threw treads all over the place, and threw away the race. Fangio won, took the World Championship, and the last race for an Alfetta. Alfa withdrew from GP racing, on a very high note. What better time?

I will perhaps drive more powerful machines. I will, perhaps, drive more exciting machines. But I doubt whether I will ever drive anything to match the 159. You can feel the history pouring out of it. I regard it as a most signal honour that I was allowed to drive it, and my thanks to Franco Perugia, Bruno and Antonio, Neil Verveij, Ray Corsi and all the others at Alfa Romeo who made it happen.

1952
FERRARI 500/625

It's a little strange strolling over to drive a blue-painted Ferrari. Somehow, it is indelibly stamped on your mind that a Ferrari should be red, with that emotive yellow and black Scuderia Ferrari badge on its flanks. Anthony Mayman's 500/625 is finished in pale blue, though, because it was raced in Grands Prix and non-championship events by Frenchman Louis Rosier between 1952 and 1954.

Apart from its colour, this car's significance is in its being a rare example of the least complicated — and among the most successful — of all GP Ferraris. The *Tipo 500s* utterly dominated that odd little period of GP racing, the two years run to unblown 2 litre Formula 2 rules in 1952–3, by winning every race they entered apart from two non-championship events in 1952 and the final GP of 1953. Nothing else could touch these straightforward four-cylinder machines, and Alberto Ascari took two consecutive World Championship titles by huge margins.

Running GPs to F2 rules came about because the previous 1½ litre supercharged/4½ litre unblown category died on its feet when Alfa Romeo retired its fabulously successful 159 at the end of 1951, leaving the Ferraris and the desperately

unreliable BRM V16s as the only serious F1 contenders for 1952. After Ferrari won the early-season F1 event unchallenged at Turin, the governing body decided that the only way to run that year's World Championship season was to open it up to F2 cars. Ferrari were wonderfully placed to make a killing . . .

The Maranello arsenal included an unblown 2 litre four-cylinder F2 car in the *Tipo 500*, the car taking its nomenclature, in usual Ferrari practice, from the capacity of a single cylinder. Designed by Aurelio Lampredi, this engine marked a sea-change from Ferrari's previous commitment to Gioachino Colombo's high-revving V12 units, the change of philosophy having been initiated when Enzo Ferrari promoted Lampredi as Colombo's successor in late 1950.

There were many advantages in Lampredi's search for simplicity: the fewer moving parts of a four-cylinder would reduce frictional power losses; it would be more reliable, as well as cheaper to manufacture; it would be substantially lighter, weighing just 348 lb to the V12's 400 lb; and its mid-range torque would suit the medium-speed road circuits then in use.

The new engine Lampredi developed early in 1951 was based

around a light alloy block, employed a five-bearing crankshaft, used two spark plugs per cylinder and carried twin overhead camshafts gear-driven from the crankshaft nose. Tested initially with two Weber carburettors, the 1,985 cc unit gave early bench power figures of 170 bhp at 7,200 rpm, a good 15 bhp more than a 2 litre V12. Fitment of four Webers in time for the 1952 season squeezed a little more power.

This engine sat in a conventional frame comprising two oval-section longitudinal beams braced by tubular cross members, this chassis being surmounted by a welded upper structure supporting attractive beaten aluminium bodywork. Unequal length wishbones and a transverse leaf spring formed the front suspension, while a de Dion tube, parallel radius rods and a transverse leaf spring took care of the rear. There was a four-speed crash gearbox mounted at the rear in unit with a ZF final drive, and hydraulic brakes with finned alloy drums provided the stopping power.

Weak though the competition was, Ferrari was absurdly dominant in the 1952 World Championship. Ascari won all six races he started, while Piero Taruffi won the Bremgarten event that Ascari miss-

The car was ideally geared for the Silverstone Club circuit, and I was able to run in third and top thanks to its torquey motor. The brakes are so good that I reckon I could outbrake almost anything from the same era.

The Ferrari 500 was incredibly dominant in 1952 and 1953, giving Alberto Ascari two World Championships during these 'Formula 2' years, Here he is winning at Silverstone in 1953.

ed. Not only was Ascari the runaway champion, but team-mates Giuseppe Farina and Taruffi followed him in the points standings, and Ferrari-mounted Swiss privateer Rudi Fischer ended the season in fourth slot.

Much the same happened in 1953, the Ferrari 500s, now producing around 180 bhp with minor exhaust and carburation changes, winning seven of the eight World Championship GPs. Ascari could manage 'only' five victories, Farina and Mike Hawthorn taking one apiece. The opposition was not *quite* so meagre that season, for Juan Manuel Fangio won the final GP for Maserati at Monza and took three

second places. This was Ferrari's only GP defeat in the two seasons of the *Tipo 500*'s reign, and a pretty fortuitous one at that — Fangio nipped through a mêlée resulting from Ascari spinning out of the lead at the final corner . . .

Ferrari built six (or possibly seven) 500s for works use, and another five for customers. The Rosier car, chassis number 0186, which I drove is one of the latter, and the Frenchman ran it with very modest success in both of the F2 GP seasons. By reputation one of motor racing's bridesmaids, Rosier's best World Championship result was only seventh place in the 1953 Dutch GP, but he often picked up prize

money in minor league races. A win in the F2 heat of the *Formule Libre* Albi GP and at the Circuit of Cadours in 1952, along with victory in Les Sables d'Olonne GP in 1953, helped pay for his racing.

In 1954, the GP formula changed from the 2 litre unblown capacity limit to 2.5 litres, and Ferrari's first entry into the fray was little more than a re-engined 500, called the 625. In effect, a 2.5 litre version of Lampredi's all-conquering 'four' was fitted into a slightly revised 500 chassis. The most striking change here was direct mounting of the front leaf spring to the bottom wishbone, whereas before it had been linked to the top wishbone. A

Left *The Ferrari 500/625 is a very good, easy car to drive fast, but its lack of top end power compared with, say, a Maserati 250F would make it most at home around a twisty track.*

Below left *A large transmission tunnel divides the cockpit, with clutch to the left and brake and throttle to the right. The low seat, left-hand gearchange and nicely placed steering wheel combine to provide an excellent driving position.*

changed carburettor mounting was another minor alteration, so, as you can see, the car was very much a stop-gap until the *Tipo 555* made its bow.

Ecurie Rosier ended up with a 625 engine in the 500, hence the 500/625 tag. It was a barren year, although there was some success early on, with Maurice Trintignant driving. He was fourth in the Argentine GP and won the Buenos Aires City GP two weeks later at the same venue; and was then promptly signed up by the works team, much to Rosier's chagrin . . .

Rosier himself then took over the driving, but lacked the *élan* of the Monegasque and eventually sold the Ferrari, replacing it with a Maserati 250F. The Frenchman's best performances that year in the Ferrari were sixth in the International Trophy and at the Pau GP, and seventh in the German GP at the Nürburgring. In all, Rosier competed in around 40 events over three busy seasons, and kept the car for occasional outings until the end of 1957.

The car then passed into the private collection of Parisian dentist Philippe Renault before being acquired by Mayman in 1981. Hall & Fowler set to work on the 500/625, and it had its first post-restoration run in 1987 at Silverstone, which is where I had my opportunity to drive

Right *On the grid for my race in Anthony Mayman's 500/625 at Silverstone. I did not get far, since the bevel gear broke just as I left the line...*

Below *One of Ferrari's few four-cylinder engines, designed by Aurelio Lampredi, powers the 500; this car takes its 500/625 designation because Louis Rosier fitted the larger 2.5 litre '625' engine allowed by new Grand Prix rules in 1954.*

it in a race.

The first impression on sitting in the Ferrari is just how comfortable it is. You seem to sit quite low in a great big armchair, with nicely positioned pedals and steering wheel. The clutch is to the left of the hefty transmission tunnel, with throttle and brakes to the right. Unusually, the gear-lever is on the left-hand side, whereas I normally expect to see it on the right on an Italian car. The gearchange of the four-speed 'box is a conventional H-gate.

Moving off down Silverstone's wide pit area is a bit disconcerting at first, as the clutch literally engages in the last 25 thou of pedal travel: you sit there, bringing back the clutch pedal and thinking you've forgotten to select first gear! But as soon as it starts to bite, there's no problem getting the car rolling.

The engine, of course, is a fairly big 'four', so it's not exactly the smoothest unit in the world, but it possesses amazing torque. Power is produced from as low down as 2,500 rpm, and the engine pulls beautifully all the way to the 6,000 rpm red line. There's no point in running that many revs in the intermediates, though, so I set myself a 5,500 rpm change-up mark and let it run to 6,000 rpm in top only. That's equivalent to around 134 mph.

So what's it like around Silverstone? Probably the best description is fabulous fun. It feels near ideally geared for this track, and I was able to run in third and top only, thanks to that torquey motor. Exiting Woodcote, the fast blind-apex right-hander before the pits, I keep the car in third all the way down to the Copse, chuck the car in, put the power down and the thing starts to drift beautifully, pulling about 4,500/5,000 rpm. There is a slight problem in that the car is picking up its inside rear wheel, and I reckon that's losing about two or three seconds a lap around here. I thought the limited slip diff was worn out, but Hall & Fowler have checked that, and it seems fine. They reckon the car needs stiffening up at the front, because once the wheel lifts, the pawl-type diff can't counter it.

Just after the exit, I change up to top: the Ferrari has a lovely gearchange, by the way. Maggotts, the left-hand sweep, is taken flat in top, and you can enter the hairpin at Becketts very cleanly in this car. That contrasts with a Maserati 250F, which is difficult to get back to the left-hand side of the circuit to set up for braking for the corner.

You hit the brakes at around 150–200 yards in the Ferrari — and they're absolutely terrific. I reckon I can outbrake anything in this car, they're that good. Because of that inside wheel problem, I tend to dive into Becketts very late and try and 'straightline' the exit. The car actually feels very good around slower corners compared with a 250F — it can't compare around quick ones, simply because the Maserati is unparalleled in that area — and the handling balance is really wonderful.

The car is very forgiving, and again, is much easier to drive than the 250F. The 500/625 has a reputation for being tricky, but I find it totally stable. You can steer it through the corner on the throttle and just play with it. If you want understeer, you can have it. If you want oversteer, just tramp on the throttle. You can do what you want with it, but the basic characteristic, I suppose, is neutral.

Becketts is taken in third, and you are back in fourth by a marshals' post which is halfway between the new entry bridge along the club straight and the exit to the corner. A quick look at the gauges — and there is certainly nothing amiss here, as the water temperature is steady at 80° C and the oil pressure at 6 kg/sq cm — and then it's time to brake for Woodcote. To reiterate, those anchors are super. I'm braking it after the 200 m board, which is about as late as I've ever managed in a car of this era. John Venables-Llewellyn came flying past me down the straight on one lap in Mayman's 250F, and I damn nearly ran into him in the corner! Drift it through Woodcote, and then you're on to another lap.

Overall, it's a very good, easy car to drive fast. At Silverstone, you lose on top end power compared to a 250F, but that isn't surprising when you consider the age of the car. I think the Ferrari, however, would be very competitive round a twistier track. I was doing 1 min 8 sec laps in practice (a shade over 85 mph average speed) and I think, with the limited slip working properly, the 500/625 could be going round in about 1 min 5 sec.

I would have liked to tell you how it went in the race, but . . . the bevel gear broke just as I left the line, which was a great pity. Maybe another chance will come one day . . .

There are more exciting looking and sounding racing Ferraris, but none has ever matched the grip which the 500s exerted on GP racing in those two F2 years. Think of Ascari — one of the all-time greats, to be bracketed with Nuvolari, Fangio, Moss, Clark and Stewart — and you always recall his total supremacy in the Ferrari 500 . . .

1954

BRM V16

I couldn't believe my ears when Tom Wheatcroft stood up at the ERA Anniversary Dinner in 1985 and promised me a drive in the BRM V16. It was a lifelong ambition which I had never thought would come true, and all to take place not 10 days after driving the sensational Alfa Romeo 159! What followed was a fascinating comparison of the two cars and the very different approaches by Alfa Romeo and BRM to competing in Grands Prix.

The most crucial difference, of course, is that the Alfa was incredibly successful, and the BRM was a total disaster. The headline to my original track test in *Classic and Sportscar* beautifully summed up the BRM in two words: 'The Howler'. The two dictionary definitions — 'maker of loud cry' and 'glaring blunder' — are equally appropriate.

To the British public, given its first sight of the new BRM in the national newspapers and motoring press after a public launch on 15 December 1949, it seemed the most stunning racing car ever produced, but the reality was a very different story. Stirling Moss was succinct: 'The BRM was, without doubt, the worst car I have ever driven in my life.'

Stirling formed that impression after being heavily involved in testing, along with Ken Richardson: 'When I was asked by Mays to test the car at Monza I felt just the same as everybody else — that this was a fantastic project. Here at last was a beautifully-built car which would challenge the Alfas and Ferraris. I went down to Monza full of optimism, but in the week that I was there I don't suppose I did more than 100 miles. The design of the engine was fantastic, the gearbox was beautiful and the brakes were really stunning, but the roadholding was virtually non-existent, the steering was dreadfully sloppy and reliability was appalling.'

As part of its publicity build-up, the V16 was given a demonstration run at the European Grand Prix meeting at Silverstone in May 1950 before being entered, at the same circuit, for its first race, the *Daily Express* Trophy in August. Both cars broke a cylinder liner during last-minute testing at Folkingham (they should have been practising at Silverstone that day), but BRM managed to get one car, to be driven by Raymond Sommer, to the start after persuasion from the organizers — the BRM would start from the back of the grid, having not run in official practice. What happened next is best described by quoting

Raymond Baxter's live broadcast on BBC Radio.

'The start to this race is one of the most sensational things I've ever seen. The BRM came out long after all the other cars were on the grid, it came round the circuit with Raymond Sommer at the wheel, the engines started up, they whipped up their crescendo of revs, down swept the flag, and away went every car except the BRM. The BRM jumped about two inches, and stayed where it was.' A half-shaft had broken when Sommer let in the clutch.

The BRM saga reaches back to the end of the Second World War, when Raymond Mays, father of the ERA, sent a circular to leading industry bosses requesting support for a new British GP contender. Oliver Lucas of Joseph Lucas and Alfred Owen of Rubery Owen promised substantial support, and within 12 months more than 100 companies had pledged sponsorship, components and development facilities. The British Motor Racing Research Trust was set up, and a company called Automobile Developments — later renamed British Racing Motors — began design work.

The heart of the car was Peter Berthon's glorious supercharged 1.5 litre V16 engine. Developing more horsepower per litre than any or-

thodox engine so far built, it certainly promised to be a world-beater as it
took shape. Its tiny cylinders —
smaller than those of an Austin
Seven — measured 49.53 mm bore
by 47.8 mm stroke, giving a capacity
of 1,496 cc. Its two alloy blocks of
cylinders were set at 135°, and each
bank had an alloy head carrying
twin overhead camshafts operating
two valves per cylinder. There was a
superb   two-piece   10-bearing
crankshaft, and cast iron wet
cylinder liners. Supercharging was
by a Rolls-Royce centrifugal blower
revolving at four times engine speed.

Being a slightly 'over-square'
design, very high crankshaft speeds
could be sustained without piston
velocity becoming excessive, so the
engine could rev to an astonishing
12,000 rpm. Power output was put
at 430 bhp at 11,000 rpm, but
towards the end of the V16's life
Mays quoted 600 bhp at 12,000 rpm.
What the figures don't indicate is
the manner with which this power is
delivered . . .

The engine was mounted so that it
sloped downwards to the rear and
was also offset from the car's

*I have never driven a car before in
which straights are even more exciting
than corners! The BRM V16's power
is phenomenal at 7,000 rpm, and
thereafter seems to double with every
thousand rpm increase.*

longitudinal axis. It nestled within a
tubular frame comprising two main
members on each side and four
cross-members. Front suspension
followed ERA practice with trailing
arms and Lockheed pneumatic
struts, while rear suspension harked
back to the Mercedes-Benz W154
with a de Dion axle, single radius
rods and pneumatic struts. Braking
was initially by three-shoe hydraulic
Girling drum brakes, but Girling
discs were later substituted.

After the Silverstone débâcle,
there came a brief ray of light when
Reg Parnell won two short races at
Goodwood in September, but no
more victories would come for two
years. In 1951, Parnell and Peter
Walker finished fifth and seventh in
the British GP at Silverstone, but
otherwise the season was a grim one
as entries for the Swiss and French
GPs were scratched, and the cars

were withdrawn with gearbox trouble only three hours before the start
of the Italian GP.

With World Championship GPs
being run to 2 litre Formula 2 rules
in 1952, BRM's search for success
had to be confined to *Formule Libre*
races, and even then the victories
were thin on the ground. Parnell
achieved a minor win at Turnberry
in August, and Froilan Gonzalez,
Parnell and Ken Wharton took the
first three places against meagre opposition in the Goodwood Trophy
race in September, but that was it.

After Alfred Owen's purchase of
BRM's assets and liabilities in October 1952, the next season
developed into a struggle between
the BRMs and Tony Vandervell's
Thin Wall Special in British *Formule Libre* events. Things at last
began to happen, with victories for
Wharton at Goodwood, Snetterton,
Charterhall and Castle Combe, but
the finest performance of the year
— and of the entire V16 tale — came
in the non-championship Albi GP in
France.

Here, for once, BRM faced international   opposition,   including

several 4.5 litre Ferraris, one of them a works car driven by Alberto Ascari. BRMs driven by Fangio and Wharton took the top two places in their heat, while Gonzalez was fifth after stopping for a wheel-change. In the final the BRM trio initially dominated until Dunlop's rubber began to suffer. Gonzalez' car twice threw a tread, but still he finished second to Louis Rosier's Ferrari. Fangio lost a tread too, the momentary loss of control causing him to brush a bank at 190 mph! The car was withdrawn with a damaged hub. Wharton's race ended when he spun at 130 mph, hit a bank and turned over, although fortunately he wasn't badly injured. For once the BRMs looked terrific in good company, and performed reliably — the trouble was that their tyres couldn't handle 580 bhp through a full race.

The V16 assumed its Mk2 guise for 1954, two new cars being built. These had a shorter wheelbase, smaller wheels and new tubular spaceframe chassis to make them lighter and more agile, thus rendering them more suitable for *Formule*

Although the V16 is vicious to handle, its brakes, Girling discs which require a good stamp on the pedal in this Mk2, are quite superb, and even better than those of the Alfa 159.

Libre 'sprint' events. The 1954 and '55 seasons weren't bad ones in motor racing's second division, with wins for Wharton, Ron Flockhart and Peter Collins, but BRM, with its sights by now set on GP racing again, was devoting all its energy to developing the 2.5 litre P25.

The V16 was one of motor racing's great 'might-have-beens'. It came good eventually, but years too late. But, for all its failures, it is undeniably charismatic, and for me this track test still rates as one of my greatest ever driving experiences.

Going back to my Alfa 159 comparison, the BRM is definitely not as good looking, and somewhat smaller in Mk2 form. Settling myself into the cockpit, I also found it less comfortable, particularly around my left leg and ankle. But you do sit lower down, owing to the propshaft being offset to the left.

In front of you is the unique strip

segment rev counter, sited centrally, accompanied by only two other instruments, the water temperature gauge on the left and the oil pressure gauge to the right. The rev counter doesn't even start its calibrations until 4,000 rpm, then sweeps on up to 12,000! The appearance is really quite spartan, with fewer instruments than the Alfa 159. A. F. Rivers-Fletcher remembers discussing the cockpit design with Berthon and deciding that a rev counter was the only really necessary instrument. From what I'd been led to expect, I wondered whether I was going to have a chance to look at the rev counter in any case!

The driving position allows you to sit with arms reasonably stretched, which is in contrast to the car as it had first appeared. Among Stirling's many complaints about the first car was the driving position, sitting right on top of the wheel. The gear lever sits down to the right of the driver, with first gear of the five-speed 'box in dog-leg position, to the left and back.

Hall & Fowler, who look after the car for the Donington Collection,

Left *The real difficulty in handling the V16 arises when the blower comes in. You really have to be awake when this happens since the power arrives with a furious bang, rather like a massive turbo gone berserk.*

Right *Froilan Gonzalez and Juan Manuel Fangio were the two most spectacular V16 drivers. This is Gonzalez winning the Woodcote Cup race at Goodwood in a Mk1 in 1952.*

had already started the engine once when I arrived to drive the car, so it only took a short push for the machine to burst into life. It didn't seem very noisy, running happily at 3,000–4,000 rpm, but after about 30 seconds I realized my ears were hurting!

At first it seemed a totally undramatic car, and very docile. Even the clutch was soft. And it drove just like a road car, all very easy through corners and with a beautifully predictable little engine — not what I had expected at all, but then I was still just warming the engine with a couple of laps at 6,000 rpm.

I could hardly wait to see if everything they say about this car is true. A little more pressure with the right foot . . .

It *is* true! The power was phenomenal at 7,000 rpm, and thereafter it seemed to double with every thousand rpm increase, right up to 10,000 rpm. And there really was no need to take the engine any higher than that . . . The noise, too, was quite staggering. I have never seen everyone at the back of the pits with their hands over their ears before!

The car is basically very stable and easy to drive until you stamp on the

Tom Wheatcroft's V16 is one of two Mk2s — both of which survive — built for the 1954 Formule Libre season. These had a shorter wheelbase, smaller wheels and a lighter spaceframe chassis.

power. Then you've got to be very, very careful. The power delivery is vicious, rather like a massive turbo gone berserk.

From 8,000 rpm there is far more power than you can transmit to the track in a corner. It becomes very much a case of lining up the car gently, getting it as straight as you can, and then really putting the power down at the beginning of the straights. The straights don't last very long . . .

The real difficulty in handling the car happens when the blower comes in. If you had good enough brakes and tyres, and the right kind of circuit, you could probably drive it above 8,000 rpm with the blower on

all the time. But when you're going through a corner at around 6,000 rpm, you've really got to be awake when the power arrives. It comes in with such a bang. It's absolutely fantastic, like somebody giving you an extra 200 horsepower in half a second flat. The effect is just the same in fifth gear as it is in second — prod the throttle in fifth half way down the straight and it just clouts you in the back. If you're not careful you could end up facing backwards instead of forwards!

My only real criticism of the car is that the gear lever travel is far too long. Not a heavy change, just too much of a stretch. On the other hand, the steering is delightful,

which came as something of a surprise in view of Stirling's harsh comments about the Mk1's steering slop. In fact, the steering linkage had been greatly improved by the time the Mk2 arrived.

The brakes, unfortunately, seemed to work only on the front wheels, which provided one or two interesting moments. I was told that they would be looked at before I would be doing my demonstration run at the VSCC Donington meeting. Quite a lot of pressure was needed on the pedal, and that is quite normal for an early disc-braked car.

Five V16s were built, three of them original Mk1 GP versions, the

Above *The Mk2 has a comfortable driving position which allows you to stretch your arms. Instruments are confined to that unusual strip segment rev counter and a pair of small gauges for water temperature and oil pressure.*

Left *A mechanic's nightmare: the incredible 1,496 cc V16 fills the front of the BRM. It can rev to an astonishing 12,000 rpm, at which point 600 bhp was produced by the end of development in 1955.*

other two 'sprint' Mk2 models. Two of the GP cars were written off, leaving three V16s which survive to this day. The National Motor Museum at Beaulieu owns the remaining Mk1 and gives it occasional airings, while Nick Mason has the other Mk2, which has been restored by Tony Merrick in recent years.

Tom Wheatcroft's car is the other Mk2, bearing chassis number 2/01 and engine number 20/2. Its racing history is documented, the record including three wins. It was built for the 1954 British *Formule Libre* season, and the Chichester Cup at Goodwood in April was the first victory in Wharton's hands. Two more wins for Flockhart followed at Snetterton and Ibsley, and the season finished with two other second places and three third places.

The car continued to race in national events for part of 1955 before being pensioned off by BRM. It remained in the Owen Organisation's hands — coming out only for rare demonstration runs — until 1981,

when Tom Wheatcroft bought it at the famous Christie's BRM auction. It now lives in Tom's fabulous Donington Collection, far and away the world's largest collection of GP and single-seater racing cars with more than 100 exhibits.

Apart from Moss, no British V16 drivers are alive now, but Tim Parnell remembers his father, Reg, talking about racing the V16: 'My father was the first British driver to be invited to drive for a continental team since Dick Seaman had driven for Mercedes. Since he drove both the BRM V16 and the Alfa 159, I suppose he was very well placed to compare them. He used to complain most about the brakes on cars: if you drove too hard in a race, you soon lost the brakes on most cars, but I remember him saying that the V16's brakes were the best he'd ever known. I remember that the car carried 75 gallons of fuel in Mk1 form, that it did under 3 mpg, and that the back wheels used to sit at an amazing angle and open out as the fuel lightened!'

A. F. Rivers-Fletcher, who spent many years working at Bourne, also has fascinating memories: 'Looking back on it, of course, it would have been much wiser to build a simpler car, but wasn't that noise absolutely glorious? I think that only Fangio used the car's full potential, and he simply loved it. I remember he drove it in the wet at Silverstone. We expected him to tool round very slowly to get the feel of the thing. No fear! He was flat-out right from the start, with the car pointing in all sorts of directions in the corners. When he came back, smiling and happy, we asked why he went so fast straight away. I remember him saying that it was the only way he could find out what happened!'

So many people have talked just like Tim Parnell and Rivers-Fletcher about the magic of the V16, and now I know just why they rave about it. I have never driven a car before in which straights are even more exciting than corners, and in that respect the V16 must be unique!

1954

MASERATI 250F

'That fantastic drive of Juan Manuel Fangio's at Nürburgring will be remembered for all time. Set the seemingly impossible task of getting back a minute in 11 laps (154 miles) from the Ferraris of Mike Hawthorn and Peter Collins, the old master did so, although his rivals were lapping as fast as the German circuit has ever been circulated. Time after time the record fell: as an exhibition of virtuoso driving it was unparalleled — and there was nothing the two British drivers could do about it . . . There has never been a man like this, whose ability far surpasses any of his rivals, enabling him to win the race of his life on the most difficult of circuits . . .'
Autosport, 9 August 1957.

Occasionally, very, very occasionally, a race develops into something quite extraordinary. At the German Grand Prix in 1957 a combination of man, machine and circuit came together to write a piece of motor racing history. The man, of course, was Fangio; the circuit, the Nürburgring; the car, the Maserati 250F.

I was at school at the time, so had to content myself with reading about it. I would love to have seen Fangio in his heyday, but it was not to be. The nearest I've come to it is watching that old film *A Tribute to Fangio*, where they strapped a camera on the back of a 250F for a few laps around the Modena track. To the enthusiast it is a splendid film, but let me make one point — only 250F drivers will appreciate quite how hard he was trying!

Obviously I was not to know that, years later, I too would be racing 250Fs, and, what's more, thoroughly enjoying myself in the process. Equally obviously, what can be said is that Fangio's exploits in 250Fs had a lasting effect on me, and this is a major reason why the model is one of my firm favourites.

I'd better say here and now that this isn't going to be a blow-by-blow, bolt-by-bolt, history of the 250F. Even now it is being written, and re-written. Maserati's paperwork was hazy, to put it mildly — ask any 250F historian, such as Cameron Millar, Doug Nye or Denis Jenkinson, if you don't believe me! So I'm going to limit myself to impressions and opinions on the model in general.

The 250F was not the most successful of GP cars, winning only eight World Championship races, four in the hands of Fangio in 1957. It was not the most powerful, either, or necessarily the fastest. Few will quibble with the comment, though, that it was one of the most beautiful racers ever, or that it was over-endowed with that peculiar quality called charisma. It has charisma oozing out of it in nearly as many places as oil did. Idiots could drive it quite quickly, and in the hands of a genius (for which read Fangio) it was unbeatable (well, nearly). Above all, it was, and is, a driver's car, fabulously satisfying. I cannot think of another machine that is more sheer, unadulterated fun than a 250F.

Memories of my times behind the wheel of a 250F come fast and furious. One that sticks for the wrong reasons was driving '2525' (all 250Fs are called by their chassis numbers). It was a fabulous car, with better handling than any other 250F, beautifully balanced. However, it was the first of the offset cars: in order to reduce seat height and frontal area, Giulio Alfieri redesigned the chassis and transmission so that the propshaft ran alongside, rather than beneath, the driver's seat. This had the desired effect, since Stirling Moss used it to win the 1956 Italian GP.

However, the driving position was very strange, to put it mildly, the propshaft running under your left knee, so that your left leg was up in the air, while your right one was down *there*. The result was that I

Above left *That fantastic day at the Nürburgring in 1957 when Fangio and his 250F pulled back a minute on the two Ferraris of Collins and Hawthorn. Here, with three laps to go, he is about to pass Collins, and Hawthorn is only a few lengths ahead.*

Left *The Piccolo goes to opposite lock the moment you show it a corner, power on or off. To go quickly a 250F has to slide, and you can drift most beautifully with total balance.*

Above *One of only two incidents, this one in a race at Oulton Park, which I have experienced with the Piccolo 250F. In both cases I ran out of steering lock when trying to hold a slide.*

Right *The 250F's 2,493 cc six-cylinder engine is one of the strongest there is: the Piccolo has needed one new piston ring and a set of valve springs in 12 years. Power output is around 260 bhp at 8,000 rpm.*

had to change gear using my left hand under my *right* knee. If you're sitting down, just try it. See what I mean? I had to brace myself into this odd position, and then would get paralysing cramp in my left hip half-way through a corner. Horrifying!

But the example that I've driven more than any other is '2534', generally acknowledged to be the last 250F made, and the second true *Piccolo*. In the Maserati scheme of things, it comes after the standard model, the offset cars, the lightweights and the V12. Thus the *Piccolo* is the smallest, lightest, shortest of the model, and has some characteristics all of its own, although at heart it's still a 250F.

The *Piccolo* is amazing. Without a shadow of doubt it is the fastest front-engined racing car in a straight line. Not necessarily round corners, but on top speed it's untouchable. I remember on one occasion at Le Mans Stirling Moss told me that no 250F had ever bettered 155 mph.

Next day, after driving the car in a Le Mans historic race, he admitted it was faster! I was in a D-type for that race, and I reckon I was running at a good 165 mph down the Mulsanne Straight, and Stirling came past me as if I was standing still. To be honest, we don't really know why: it seems to be a fluke engine in a fluke chassis, which is no reflection on engine builder Cyril Embrey or the JCB mechanics.

It's a funny thing, but nowadays the car is several seconds a lap faster than it was when I first started racing it in the early 'seventies. There are a number of possible reasons for this: I'm getting older and better, or more foolish, or — most likely — the track surface and tyres have been 'improved'.

I'm not sure that 'improved' is the right word here. Modern compounds may lower lap times, but Charlie Lucas (another 250F devotee) and I came to the conclusion that the older ones were better — slower, but better. Essentially,

this is because the 250F was designed to slide, and if you increase tyre grip all sorts of strange things happen. Chassis twist, suspension deflection, and so on. With the older tyres you could just glide through corners, whereas the newer ones make life more twitchy.

Some drivers tend to be a little frightened by the 250F because they are not used to a car which is continually sliding. To go quickly in a 250F, the car will slide, *has* to slide — that's the way they were, and that's the way it's gotta be . . .

You can drift (remember the classic drift?) an early 250F most beautifully, with total balance. No car can touch it through a fast corner like the one at the end of the straight at Paul Ricard — a 130 mph corner if ever there was one — or the pre-chicane Woodcote at Silverstone.

On the other hand the 250F doesn't like slow corners, basically because of a rather appalling lack of traction at the back, the *Piccolo* being worse than the others in this respect. Which brings me back to the *Piccolo* once more, and its oddities.

I'm often asked if the *Piccolo* is twitchier than the others. It's *not* twitchy, not in the slightest, it's just that it goes on to opposite lock the moment you *show* it a corner, power on or off. It's the classic case of steering on the throttle, once you've set it up into the corner of course. From then on the tail just hangs out, the degree of tail-out depending on the amount of wellie you're prepared to give it. One of these days I might even try something I've been considering for some time, which is to take it round a right-hand circuit without ever steering to the right!

Which brings me to the vexed question of incidents, of which I've had two in public, one at Oulton Park years ago, the other at the VSCC Hawthorn meeting at Silverstone in 1982. In both I was in complete control throughout the whole episode, and if the wall at Silverstone had been three feet further away I would have got away with it (perhaps the people at Silverstone might like to take note of my suggestion).

More important, if there had been another inch or so of lock I'd have been able to hold it. Unfortunately there wasn't, I hit the steering stops, and just couldn't turn left any more. I don't really consider it a driving error — well, obviously it *was* an error, but not a stupid mistake. Anyone at that Silverstone meeting might remember that I didn't stop, a bad decision in retrospect, since, at the next corner, I discovered that the car wouldn't turn right on account of the wheelbase being somewhat shorter on one side than the other. To be honest, I felt so embarrassed, I'd have *carried* it around rather than abandon it.

The point of all this is that in some 12 or so seasons of racing a 250F, this isn't a bad record, and shows just how inherently controllable and stable the car is.

One other peculiarity of the car must be mentioned under the heading of handling, and that's its behaviour through the chicane at Thruxton. You come in on a tight right-hander, then immediately switch to a left-hander, followed by another right-hander, and once you've gone in it's flat from then on all the way out. Now, in the *Piccolo* that final transition to the right is very difficult, because the chassis is still flexing and steering isn't, so it just distorts and tightens up. The only really adverse effect it has is on the nerves . . .

Talking of steering, you can't call that of the 250F 'fingertip', because it's actually quite heavy, even without the peculiarities of the Thruxton chicane, and fairly direct. Climbing from the Ferrari 246 Dino into the 250F, I used to think the latter was a load of rubbish at first, because it wasn't nearly as sophisticated. But then after a few laps I would prefer the 250F to the Dino, as the physical inputs from the steering are so much higher.

The brakes, for example, are glorious. I reckon the *Piccolo* will out-brake anything else on the circuit. There are one or two tricks to making them work, though: for example, it is critical to match drum to lining. We set up a profile grinder to do just this, but I can't say it was a popular machine since the air around it became heavy with asbestos dust! Another trick we learned was to use a soft lining, so soft that you can pick it off with your finger nail when it's first fitted. The secret is that it cures itself with heat, and in so doing forms itself nicely to the drum, giving all-round contact and a super, progressive feel, not to mention very good stopping ability. If you use a hard lining you can get localized hot spots and terrible vibrations, as well as the necessity for a new drum liner.

Without a doubt one of the nicest things about the 250F is the four-speed gearbox — in fact I'll go further and say it's one of the best in any racing car. What else is there to say? As far as gear ratios go, we kept the same ones in for all British circuits, only putting in higher cogs for Le Mans, Paul Ricard and other fast tracks.

And then, of course, there's that marvellous 2,493 cc straight-six engine, producing around 260 bhp late in its life. It had twin overhead camshafts operating two valves per cylinder, carburation was by three twin-choke Webers (although the factory experimented with fuel injection) and there were twin spark plugs for each cylinder.

It is astonishingly strong (that in the *Piccolo* has had one ring go, and a new set of valve springs, and that's it in an engine with probably more racing miles under its belt than most others). It has simply amazing torque from 4,000 rpm on, so there's really no point in revving it over 7,000 rpm in the gears, although on the straights I take it up to 8,000 rpm, and have seen 8,200 rpm at Silverstone, which is very fast, believe me — you *know* when you've reached it!

On top of that it's beautifully smooth, and of course has one of the most spine-tingling barks of any car. It's untemperamental, too, but starting can be difficult unless you put one hard and soft plug in each cylinder. And it's essential that it is warmed up properly: there are five gallons of oil swilling around between engine and tail-mounted oil tank, so I reckon on at least a 20 min warm-up before even venturing on to the circuit.

To me, the 250F is one of the greatest, a classic among classics. As the old song (nearly) says, lovely to look at, delightful to drive and heaven to hear, a combination like this is quite the best thing there is. It doesn't take long behind the wheel of one to know what made Fangio tiger the way he did that day at the Nürburgring.

Finally, I must take this opportunity to thank Anthony Bamford for making it all possible, and to his team for keeping me and the car on the road. I owe an immense debt of gratitude to them that I doubt I will ever repay.

1954
JAGUAR D-TYPE

From the moment the first pictures of 'Jaguar's new competition model' were leaked to the motoring press in early 1954, it was obvious that a truly great racing car had been born. Like countless others, I gawped at the fuzzy shots of the still unpainted car and fell in love with it there and then.

You knew — you just *knew* — that it would be successful. It was, of course, perhaps even more so than its originators intended, for its sole function was to win one race — Le Mans. This it did three years in succession, 1955, 1956 and 1957, but it also won innumerable other races all over the world, invariably in private hands (the works, surprisingly, entered relatively few races).

This, though, is not the story of the D-type in general, but one car in particular which I have driven several times over a period of 15 years: chassis number XKD606, now owned by Anthony Bamford. However, a brief history of the model is required to put 606 into perspective.

Jaguar had won Le Mans in 1953 with the C-type. Late in that year a new model was drawn up, lighter, smaller, more nimble, better streamlined. In-house it was called the 'D' but wasn't given an official designation until Harold Hastings

of *The Motor*, apparently, called it that in his report of the 1954 race. Since Jaguar didn't have a bottomless pocket for their racing activities, the new car had to incorporate various production items — surprisingly many compared to the machines that flowed from Ferrari, for example.

Thus the engine was the indomitable 3.4 litre twin-cam straight six. In the D-type it was dry sumped for a lower bonnet line and to prevent oil surge, and produced 250 bhp at 6,000 rpm (and an astonishing 248 lb ft of torque at a low 4,500 rpm), thanks in part to bigger valves and triple Weber DC0E 45 mm carbs. The front suspension followed XK practice with twin wishbones and longitudinal torsion bars, and the XK140's rack and pinion steering was used.

The chassis, though, was something completely different. Breaking new ground, the centre section was of monocoque construction, whereby bulkheads fore and aft were joined by longitudinal tunnels: the outer skin wrapped round them like an aircraft fuselage, and indeed there was much aircraft influence in its construction. A multi-tubular spaceframe speared through the front bulkhead and keyed to that at

the back, the whole providing a mounting for the engine and front suspension. Since Le Mans, with its billiard-table smooth surface, was the aim, a sophisticated rear suspension was unnecessary, so a live axle was retained. It was mounted directly on to the rear bulkhead by a pair of trailing arms on each side, the lower ones operating the transverse torsion bar spring, with further location by an A-bracket. (In fact, the car could be moved with the whole of the tail section removed!)

Other features included a triple-plate clutch, Jaguar's own four-speed gearbox, a variety of rear axle ratios, disc brakes which Jaguar had pioneered, and Dunlop light alloy wheels and knock-off hub-caps.

But it was the shape — ah, the shape — that made the D-type so instantly distinctive. The work of the gifted Malcolm Sayer, the svelte panelling wrapped as tightly as it was possible to get around the mechanicals and wheels. Sayer was not only a good aerodynamicist but, along with Sir William Lyons, had an eye for a line, and there isn't one misplaced in the D-type. Like the Type 35 Bugatti or the Ferrari GTO, it was a classic case of what looks right *is* right, even though Frank Costin may disagree!

Three D-types were entered for Le

Mans in 1954 and, contrary to what most people believe, *didn't* win. That honour fell to Gonzalez and Trintignant in a Ferrari, but the Rolt-Hamilton car, registered OKV 1, came home a fighting second, and from that moment on the D-type's reputation was assured. Not many cars achieve instant fame by finishing second . . .

Le Mans 1955 promised to be one of the all-time great races. Mercedes had returned, with their complex, sophisticated 300SLRs, complete with airbrake to try to remove some of the D-type's disc brake advantage, while Ferrari had a set of fearsome 4½ litre cars. Nor could Aston Martin or Maserati be discounted. The opening laps indeed proved sensational, with Fangio and Hawthorn fighting tooth and nail, seldom a hair's-breadth apart, for all the world as if they were repeating the epic 1952 French GP: this was racing at its very finest. Then, of course, tragedy struck in motor racing's greatest disaster when Pierre Levegh's Mercedes

plunged into the crowd. The atmosphere evaporated, Mercedes withdrew their cars, and it was a subdued and saddened Hawthorn and Bueb who reeled off the hours to cross the line first. Jaguar's first D-type Le Mans win was not the victory it could have been.

The 1955 D-types run by the works were modified from the previous year. The most obvious change was a longer snout, adding some 7½ in to the overall length of the car and giving rise to the name 'Long-nose', coupled with a higher wrap-around windshield blending into a fared-in tail fin. Under the new bonnet was the familiar 3.4 litre six, but with a new head whose larger valves required a wider angle between them (the 'wide angle' or

Malcolm Sayer produced a stunningly seductive shape which helped the D-type to reach close to 180 mph on the Mulsanne Straight. Wind buffeting is not severe as long as you keep your head down.

35/40 — from the valve angle — head). This engine pumped out 270 bhp at 6,000 rpm, and 256 lb ft of torque at 4,500 rpm.

Jaguar returned to the Sarthe in 1956 with a new team of works cars, chassis numbered 601 to 606. All were as the 1955 cars but a couple were equipped with fuel injection to give 272 bhp at 5,750 rpm, and 270 lb ft of torque at a very useful 4,000 rpm. To meet new regulations there were full-width windscreens. To recoup some of the drag lost because of this, plastic tonneau covers, stretching from the top of the 'screen to the rear bulkhead, were fitted. At speed they ballooned up to give a better airflow.

'Our' car, 606, was due to be driven by Ulsterman Desmond Titterington and the famous Belgian journalist Paul Frère, but Titterington ran off the road in practice so 606 was replaced by 603 in the event.

The race itself was a near disaster for Jaguar: in the opening laps Frère spun on the streaming wet track and struck the bank in the Esses very

hard indeed. Fairman, in another team car, spun to avoid him, but was then attacked by de Portago's Ferrari. Exit two D-types. The sole surviving works car, that driven by the previous year's winners Hawthorn and Bueb, suffered from a cracked fuel injection line which dropped them down to twentieth at one point: they eventually finished sixth.

However, not all the Jaguar luck ran out. One of the privateer entries in D-types that year was XKD 501, an ex-works 1955 short-nose car. The entry was in the name of Scotland's Ecurie Ecosse, which enjoyed a particularly close working relationship with the factory, and the drivers were Ninian Sanderson and Ron Flockhart. This pairing took up the cudgels and, in a race-long battle with Moss and Collins in an Aston DB3S, finished a bare 10 miles in front to give Jaguar its second D-type victory.

Jaguar withdrew from racing at the end of 1956, to concentrate on its

The D-type has all the qualities needed to win Le Mans, but it is not so happy on a twisty circuit; its beam axle rear suspension hops up and down so that you lose both forward and sideways grip.

production cars. However, two cars, 603 and 606, were sold to Ecurie Ecosse to run as a quasi-works team. With them came a bigger-bore engine, up from 83 mm to 87 mm, a corresponding increase in capacity to 3,781 cc (3.8 in common parlance) and, of course, more power: 306 bhp at 5,500 rpm, and a massive 312 lb ft of torque at 4,500 rpm when fitted with fuel injection.

The opposition that year was impressive. From Aston came the DBR1s and a DBR2 complete with 3.7 litre engine. Ferrari fielded no fewer than 10 cars, including a couple of 4 litre V12s to be driven by Hawthorn, Musso, Collins and Phil Hill. Maserati came with the awesome 450S, Costin-designed, Zagato-bodied, coupé.

You might be forgiven for thinking that the D-types would be out-dated in such company, looking for placings rather than an outright win. And so it seemed at first, with the Ferraris and Maseratis battling away at the front in those initial, hectic, hours. 'Battle', though, was the operative word: with so much in-fighting they wore each other out, and gradually their attack faded. By midnight, half distance, D-types filled the first four places. At the end of the 24 hours, Ron Flockhart and Ivor Bueb in 606 led a Jaguar procession across the line, with D-types in second, third, fourth and sixth positions. The winning average was a new record, 113.8 mph.

Come forward, now, 16 years, to 1973. That year was the 50th anniversary of Le Mans and l'Automobile Club de l'Ouest organized a couple of races for historic cars. Shortly before, Anthony Bamford had acquired 606, and we entered the post-war historic event.

You can imagine my feelings: like

every kid in the 'fifties, my one ambition, my ruling passion, was to drive a D-type at Le Mans. Here I was, doing so, *and* in a winner at that . . . I was also entered in the real 24 hours along with Neil Corner in a JCB Daytona, so it was a busy weekend! We qualified the Daytona at 4 min 18 sec, and the D-type at 4 min 43 sec, which gives you some idea of the speed differential in 16 years (but note that the D-type's time was better than some of the Porsche Carreras in the main event). Neil was in another JCB car, a SWB 250GT, in the historic race, but the organizers imposed a 2 min penalty on the Ferrari because it was officially too young.

The D-type is not really suited to British circuits, but at Le Mans it immediately felt right — perhaps it was just psychological, this feeling, but I don't think so. Anyway, the start was interesting in that it was of the old-fashioned type, where you had to run across the road. This was all very well, but in the days when this

The D-type is a relaxing car to drive, as it needed to be for endurance races. Its steering is delightful, and the power-assisted brakes — with a dead feel, not unlike those of a Citroën — require little effort.

was standard the road was considerably wider: by 1973 it was narrow and Armco-lined. I was about fifteenth or so on the grid, and decided it would be expedient to get away quickly. Consequently I ran like hell for the car, and in the ensuing mêlée found myself 50 yards or so in the lead. Definitely one of my better moves.

I took it a bit carefully through the Esses (remembering Frère in 1956!) and Richard Bond in a Lister passed me. Out on to the Mulsanne Straight we went, and then matters became fascinating. By Les Hunaudières we were travelling side by side at about 150 mph. Bond was hanging on for all his worth: the front of the Lister looked as if it was about 6 in higher than normal, giv-

ing the effect that it would take off and loop the loop. I just drove straight past him, the D-type so stable that I had time to take my hands off the wheel and pass on assorted V signs . . .

That has to be the D-type's greatest strength — straight line performance. I was fascinated to see a story in *Autocar* a couple of years ago where a D-type was put through a wind tunnel. They recorded a drag factor (Cd) of 0.49, which was highly disappointing — even modern saloons, complete with jagged underbodies and various external excrescences, can manage something in the mid-0.3s. They also recorded quite high front and rear lift, and I cannot but agree with their conclusions: 'We couldn't help wondering whether the car's ride height front and rear — and therefore its pitch attitude — was as it should have been or was for stability at those tremendous Mulsanne straight speeds.'

Whatever, at one point, perhaps

with a following wind, I saw 6,200 rpm in top on the Mulsanne. Someone calculated that this was a true speed of 178 mph, which believe you me is staggeringly quick. What's more, its stability is uncanny: I could go through the kink at the end of the Mulsanne straight without

even *thinking* of lifting, whereas the Daytona had an aerodynamic problem at the back and it was like walking the proverbial tightrope. I suppose the D-type shows the difference between aerodynamic efficiency, the car's sheer ability to slip through the air with the greatest of ease, and

Shortly after my first Le Mans outing in 1973 with XKD606, Noel Edmonds drove the car at Silverstone in the JCB historic car race supporting the British Grand Prix. I guess I was briefing him here...

At Le Mans for my second D-type outing there, in 1978. I had won in 1973, but this time I spun out of the lead at the last corner and let Stirling Moss's Maserati 250F through to win.

aerodynamic stability wherein it isn't deflected from its path. And it must be fairly efficient: after all, 170 mph on 300 or so bhp takes some doing . . .

The race became interesting about half way through when an errant Frenchman in a Porsche threw himself at me through the Porsche complex. I went off on the inside and caught the driver's side tail a mighty bang — the car nearly overturned. A quick trip to the pits was called for, and from then on I really motored — the damage was fairly minimal. With various people dropping out in front I eventually found myself right behind Neil Corner in the 250GT on the last lap.

Autosport's description of that last lap shows how close it was: 'Both JCB cars flashed down the Mulsanne side by side with Willie taking the lead until Mulsanne corner when he found it all so amusing he spun and continued behind the Ferrari. For the rest of the lap Green gave chase and reached the finish by diving from behind the Ferrari and virtually staged a dead-heat had it not been for Corner's penalty. So on the road the Ferrari won, and Green won officially, but whatever it was a JCB domination'. That had to be one of my most satisfying results ever. A win in a D-type at Le Mans . . .

We were back again in the D-type for another historic race in 1978. The car was untouched apart from the repair to the accident damage and an oil change. This time I was even quicker — I put in a 4 min 36 sec lap — and was concentrating wonderfully. I had a similar problem with the brakes that had caused the Mulsanne moment the year before (one of the rear pads was expanding so much from the heat of stopping the car from 170 mph that it was sticking, rather like an unwanted hand-brake turn!) and I was just pipped by Stirling Moss in the 250F. In fact, I was in front coming into the last corner, but was, shall we say, distracted by Mossy and spun, so he slipped through to win. Still, one first and one second in a D-type at Le Mans isn't a bad record.

The car has delightful steering and front suspension, but you're stuck with that beam axle at the rear, which is a bit tedious when you're trying to change direction. In a bumpy corner it hops up and down so you lose both forward and sideways grip, while on smooth corners it lifts an inside rear wheel and all that lovely torque slips away. At Le Mans, of course, it doesn't matter, and it creates no problems, but even on a smooth circuit you are dependent on having an efficient and operative limited slip differential.

And what can you say about that magnificent engine! Onlookers are staggered when it starts at the first touch of the button and sits there idling quietly away to itself. At the one extreme it's uncannily untemperamental — you could stuff it straight into your XJ and use it for shopping. Use it though, and it really comes alive. There's superb torque from about 3,000 rpm, and by 4,500 rpm it's pulling like a steam train. You really should respect the 5,800 rpm rev limit, and it was a bit naughty of me to take it as high as 6,200 rpm. At 6,300 rpm valves touch and — bang. Don't over-rev it, though, and it should last forever.

The brakes are odd. They are power-assisted by an hydraulic servo driven from the back of the gearbox which works only when the car is rolling. In action they feel particularly dead, not unlike those of a Citroën. It's not something I really like, but it does make for a very relaxing car to drive for 24 hours in that you don't have to apply tremendous pedal pressure at the end of the straights. This is important — after 12 hours with the Daytona my right foot was so bruised I could barely walk.

The gearchange, via a little lever tilted forward at quite an acute angle, is heavy — second especially — but has a short throw and is positive and direct. The clutch, too, is surprisingly light — Jaguar really made sure the D-type wouldn't wear you out through sheer physical effort. The driving position suits me

The Anthony Bamford D-type, XKD606, was sold by the works to Ecurie Ecosse for the 1957 season and given a 3.8 litre engine. Driven by Ivor Bueb (pictured here) and Ron Flockhart, it achieved the last D-type win at Le Mans.

The 1957 Le Mans winner as it is to-day, still wearing that distinctive Ecurie Ecosse blue; it is among the most original of D-types.

A glorious sight is revealed when the one-piece bonnet is hinged forwards. In definitive 3.8 litre form with three Weber 45DCOE carburettors, the famous twin-cam XK engine produces just over 300 bhp.

fine, and wind buffeting isn't bad as long as you keep your head well down.

Interestingly, the D-type chassis feels much more rigid than that of a lightweight E-type. The only visible difference is the D-type's bracing bar between front and rear bulkheads by your left shoulder, and I suspect this plays a very important part in structural rigidity.

The D-type is one of the ultimate racing cars. Simple, enormously fast and utterly reliable, it combined all the qualities required to win one of the most prestigious races ever devised — Le Mans. And it looks sensational, sounds as magnificent as it looks, and behaves as magnificently as it sounds. What more is there to say?

1957
MASERATI 450S

This track test was one of those moments of sheer opportunism which began, in time honoured fashion, over a beer. One evening I was chatting to Stephen Griswold when the subject of his latest restoration came up; before I knew it I had been invited to drive what is probably the most powerful front engined sports racing car ever. I had to present myself at Silverstone the next day ...

The reason for the rush was that this very special Maserati 450S, with its 6.4-litre 'marine' engine, was due to be despatched to its owner, Peter Kaus, as soon as Griswold had given it a clean bill of health. That meant a shakedown session at Silverstone, where I would have the chance of a few laps during the day.

To start at the end of the story, so to speak, this particular 450S evolved into its ultra-powerful current form long after the works 4.5 litre cars were outlawed by the CSI's new 3 litre limit imposed for the 1958 season. Several cars — including this chassis '4506' bought by John Edgar in 1957 — went big-banger racing in America, and were modified along the way. When Maserati produced a *Tipo 59* V8 enlarged to 5.6 litres for powerboat racing, developing 520 bhp at 7,000 rpm, Edgar's car was one of two 450Ss

(Jim Hall's was the other) to be fitted with the big engine. In 1962, Maserati produced an even larger 6.4 litre marine V8, dubbed the *Tipo 62,* and Joel Finn installed one of these when he was having 'our' car restored. In today's specification, therefore, this 450S isn't strictly original, but it is formidable ...

The 450S was truly the zenith of 'fifties sports car racing, but it so nearly didn't happen at all. Maserati knew in 1955 that its six-cylinder 300S was no match for the Mercedes-Benz 300SLR, the Jaguar D-type and Ferrari's various weapons, and began to consider how to get back into the fight. Chief Engineer Vittorio Bellentani laid down his initial thoughts for a 4.5 litre four-cam V8, but in the wake of the Le Mans disaster it was put on ice while sports car racing found its feet once more.

Then an order from American entrant Tony Parravano for a new engine to be designed by Maserati for his Indianapolis Kurtis Kraft gave the project new impetus late in the year, and Giulio Alfieri, newly arrived in Modena as Bellentani's successor, set to work on a detailed design, which would be the company's first V8 since 1935. The 4,474 cc (93.8 mm bore × 81 mm stroke) V8 which emerged was

undeniably state of the art.

Its pair of cylinder blocks, set at 90°, each carried twin overhead camshafts operating two valves per cylinder, the camshafts being driven by a train of gears from the crankshaft nose. Two spark plugs fired each cylinder — as a fail-safe, one set was driven by a magneto, the other by a pair of coils and a distributor. Carburation was provided by four twin-choke downdraught Webers tucked within the vee.

Progress on the new V8 was slow, and it wasn't until mid-summer of 1956 that the first unit ran on the bench. It was worth waiting for, those early tests revealing immense flexibility and a power peak of 400 bhp at 6,800 rpm. The first engine was installed in a modified 350S chassis and ran in practice for the Swedish Grand Prix at Kristianstad, where its drum brakes quickly gave up the ghost under the barrage of power. Formula 1 commitments precluded any further development until the winter of 1956–7, but the works embarked on the 1957 Sports Car World Championship season with unbridled confidence.

Valerio Colotti designed a new chassis based on 300S experience, beefing up the tubular spaceframe to cope. Power was fed through a

new five-speed transaxle with the gearbox section ahead of the final drive, and a de Dion rear suspension tube was set aft of this unit.

Maserati's buoyant mood was fully justified at the first race of 1957, the Argentine 1,000 km, when Juan Manuel Fangio and Stirling Moss led with ease until the 450S's transmission failed. Two months later at Sebring for the 12 Hours, Fangio and Jean Behra devastated the opposition by leading throughout and shattering lap and distance records. The 450S had well and truly arrived.

The big one, as far as Maserati were concerned, was the Mille Miglia, which the Modena company had never won. Lots of lire were thrown at an intensive pre-race testing programme, which included a complete 1,000-mile practice run in the untouched Sebring winning car. A bolt in the rear suspension broke after 400 miles, but otherwise the already tired car acquitted itself well while being hammered by Behra. Moss also did some test runs, trying a clever two-speed 'overdrive' which gave a 185 mph top speed for the fast sections, or a lower geared

The Maserati 450S has so much power that the handling is destroyed when you put the boot in through a corner. Driving one in the dry is a bit like coping with any other rear-driven racing car in the wet.

160 mph top speed set of ratios for the mountains. Maserati would start the Millie Miglia as firm favourites.

Sadly it all turned sour as quickly as milk on a hot day. During a final shakedown test on the Friday before the race, Behra hit a lorry and his car was damaged beyond immediate repair. That left Moss and Denis Jenkinson — winners in 1955 with Mercedes-Benz — to fly the flag alone.

Jenks later described in *Motor Sport* the early miles leaving Brescia, writing that he had 'swallowed hard as I saw that Moss was pulling out the overdrive gear ... and we were up at 6,700 rpm in overdrive fifth ... here we were doing approximately 168 mph just as we were leaving town, on a straight of barely two kilometres. We looked at each other and grinned...'

But only seven miles into the race Moss hit the brakes to haul in the big

car from around 130 mph, dropping down to 80 mph for a left-hand corner. Jenks felt Moss check the car, 'and then it seemed to accelerate and I saw that he was deliberately sliding the car into the inside of the corner as we approached and my first thought was that it had jumped out of gear. This thought was heightened when I saw him make a violent grab at the gear lever while the car was sliding across the corner, and then he stopped working on the wheel and we slowed up. I thought "Well go on then, accelerate," but he didn't ...'

Stirling was pointing at the floor instead, where the brake pedal lay broken. A flaw in the pedal arm — there was speculation about sabotage — had scuppered the best-laid plans.

Maserati needed a good result at the Nürburgring to pick themselves up again, but both cars failed. And so to Le Mans, where Behra and André Simon shared a regular open car, while Moss and Harry Schell piloted an ungainly brute of a closed coupé styled by Frank Costin and built by Zagato. Reserve driver Fangio set a pole position time in the

open car, but both cars retired from the race with the same problem — seizure of a half-shaft universal joint.

Only the Swedish and Venezuelan GPs remained, and Maserati needed to win both to take the world title. The two 450Ss dominated at Kristianstad until Schell retired with another UJ seizure, but Moss and Behra survived to win at record speed. Everything hinged on the battle with Ferrari at the final round at Caracas in November.

Three 450Ss took the start, Temple Buell's new car for Masten Gregory and Dale Duncan joining the works pair driven by Moss, Schell and Behra, with a 300S for Jo Bonnier as further back-up. Rarely has a championship challenge been so calamitous. Gregory was out on lap 2 after rolling Buell's car, Moss led until a collision when an AC Ace veered into his path, and then Behra's car caught fire in the pits, burning his hands. Moss and Schell brought the damaged car back into contention, but the final ironic touch came when Bonnier's 300S lost a wheel just as Schell was preparing to pass, the 450S slam-

ming into a wall and bursting into flames … Ferrari took the first four places, and the title.

Chassis '4506' looked magnificent when I set eyes on it at Silverstone, fresh out of Griswold's workshops. It's a gorgeous looking car in that special Maserati shade of burgundy red, and I couldn't wait to get a taste of its charisma for myself. Once I'd strapped myself in my first impression was that the seating position seemed very low, and that the car looked huge and heavy to handle. On the move, though, I found that the controls were quite light, but I disliked the upright seat and the wooden steering wheel rim, which was so slippery that you could inadvertently let go of it. One interesting detail I noticed as I was checking round the cockpit before driving off was a small peep-hole behind my right shoulder so that you could check the tyre wear dur-

ing a race. A necessary tweak, I thought, imagining all the power that would have gone through the rear wheels with the ordinary 4.5 litre V8 of its heyday, let alone this 6.4 litre monster.

As I expected, the handling was neutral until I put my boot in — that just destroyed it. You would set up the car in the middle of a corner at, say, 3,000 rpm, put the welly in, and the back end would just *go*. It was not as if the tail suddenly stepped sideways a little: the immediate wheelspin meant that the effect was far more dramatic than that. Coming out of Woodcote, it felt as if the rear wheels didn't start to bite properly until halfway down the pits straight. I would say that there's around 400–450 bhp available (Steve agreed that it's in that region), but the incredible torque is the most striking characteristic. Although the engine is red-lined at 5,700 rpm, the torque seems to peak at around 3,000, and you don't need much more than 4,000 anywhere at Silverstone.

I'm not sure whether this kind of power is more than the chassis can handle, but it was certainly more

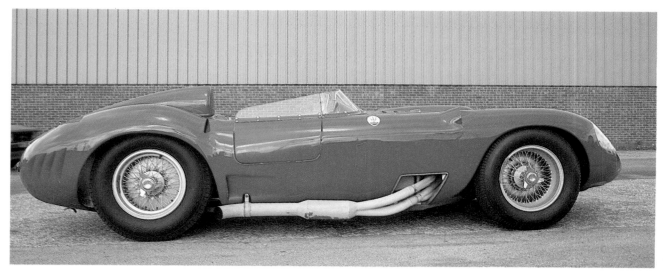

Above *The 450S was the peak of 'fifties sports car development, and but for disasters on the Mille Miglia and at Caracas it should have won the 1957 Sports Car World Championship for Maserati.*

Left *It is as brutal as it looks. I drove the 450S on a shake-down run straight after Stephen Griswold's restoration in 1984, and today it lives in Peter Kaus's fabulous Rosso Bianco Collection in Aschaffenburg, near Frankfurt.*

than the driver could in this instance. Power is way in excess of roadholding because of the narrow tyres, and, now I think about it, there are very few racing cars which push so much power through so little rubber. I can't imagine what it would have been like to drive a pre-war Mercedes-Benz or Auto Union! Mind you, I think the 450S could have done with different tyres: this one was all wrong because there was more rubber on the front than the back.

The gearing was very high, good for 185 mph in fifth I should say. I never got into fifth, even though I was changing at 4,000 rpm. I had been told to expect a noisy gearbox,

but I didn't find it so. I used only the middle three gears, but I reckon I could have gone just as quickly with only third and fourth. It reminded me, in fact, of the CanAm McLaren M8F I once drove, for that also had so much torque that the gears were almost a luxury! The linkage fell off when I drove the McLaren so I had to leave it in top, and I went 2 sec a lap quicker!

The brakes are adequate for the power, but felt as if they were fading out through lack of hydraulic travel. And the old bugbear of driving a car like this in an open test session cropped up. All and sundry were out on the track, and some of those little heroes — making no allowance for

the fact that I was driving a ton of uncontrollable machinery — did odd things like driving round the outside of me through a corner, which isn't wise when the car is in the middle of a great opposite-locking power slide ...

When I came in after only about 20 min in the car I knew that I'd been driving quite a handful: I wasn't exhausted, but I would have been after half an hour. It was like fighting a battleship. This time I didn't envy the car's owner, for Peter Kaus was due to do the anniversary Mille Miglia in it. I wouldn't have set out over 1,000 miles without a team of 20 drivers!

Obviously this car has more

That wonderful V8 engine, topped by four twin-choke Webers tucked into the vee. Maserati raced these cars in 4.5 litre capacity, but during the 'sixties this 6.4 litre 'marine' version — the largest Maserati V8 ever — was fitted.

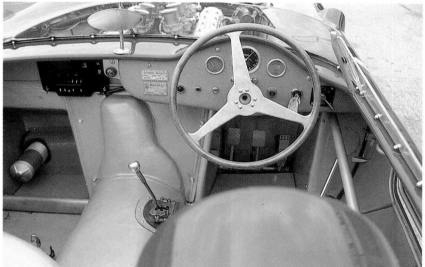

The controls are light, but I disliked the upright seating position and slippery wooden steering wheel. Transmission is by a five-speed transaxle.

power than the 1957 team cars ever knew, and *they* were the most powerful sports racers of their day. Latterly I can remember Charlie Lucas having a good old go in John Fellowes's 450S, but I can now understand why John never drove very quickly. Driving one in the dry is a bit like coping with any other rear-driven racing car in the wet ...

For all that, though, it was a wonderful experience to drive a 450S for the first time. Luckily, Peter Kaus believes in airing his best cars regularly, so this 450S has been seen in public plenty of times — including twice on the Mille Miglia retrospective — since my drive in it.

He has so many cars, over 200 at the last count, that in 1987 he opened the Rosso Bianco Collection in Aschaffenburg, near Frankfurt. Maseratis, and sports racers in particular, figure large in his enthusiasm, and the 450S is among the cars you can see in this spectacular museum. It's well worth a visit.

1957

VANWALL

It has been my great fortune to drive some of the finest racing cars the world has ever seen, but none has the special aura, the mystique, the magic of the legend called Vanwall. To youngsters, the name may be just one among many in the list of historical records. To those who were around in the heady days of the late 'fifties it meant British supremacy, the proud wearing of British Racing Green, the first of a long line of British World Championships (Vanwall won the first FIA Constructors' Cup in 1958). But, unlike the Maseratis and Ferraris and Coopers that escaped the factories, the Vanwalls, once retired, never returned to the tracks apart from all too rare demonstrations.

They are thus among that select breed — the pre-war Mercedes and Auto Unions, the Type 159 Alfa Romeos — that have retained an air of glory, of domination, that puts them above and beyond most people's dreams. And, to the best of my knowledge, no one has ever carried out a full-blooded track test. I don't think I need explain any further why I regard it as a very special honour that I was allowed to take the wheel for some no-holds-barred (well, few-holds-barred) lappery of Silverstone's Grand Prix circuit.

The Vanwall grew out of Tony Vandervell's enthusiasm for Grand Prix racing and his passionate desire to see a British-built car beat the Continentals. At first he directed his energy and money into the BRM team, but he became so impatient with the delays in completing the first V16 BRM that he went off on his own with a 4½ litre V12 Ferrari hybrid which he named the Thin Wall Special after the steel-backed bearings he manufactured. He hired Reg Parnell to drive it, and one early success came in the torrential rain of the 1951 International Trophy at Silverstone. Parnell led the Alfas, Maseratis and Talbots through an incredible rainstorm, taking victory when the flag was hung out after only six laps. The Thin Wall Special won many *Formule Libre* races during 1952–3, when GP rules accepted only 2 litre unblown Formula 2 cars, but the success of Ferrari's little four-cylinder cars in Ascari's hands set Vandervell thinking about his own GP future.

He decided to make a car of his own, using a new four-cylinder engine, to beat 'those bloody red cars'. The 'Old Man', as he was known, also happened to be a director of Norton motor cycles, and knew that research carried out by BRM on Norton's behalf could be applied to his new engine. BRM had experimented successfully with water-cooling on

one of Norton's famous twin-cam single-cylinder 500s, and the 'Old Man' conceived the idea of a 2 litre F2 engine with four of these cylinders on a special crankcase.

To save time and money, the iron block and crankcase of a Rolls-Royce military engine was modified and cast in light alloy. While the twin-cam top end broadly followed Norton design, there was a new one-piece alloy cylinder head. The 85.9 mm × 86 mm cylinders had cast aluminium water jackets, there were magneto-sparked twin plugs to each cylinder, and initially fuel supply was by four Amal racing motor cycle carburettors, with fuel injection a future objective.

Having given a promising 235 bhp at 7,500 rpm on the brake, the engine was installed in a Cooper-built tubular spaceframe chassis, suspended on transverse leaf springs combined with Ferrari front wishbones, steering and de Dion rear end, and using Vandervell's own Goodyear-designed disc brakes. To save time, the British-built four-speed gearbox borrowed the design of a Ferrari unit.

The car wasn't finished when the F2 period ended at the close of 1953, but Alan Brown gave the prototype — the first Vanwall — its race debut in the 1954 International Trophy,

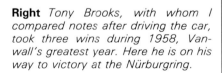

Above *In spite of braking problems and an almost total lack of fine tuning when I drove the Vanwall in 1983, it was putting up times competitive enough to suggest that it could win British historic races.*

Right *Tony Brooks, with whom I compared notes after driving the car, took three wins during 1958, Vanwall's greatest year. Here he is on his way to victory at the Nürburgring.*

running encouragingly well in fifth place in the final until an oil pipe broke. Peter Collins drove the car in a few GPs, and by the end of the year its engine had been bored out to 96 mm to reach the 2½ litres allowed by the new F1 regulations. Vanwall was ready for its first serious GP season.

The 'Old Man' signed Mike Hawthorn when Collins absconded to BRM in 1955, and put Ken Wharton in a second car. Two new chassis were built, these being much improved: the engines were fitted with Bosch port fuel injection, the chassis now had coil front springs instead of

transverse leaf, the rear disc brakes were moved inboard and the bodywork was cleaned up. But it was such a dismal GP season for Hawthorn that he asked to be released from his contract. Ninth place in the British GP was the fledgling Vanwall team's best result, although Harry Schell (Hawthorn's successor) scored minor wins at Crystal Palace, Snetterton and Castle Combe. The 'Old Man' thought it disastrous, but he wasn't one to give up. He took drastic action.

Over the winter of 1955-6, Colin Chapman was commissioned to design an all-new tubular spaceframe

chassis and improve the de Dion rear suspension. Frank Costin worked on aerodynamics and produced the glorious long-nosed, high-tailed 'teardrop' shape that would become a Vanwall hallmark. Harry Weslake instigated engine improvements, including invaluable gas-flowing, to push power to 280 bhp. All the right people were involved ...

The trouble with 1956 was desperate unreliability. The highlight was Stirling Moss's one-off drive to win the International Trophy, but there were no other victories that year for regular drivers Schell and Maurice Trintignant. The

Above *Although many photographs show the Vanwall to have been an understeerer, I found it beautifully neutral in its handling, and at its best through long, fast corners.*

Left *The Vanwall's distinctive cigar shape, designed by Frank Costin, is an evocative sight in British Racing Green. Vanwall achieved in four seasons what BRM had been trying to do in a decade.*

Above *From humble beginnings — a modified Rolls-Royce military block and crankcase cast in light alloy and a twin-cam cylinder head derived from Norton motorcycle design — the four-cylinder engine was developed by Harry Weslake to produce 280 bhp.*

Right *I have never seen such quality of engineering on a racing car. Every component gleams, welds are even along their length and suspension arms are polished and beautifully machined.*

The instrument panel is plain, with a large rev counter and four small gauges for oil pressure and temperature, fuel pressure and water temperature. An eye-ball fresh-air vent can be seen by the left-hand driving mirror.

cars were fast — witness Schell's challenge to the leading Ferrari trio at Reims — but invariably fell apart.

But Vanwall's challenge grew still stronger in 1957 when the 'Old Man' signed two British aces, Moss and Tony Brooks, to drive his British Racing Green cars. It was a much more competitive and reliable season, with the glorious win in the British GP shared by Moss and Brooks the undoubted highlight. Brooks was still only partially fit after an illness which had kept him (and Moss, incidentally) out of the two previous GPs. When the ignition failed on Moss's car, Stirling took over Brooks's machine and fought his way through from ninth place to the front. It was a glorious maiden victory for Vanwall on home ground — those 'bloody red cars' were defeated at last. Following another win at Pescara, Moss went to Monza, the very lion's den, and beat the Ferraris again. Suddenly it had all come good for Vanwall, the 'Old Man' achieving in four seasons what BRM had been trying to do since 1950.

Problems in adapting engines to the AvGas fuel required by new FIA rules gave Vanwall a slow start to its fifth (and final) season. Eventually 270 bhp was achieved, a drop of

15 bhp from the best alcohol-assisted output, but all the teams faced the same challenge. Vanwall missed the first race in Argentina (where Moss won in a rear-engined Cooper) because of this, and then at Monaco the whole team retired. Thereafter, however, Vanwall entered its most glorious phase, winning six of the next eight GPs. Moss won in Holland, Portugal and Morocco, and Brooks took victory in Belgium, Germany and Italy. Such was the points structure of the World Championship that Mike Hawthorn (in a Ferrari) ended up with the title despite winning only one race to Moss's four.

Sadly, there was a tragic end to this wonderful season, for Stuart Lewis-Evans suffered fatal burns when his Vanwall crashed in the last race at Casablanca. The 'Old Man' took this very hard, and on top of the strains of these intense years it had an adverse effect on his health. After serious warnings from his doctors he took their advice and withdrew from motor racing in January 1959. His team of engineers was gradually dispersed, but the racing organization lingered on long enough to build a lowered version of the 1958 car and a 2.6 litre rear-engined Inter-Continental one-off,

neither of which succeeded.

The first thing that struck me when I looked over the Vanwall I was about to drive was that the standard of engineering is the finest I have ever seen, bar none. Every component gleams, looking as if (as indeed was the case) no expense was spared in producing it. Welds are absolutely even along their length, suspension arms polished and beautifully machined, bodywork totally ripple-free. The car is a tribute to those who built it and those who look after it today.

Before recording my impressions, a word or two of explanation. First, it had come 'straight out of the box', as it were, and no attempt had been made to sort it. Under those conditions you cannot expect a car to be *à point* instantly, and the Vanwall wasn't — but it was closer than most others I've driven under similar circumstances. Secondly, I was intrigued to discover what Tony Brooks thought about it some 25 years on, and have included his comments where appropriate — they were recorded, by the way, *after* I drove the car, so I wasn't influenced by his opinions.

You climb in by standing on the rear wheel and lifting your legs over high sides. Once in, the cockpit is spacious, with assorted chassis tubes and cooling ducts either side of you. There are two eye-ball fresh-air vents each side of the dashboard, fed by intakes in the nose of the rear view mirror fairings. In front of you is a plain instrument panel with a huge tachometer and gauges for oil pressure and temperature, fuel pressure and water temperature. The only problem I encountered in the cockpit was that the steering wheel was too big for my tastes — a smaller one would have made life easier, and apparently there *are* smaller ones available, with three or four spokes to choice as well.

Contemporary photographs of Vanwalls show the drivers sitting higher than in the Ferraris and the Maseratis because the gearbox is underneath the seat. This is no problem, and the driving position suited me well — I didn't need padding or seat adjustment as I have done in one or two other cars. The high cockpit sides protect you well from the airstream too (Tony Brooks: 'It was nice not to be buffeted around, not to have the wind get under your helmet peak and try and rip it off. It helped concentration. On slow circuits, though, it could lead to a build-up of fumes — but the Ferrari was even worse in this respect. It once made me physically ill').

The five-speed gear-change is so arranged that first is a dog-leg, left and back, the other four gears being in the normal H pattern. In practice first is used only for full-bore racing starts with a full tank of fuel as far as I can see: you're normally push-started in second and as long as the car is moving you can pull away quite happily in that gear.

The change itself has come in for some criticism over the years (Tony Brooks: 'The worst feature was the gearbox, heavy and awkward, more like a pre-war Bentley than a GP car. Compared to the Vanwall's, the Ferrari's was like a knife through butter'). I must confess I was a little surprised at this, since I found no problems with it and, frankly, I've

driven worse. Perhaps the travel was a bit long, and it wasn't as instant as that of a 250F or Dino, but then very few are. Of course I only drove the car for a few laps — over the course of a full GP it may be different.

The Vanwall engine was Tony Vandervell's passion, the one thing he cared most about in his cars, and it shows: it is superb. I found it surprisingly smooth for a big four-cylinder, but there's much more to it than that. On the one hand there is a lot of torque low down, so you can put up quite respectable lap times without over revving it, but on the other hand power comes in noticeably at 6,000 rpm (I imposed a rev limit of 7,000 rpm on myself, although I believe it is safe to 7,500 rpm or so). Thus the engine combines the best of both worlds, with a lot of pull at the bottom end, yet a willingness to rev at the top (Tony Brooks: 'The Vanwall was a big four, the Ferrari a V6 and a year later, so although the Vanwall felt more torquey, the Ferrari was smoother and faster'). On this we agree.

Again, contemporary shots show that the Vanwall was an inveterate understeerer. To me, it was beautifully neutral and, like most cars of this era, the attitude is dependent on the throttle — you steer it by judicious use of the accelerator pedal. For some reason very few cars understeer with me and the Vanwall was no exception. It is, however, at its best in long fast corners such as Abbey, when it holds its line very well.

On slower corners it seems to lift an inside rear wheel and — the only way I can describe it — almost 'overbalances' as it were. It is quite unlike the 250F — the Maserati hangs its tail out as soon as you blink at it, whereas the Vanwall repays neatness and tidiness. (Tony Brooks: 'It was not as forgiving as a 250F — you had to drive it precisely, almost geometrically precisely. You couldn't throw it around in slow corners as you could the 250F. It felt rather heavy — it was

not a "lively" car. But if the Maserati handled better, the Vanwall was more powerful, more aerodynamic, so though it may have lost a bit on slow circuits it was better on fast ones'). On the whole, again we are in agreement. Although hanging the tail out may be more fun and make for a more nimble car, it may not always be the quickest way.

The one aspect of the car I cannot really comment on is the braking because a fault in a caliper meant that one of the front brakes wasn't working at full efficiency, and there was a tendency for the car to turn sharp left when the appropriate pedal was pushed.

Summing up, Tony Brooks said: 'It was not an easy car to drive quickly. Overall it was very efficient but at the same time it was hard work.' Admittedly I haven't put in the mileage he has in the car, nor was I driving it at ten tenths, but in my limited experience I found it superbly enjoyable. Even more exciting than that was the fact that, in spite of the problems with the brakes, and the almost total lack of fine tuning, I was putting up competitive lap times. It wouldn't take very much work to see it sorted well enough to win historic races, and it then really would be a crowd puller. Just think how glorious it would be to recreate those 1957–8 seasons, the last in which front-engined cars dominated.

I was very grateful to Jon Simpson, John Collins, Sean Powell and Roy Peters of Vandervell, not only for a memorable day, but also for their superb standard of workmanship, and to ace restorer Tony Merrick for beavering away to make it possible. As a postscript, the car I drove was one of four in the Vandervell collection which were subsequently sold lock, stock and barrel to Tom Wheatcroft in late 1986. Today you can see all four — the Thin Wall Special, two 'teardrop' cars and the rear-engined Inter-Continental — in Tom's fabulous Donington Collection.

1957
ASTON MARTIN DBR1

For one issue of *Classic and Sportscar* back in 1982 I drove three Aston Martins — a 1935 Ulster, a 1955 DB3S and a 1982 Nimrod. It was a nice little line-up, but any Aston Martin enthusiast would have spotted an immediate gap — the most important sports racing Aston of all, the DBR1. Soon afterwards, I was able to put that right when the opportunity arose to drive Bill Symons's car, DBR1/4. It would make an interesting comparison with the DB3S which preceded it.

The DBR1 was the car which really put Aston Martin on the sports car racing map by winning Le Mans in 1959, and taking that year's

World Sports Car Championship as well. Its roots, though, go right back to the end of the 1940s, when David Brown, the new post-war owner of Aston Martin, began to entertain the idea of winning Le Mans.

The company's first Le Mans foray under David Brown came in 1949 with three DB2s, one of which survived to finish seventh. The legendary John Wyer joined the team for 1950 — temporarily at first, but he stayed for 13 years! — and Aston Martin went racing seriously, two DB2s finishing fifth and sixth at Le Mans. Better. For 1951 two lightweight DB2s and the fifth-placed car from the year before were entered, taking third, fifth and seventh places. Better still.

Professor Robert Eberan-Eberhorst, meanwhile, was working on a proper sports racer (rather than a modified production car), the DB3, which was entered for Le Mans in 1952. The race was an unmitigated disaster, two cars retiring at 10 and 31 laps, the third rumbling on for 20 hours before breaking. Ironically enough for a car from a firm with strong connections in the gear industry, two of the cars were eliminated with final drive failure. Even more ironically, if later racing Astons ever had a weakness, it was always in the gearbox . . .

Eberan-Eberhorst's chassis for the DB3 was a ladder type, with two 4 in tubes running down each side. Front suspension followed Auto Union (for whom von Eberhorst worked pre-war) practice in having trailing arms and transverse torsion bars, while a de Dion tube was used at the rear. Brakes were drums all round (inboard at the back) and towards the end of the car's life the six-cylinder engine was bored out to 2,922 cc, which was perilously close

to its limits. Since other teams, like Jaguar, had larger and more powerful engines, this was to be one of Aston's greatest handicaps for many years, and it was only with the arrival of the CSI's 3 litre rules for 1958 that Aston found itself on a genuinely equal footing.

Neat though the DB3 was, it turned out to be too heavy and ponderous. Although Eberan-Eberhorst didn't take kindly to the idea, Willie Watson, a senior design engineer, undertook to redesign the DB3, and so the DB3S was born. Most of the significant dimensions, including metal thickness, were reduced, the de Dion suspension was reworked and a gorgeous open body designed by Frank Feeley was fitted. The DB3S is rightly regarded

Below left Once you have the hang of the Aston Martin DBR1 you can chuck it around corners with some abandon, which is one reason why the car always excelled on 'driver's circuits' like the Nürburgring.

Below The DBR1's 2½ litre engine (a 3 litre used to be fitted until a former owner exchanged it for a Grand Prix unit) feels underpowered, but my main criticism is the car's pig of a gearbox — quite the worst I have ever used.

It seems odd to praise a racing car for its ride quality, but the DBR1 is so comfortable that I could easily imagine climbing into it cold and running a 1,000 km race.

Apart from the famous win scored by Carroll Shelby and Roy Salvadori at Le Mans in 1959, the DBR1 is best remembered for its string of three victories in the Nürburgring 1,000 km. This is Stirling Moss on his way to the third, in 1959.

Bill Symons' DBR1 gained a 2½ litre engine in the late 'sixties, and consequently has only 230–240 bhp. The correct 3 litre six-cylinder would make it very competitive in today's historic racing.

In comparison with the DBR1, the DB3S which I drove two years earlier was a more sensitive car with a better gearbox, but I prefer the later car's impeccable handling manners, comfort and build quality.

as one of the most beautiful sports racers ever.

The 1953 Le Mans was a disaster, all three DB3Ss retiring, but Aston won all the other races it entered that year, including the Goodwood Nine Hours and the TT. The following year's Le Mans was even worse, but, as Wyer has since pointed out, Aston was by now overstretching itself with its racing programme.

To overcome the problem of engine size, a 4½ litre V12 was built, but it proved to have a weak bottom end. It was fitted to an enlarged, and heavy, DB3S chassis, and called a Lagonda. The alternative route to more power was supercharging, so a Wade blower was fitted to one DB3S. Thus the 1954 Le Mans team comprised the Lagonda, two DB3Ss with coupé bodywork (hopefully to make them faster), a supercharged DB3S and a regular DB3S. None survived, and the two closed cars both crashed — Wyer has always thought that suspect aerodynamics were the cause.

With Wyer taking things at a more acceptable pace in 1955 and 1956, the DB3S was gradually improved. Paul Frère won at Spa in 1955, and Peter Walker/Dennis Poore took the Goodwood Nine Hours again. Two of the three DB3Ss entered for the tragic 1955 Le

Mans retired, but Peter Collins and Frère motored home to a fighting second place.

By 1956 the DB3S's bodywork had been tidied up, but still Aston's successes came generally when the larger-engined, faster cars retired. There was a third Goodwood Nine Hours victory, and Stirling Moss and Collins achieved another second place at Le Mans, but by now it was clear to the public that Aston needed a new car. Fortunately, they had produced just such a thing in the DBR1 at the 1956 Le Mans . . .

Ted Cutting, newly appointed to head racing car design, began to draw up the DBR1 in July 1955. Out went the ladder chassis, in came a spaceframe. Since the DB3S had splendid roadholding and handling, suspension remained the same, with trailing arms and torsion bars up front, de Dion at the back. Cutting's body was smoother than Feeley's, and was made from strong aircraft quality aluminium sheet.

The engine was revised so much as to be virtually new. Initially, DB3S 12 plug heads were retained, but the bottom end was changed completely. W. O. Bentley's 'cheeses', semi-circular devices which wrapped around the main bearings and allowed the crankshaft to be inserted into a rigid barrel-type

crankcase, were discarded in favour of more orthodox main bearing caps in a new alloy crankcase. Crankshaft and con-rods were taken from the DB3S, but camshaft drive was changed from chains to gears. When a wide-angle head was later developed, power was given as 267 bhp in conjunction with a four main-bearing crankshaft, although seven bearings were used from 1958 in some engines.

That Le Mans appearance was the DBR1's first and only outing of 1956, and, since it was a prototype rather than a production car, it had to run to a 2½ litre limit. Tony Brooks and Reg Parnell did well, reaching fourth place until the engine ran its bearings after 20 hours.

The DBR1's first full season was in 1957, and after a couple of minor British events with the 2½ litre engine it ran with a full 3 litres at Spa, where Brooks and Roy Salvadori romped home first and second. This was followed shortly after by one of the DBR1's greatest wins, when Brooks and Noel Cunningham-Reid (a relative newcomer) led the Nürburgring 1,000 km from start to finish.

Hopes were high for Le Mans after this result, so two DBR1s and a DBR2 (powered by an early version

of the 3.7 litre engine destined for the road-going DB4) were entered. Again disaster befell the team. Brooks crashed out of second place at half-distance at Tertre Rouge while searching for a gear, and the other two cars (driven by Salvadori/ Les Leston and the Whitehead brothers) suffered transmission failure.

The splendid news for Aston Martin in 1958 was that the World Championship was limited to 3 litre cars — the team had been soldiering on with cars of just this capacity. Maserati had withdrawn from racing, near bankruptcy, and Stirling Moss was back at Aston.

Two DBR1s were entered at Sebring, but both Moss and Brooks retired with the inevitable transmission failure. Moss took one car to the Targa Florio, and again gearbox trouble caused his retirement (after setting fastest lap). The Nürburg-

Exquisitely beautiful, Aston designer Ted Cutting's body for the DBR1 was made from strong aircraft quality aluminium sheet. In terms of workmanship, the car rivals the Vanwall for quality.

ring 1,000 km saw a win as fantastic as the previous year's, with Stirling on tremendous form. The Salvadori/ Carroll Shelby car retired with transmission problems, while Brooks was punted off by another car.

Yet again the cars failed at Le Mans, DB's great ambition: Stuart Lewis-Evans crashed, the Moss/ Jack Brabham car blew up and the Brooks/Maurice Trintignant car retired with those ever-present transmission faults. The Whitehead brothers, however, saved Aston's bacon by finishing second in an old DB3S, the very same car which had also finished second in 1956. The season closed for Aston with a

1–2–3 at the TT, although this was only a half-distance, half-points affair.

And so to the season when it all came good. After nine frustrating attempts at Le Mans, the obsession which Brown and Wyer felt for this race would finally be quenched. They started the season planning only a single outing at the Sarthe circuit, but the Sebring organizers enticed them to send a singleton car over to America for Salvadori and Shelby — it retired with a clutch problem. Then Stirling persuaded them that the Nürburgring 1,000 km was really too good to miss, and, despite an off-course excursion by co-driver Jack Fairman, he gave Aston its third successive win at the circuit.

Three cars were prepared for Le Mans: DBR1/2 for Salvadori/ Shelby, DBR1/3 for Moss/Fairman and DBR1/4 (a brand new car) for

Trintignant/Frère. As the Ferraris were quicker in practice, Wyer decided that one car, the Moss/Fairman machine, should set out as a hare and try to extend the Ferraris beyond their limits, while the other two paced themselves. The plan was successful: Moss retired from the lead quite soon, but the damage to the Ferraris had been done. The Hill/Gendebien Ferrari gave the leading Aston, driven by Salvadori/Shelby, quite a run for its money, the two cars changing places at the front several times, before the Ferrari expired at noon on Sunday, leaving the two surviving Astons to cruise home to a glorious 1–2, Salvadori/Shelby in front. After 10 years of trying, Aston Martin had finally pulled it off.

By now it was apparent that the World Championship lay within Aston's grasp — a win in the Goodwood TT would clinch it. The same three cars were entered, Moss/Salvadori in DBR1/3, Shelby/Fairman in DBR1/2 and Trintignant/Frère in DBR1/4. It was a close run thing. Moss, as ever, shot into the lead and held it until Salvadori took over. When Salvadori came in there was a terrific flare-up: fuel had spilled on to the car, there was a flashback from the exhaust, and up it went. It was almost an exact repeat of a fire at the same race for the same team back in 1952.

When the furore had died down, Moss climbed back into the Shelby/Fairman car and took it through to the lead and a win, the Trintignant car finishing fourth. It was enough to give Aston Martin the World Championship. On this crest of a wave, David Brown announced the team's retirement from motor racing.

The car which I drove, DBR1/4, was thus the last team car to be built, and took second place at Le Mans and fourth at Goodwood. It was then put under wraps at Astons until 1961, when it was loaned to John Ogier's Essex Racing Team for that year's Le Mans. Fitted with the regulation high windscreen, it was

driven by Salvadori and Tony Maggs, and joined in the race by the Border Reivers DBR1 driven by Jim Clark and Ron Flockhart (this latter car, incidentally, had finished third in the 1960 Le Mans, driven by Clark and Salvadori). Both Astons made a superb start, and in the early stages battled furiously with a Ferrari 250GT. DBR1/4 then settled back to run between sixth and fourth places until a leaking fuel tank put it out in the 18th hour.

The car then went on display at the National Motor Museum between 1963–68, whereupon it came into Peter Brewer's hands. He extracted the 3 litre engine for a DBR4 single-seater, replacing it with a $2\frac{1}{2}$ litre Grand Prix engine which has remained in place to this day. The car then came back to Aston Martin, and in 1972 William Willson, head of Company Developments in Newport Pagnell at the time, ordered a complete restoration.

As the car seemed too good to languish in a museum, Aston Martin approached the AMOC with the suggestion that one of its members should race the car in historic events. Brian Joscelyne had a season with it in 1973, but at the Le Mans *Cinquantenaire* race for historic cars he hit that perennial problem of being unable to find a gear, damaging the car as it left the track. It was repaired in time for more racing in 1973, and in 1974 Bill Nicholson, an Aston employee, had a few outings in it. When Aston Martin called in the official receiver in 1975, the car was sold to its current owner, Bill Symons.

The first thing that strikes you about the car is the incredible workmanship and detailing that has gone into it — I was reminded quite strongly of the Vanwall in this respect. Almost every part is stamped 'DBR1-4', and there are numerous little touches — the polished suspension arms, and so on — that set the car apart. The same ethos must have suffused the air both at Newport Pagnell and at Acton in the late 1950s. Only perfection was acceptable to the two

magnates running the companies, David Brown at Aston and Tony Vandervell at Vanwall. Today the car is a credit to the owner and John Pearson, who, in his own words, 'just rubs a rag over it', but who in fact does a great deal of the preparation. From its smooth, oval grille to its shapely tail, you can tell this is a purpose-built machine.

It was said that 'Bert' Bertelli, who designed the pre-war Ulster, insisted that, if his cars were to be driven for long distances, they had to be comfortable. That legacy lives on, for the cockpit of the DBR1 is very comfortable indeed — I felt I could climb in cold and run a 1,000 km race straight off. Among other things that contribute to the long-distance abilities of the car is a surprisingly good ride, not something you usually comment on in a racing car, but a useful, even vital, factor if you're sitting behind the wheel for long stretches.

The starting procedure is slightly odd, in that you press the starter, *then* switch on. This prevents any blow-back, and it must be said that the engine caught and ran the instant the switch was flicked, settling down into that particularly emotive and beautiful growl of a straight-six.

On the day I drove it, Bill and John were investigating a mysterious misfire which occurred at high revs, so I didn't drive as many laps as I should have liked, and kept the rev limit down to 6,500 rpm or so, even though maximum power from the $2\frac{1}{2}$ litre engine occurs at about 7,500 rpm. Still, the lower revs were more than enough to give me an idea of what the car is about.

The first — and most adverse — impression was that the gearbox is an absolute pig. I've driven some awkward 'boxes in my time, but that in the Aston takes some beating. It was a David Brown copy of one used at the time by Maserati — the Italians got it right, but the Brits got it all wrong. In particular I had a moment or two trying to come down from fourth to third while turning into a corner — not the best of times to find yourself gearless! Even if you have the revs right, it just baulks and refuses to engage. This was annoying to me, and even Bill and John admitted it wasn't the easiest change around. Both, however, have got the hang of it, and it seems it's just a case of practice making perfect. I'd need more practice — and it's not surprising that one of the most frequent causes of retirement of the DBR1s in their day was gearbox malfunction!

The other flaw in the car as it is at the moment is that the 2½ litre engine, though probably giving some 230–240 bhp, is very much a GP unit, feeling underpowered and lacking torque. The car cries out for the 3 litre engine, which would make it really competitive.

The lack of torque is emphasized somewhat by the tall gearing the car is pulling at the moment — I never even used fifth, and that, remember, was keeping the revs down. It's a pity we didn't have the full Silverstone circuit to conduct our lappery: I've a feeling the car would have come out with flying colours. Still, there's enough power to put up respectable times, and the engine is beautifully sweet and smooth. Noise, of course, is one of the major factors in any car as far as I'm concerned, and that straight-six is, like so many others, pure music.

To be honest, the Club Circuit at Silverstone, with its three tightish corners and fast left-hander at Maggotts, is not the ideal stamping ground for a DBR1, but its handling features are still apparent. To realize the car's full potential, you really need wide open spaces and sweeping curves, as at Goodwood, or fast, twisting roads such as at the Nürburgring.

Without a doubt, handling and roadholding are what the DBR1 is all about. The steering has that typically Aston characteristic of plenty of castor, which means strong self-centring. That allows you most definitely to steer on the throttle. As set up at the moment, there is perhaps a shade too much oversteer: a little less might not look so spectacular, but would mean higher cornering speeds. Nevertheless, once you have the hang of it you can chuck it around corners with some abandon — which is another reason why it shone, and would still shine, over the old Nürburgring circuit. When Astons won it was invariably through roadholding rather than an excess of power, and that partly explains why they shone on 'driver's circuits' and why it took them so long to win at Le Mans.

It is worth adding a few notes about the DB3S, an example of which I drove two years earlier. This was DB3S/8, one of the team of three built for 1955 and one of 11 works cars built in all. Somehow it missed being registered in sequence with the other two (62 EMU and 63 EMU), carrying the number 743 HYX. It won its first race, Frère driving at Spa, retired from Le Mans, and then won the *Daily Herald* International Trophy at Oulton Park in Parnell's hands. It then went to America, where its history is not recorded, before returning to Britain to Roger St John Hart, who in turn sold it to the Midland Motor Museum at Bridgnorth.

My main memory of the car is its handling response, which is just as refined as the DBR1. Although the DB3S seems on paper to be similar to the Jaguar D-type, what it loses on power against that car it partially regains in handling. On a twisty circuit, like the Nürburgring, it would comfortably beat a D-type. The DB3S is a beautifully sensitive and alive car which begs to be driven well.

The differences between DB3S/8 and DBR1/4, with its 'under-sized' 2½ litre engine, were rather disguised in power terms, but I do remember the earlier car having one of the noisiest engines I've ever sat behind. The 2,922 cc straight-six is totally untemperamental and very tractable. Where the DB3S differs most is in its gearbox, which although a similar David Brown four-speed, feels very much sweeter. It has a heavy change, but the action is positive, with lovely short movements and unbeatable syncromesh.

Much as I loved the DB3S, it was the DBR1 which made the stronger impression on me. Its combination of road manners, comfortable ride, pleasant cockpit and quality of build makes it one of the ultimate long-distance sports racers. It was tremendous fun through the only really fast corner, the sweeping left-hander at Maggotts, and it was here, just for a few seconds, that the DBR1 was suddenly, briefly, in its element.

1958

FERRARI
250 TESTA ROSSA

I must confess I find it mildly amusing to go to a race meeting at which there are modern saloon car events, and see just how many of the entries are trailered to and from the circuit. I mean, if they're so-called 'standard' cars, they ought to be capable of coping with give-and-take traffic without any major dramas . . .

By contrast, the particular Ferrari 250 Testa Rossa which I've driven several times, the subject of this track test, is both tested and taxed, and is used quite frequently on the road. Now obviously it is used only on high days and holidays, since weather protection is minimal (nonexistent, actually) — as it is also rather rare and valuable, road slush is not good for it.

The point I am trying to make is that it is totally tractable (provided you're reasonable and avoid mile-long traffic jams) on the one hand, yet an effective racing car on the other — in its day, it was *the* car to beat. Can you imagine someone trying to trickle along in, say, the current Le Mans Jaguar?

The 250 Testa Rossa was born out of the CSI's new 3 litre rules for the World Sports Car Championship in 1958, although its engine was a development of the fabulous 60° V12 engine which had won four of the five titles between 1953–57, and

which had roots going right back to the very first 1½ litre V12 designed by Gioachino Colombo. All Ferrari had to do, in effect, was scour its parts shelves to make the Testa Rossa.

Ferrari's engineers, headed by Andrea Fraschetti, were given a brief that the new car should be light, powerful, and — above all — robust. It would weigh between 1,800–1,900 lb, develop around 300 bhp and be rugged enough to appeal to private customers. This last requirement was an important commercial consideration for Ferrari, and the sums were helped by the SCCA's inclination also to create a 3 litre class in American sports car racing. If Ferrari could build a relatively straightforward and competitive 3 litre sports car for World Championship events, the same machine could double as a sports racer for the American market.

Three options for this car's power unit were available, two of them V12 permutations. The most powerful would be the four-cam V12 used in existing 315 and 335S sports racers, but its complexity, weight and cost made it a poor choice for customer use. Vittorio Jano's V6 Dino engines were being developed rapidly for Formula 1 use, but again their elaborate four-cam layout and

— at this stage — unproven reliability made them unsuitable. The most sensible option, instead, was a full-race development of the reliable and well-proven 3 litre 250GT V12 two-cam engine. The biggest change for the Testa Rossa was separate intake ports for each cylinder, a feature which not only improved breathing, but also allowed the spark plugs to be moved to the outside of the head, next to the exhaust ports.

Two Testa Rossa prototypes using this two-cam 3 litre V12 were run during 1957 alongside existing works cars. The first to appear, at the Nürburgring, used the 92.5 in wheelbase, de Dion rear suspension chassis which was usually powered by 3.8 litre 315S or 4 litre 335S four-cam V12 engines. The second Testa Rossa prototype appeared for Le Mans, this one based on a longer, stronger chassis as used in the older four-cylinder Testa Rossa, fitted with a live rear axle and coil spring suspension. This second prototype was significant for its frontal styling, using front wings which were virtually separate from the centre of the body to allow air to gush on to the front drum brakes. This was the real birth — as opposed to the gestation — of the 'Pontoon-Fender' Testa Rossa.

Driven by Olivier Gende-

Although I have never driven the 'Pontoon' Testa Rossa in a circuit race, I have plenty of experience of it on road and track, including the Mille Miglia retrospective during which it was superbly comfortable.

Ready for the open road with a taxed and registered Testa Rossa: it is incredibly tractable for a World Championship winning sports car. Can you imagine trickling along in traffic in a current Le Mans Jaguar?

Although the 'Pontoon' Testa Rossa, with its live rear axle, does not handle as well as the 1961 car which I raced, it is totally predictable.

The 'Pontoon' bodywork was abandoned for works Testa Rossas during 1958 because it generated too much front-end lift — that bridge-piece connecting wings and nose looks as though it should produce downforce, like a Formula 1 car's canard fins.

bein/Maurice Trintignant, the 'Pontoon' Testa Rossa ran well in second place at Le Mans until a piston burned through. With confirmation in September 1957 of the forthcoming 3 litre rules, Ferrari's attention was directed entirely on the new cars, the other prototype also acquiring a 'Pontoon' body. In this near-definitive form, both Testa Rossas ran at the notorious Caracas season finale, finishing third and fourth in a race which saw Maserati opposition wiped out in a series of catastrophic accidents.

By the time 1958 plans had crystallized, there were two types of Testa Rossa, one for works use, the other for customers. Both had 73 mm × 58.8 mm V12 engines displacing 2,953 cc, and power was quoted as 300 bhp at 7,200 rpm. The red-crackle paint finish on the cam covers gave the car its name, which translates to 'Red Head' — this wasn't the first Ferrari engine to have this feature, but the name stuck.

The rest of the car was fairly typical of Ferraris of the period: there was a tubular ladder-type chassis, independent front suspension by coil springs and wishbones, a live axle at the rear with semi-elliptic springs and trailing arms, and massive, finned drum brakes all round (Ferrari was unbelievably slow to adopt discs!). Works cars

gained a major modification developed after winter testing revealed excessive nose-heaviness — the front-mounted gearbox and live axle were replaced by a transaxle gearbox at the rear and a de Dion tube.

Clothing this conventional mechanical specification was that voluptuous 'Pontoon' body, designed and built by Scaglietti. Although that characteristic separate-winged nose style looked superb, it disappeared from the works cars during 1958 because of its questionable, lift-generating aerodynamics. Most of the customer cars had the 'Pontoon' style, and still do.

By the end of 1958, the Testa Rossa had proved its worth by winning the World Championship by the massive margin of 38 points to Aston Martin's 16. Ferrari won four of the five championship rounds (Buenos Aires, Sebring, Targa Florio and Le Mans), and took three second places, two thirds and three fourths. With Maserati absent owing to its parlous financial state, and the ageing Jaguar D-types now being run by privateers like Ecurie Ecosse, Ferrari's only real opposition came from Aston Martin, who won at the Nürburgring. Not that lack of opposition should take anything away from the Testa Rossa's charisma . . .

The Testa Rossa would continue

to win World Championship races for the next three years, although by the end of that period it behaved and looked nothing like the original. As the first and most successful of the line, it is the 'Pontoon' car which is best remembered now.

To me and to many others, the original 250 Testa Rossa is one of the most beautiful Ferraris the *Commendatore* has ever made, and that is really saying something when you think of some of the exquisite machinery that has emanated from Modena. There is something about that distinctive, curvaceous front that is not just lovely to look at, but has echoes of earlier cars — the pre-war 1750 Zagato-bodied Alfa Romeos, for example.

Those front wings, with their subtlety yet strength of line, are the product of immensely skilled sheet metal workers. After driving the car, I tried to think of other machines which feature those sculpted scoops behind the front wheels — there's the Aston Martin DB3S, of course, but I reckon that the OSCA coupé which appeared at Le Mans in 1953 has to be the earliest. I'm not sure what effect the nose shape has on the car's aerodynamics. The way it looks, the bridging piece between wing and nose should produce downforce like a modern F1 canard wing, but it's common knowledge that Ferrari

Left *The car has such presence. Even as Ferraris go, the 250 Testa Rossa is one of the all-time greats. It was a suitable choice for my very first* Classic and Sportscar *track test.*

Right *A grimace for the photographer as I sit on the grid for a Lloyds & Scottish Historic Car Championship race at Silverstone, at the wheel of the 1961 'shark-nose' Testa Rossa.*

found just the opposite . . .

It seems impossible that this car and the 1961 'shark-nose' Testa Rossa I drove in the Lloyds & Scottish Historic Car Championship in 1981 are just three years apart in age. For a start, the 1958 car has a much more spacious and comfortable cockpit and, of course, a somewhat higher seating position so that you look over, rather than through, the windscreen. The 1961 car has one that lies nearly flat and on top of that is convex-curved. If you try to look through it, everything becomes distorted. I can distinctly remember sitting up suddenly to look over the thing and finding the next corner some 50 yards closer than expected!

Again the 1961 car has the traditional 'Italian ape' driving position, with your knees up under your chin somewhere and the wheel about a mile away, but there are no such complaints about this car. There's plenty of room around the pedals (but don't try driving it in wellies!) and the seating position is much more accommodating to my shape. The gear-change, using that delightful, *engineered* lever, is — what? Unremarkable is probably the best word. It's just a nice, positive, faultless four-speed 'box made for racing.

I have never driven this 'Pontoon' Testa Rossa in anger in a circuit race. Although it would have been eligible for the old Lloyds & Scottish series, I think that it would have been overwhelmed by the more developed and bigger-engined Lister-Jaguars that we used to see in such numbers. That would have been a shame, because I don't like to see Ferraris not winning . . .

I have, however, driven it on both road and track. You may have noticed that it's left-hand drive, which most people would say is a disadvantage on clockwise circuits. I happen to think the opposite: I prefer to sit on the outside as I believe you get more feel. Unless, of course, you're in something like the 1961 car where you cannot see over the nose to place the car properly!

What I have discovered about the 'Pontoon' Testa Rossa is that I like it very much. Its handling is nothing like the later car, its live rear axle (albeit a well-located one) making a considerable difference compared with the 1961 car's independent rear suspension. Like the D-type Jaguar, for example, it will lift an inner rear wheel in a tight, hard corner, but the handling itself is totally predictable. With its successes on some of the more bumpy circuits, the combination of ride and handling must be good. The tail may tend to hop around and become a little skittish, but with its predictability this is no problem.

The brakes are fine, although they are now non-original discs — a previous owner must have found the old finned drums inadequate. They may not be as good as the D-type's discs, but they have much more feel and pull the car up four-square.

But the heart of any car is the engine, and that of the Testa Rossa is no exception. It's been said before many times, I suppose, but that V12 is quite wonderful. The fact that it can be driven on the road so fuss-free and undramatically shows how tractable and torquey it is, yet at the other end of the scale, using all the 7,000, 7,500 or even 8,000 rpm of which these engines are capable, there is enormous power: it is a forgiving yet almost unburstable power unit. And all the while there is that unique, magnificent engine note which, once heard, is never forgotten.

How quick would it be on a circuit? This is a moot point, but if we take the full Grand Prix circuit (including the old Woodcote chicane) at Silverstone, I lapped there in the 1 min 42 sec bracket in the later car, and, judging by that, I reckon the 250 Testa Rossa would probably turn in times around the 1 min 49 sec mark. By any standards, that's not bad.

Five years after I wrote about the Testa Rossa in *Classic and Sportscar*, Anthony Bamford and I took

Bouncing over a Silverstone kerb in the 1961 Testa Rossa. Notice the curvature of the windscreen: everything is distorted when you try to look through it, which makes placing the car very difficult.

More glowing words have probably been written about Ferrari V12 engines than any other subject under the motoring sun: the Testa Rossa's 3 litre unit is fuss-free, tractable, intoxicating and torquey.

part with it in the 1987 Mille Miglia retrospective, which can only be described as a thorough test. Apart from fitting the seats from Bamford's 1963 GTO, the car was prepared to its standard specification by Brian Morley.

Just like the Jaguar D-type at Le Mans, the Testa Rossa was totally in its element, and the further we went the better it felt. The car was so comfortable that I could easily have driven the 1,000 miles on my own — on closed roads! — and on the long straights back to Brescia it pulled well over 150 mph.

The 250 Testa Rossa has to be one of the all-time great sports racing cars, even as Ferraris go. It has the looks, and such beautiful looks too; it has that fantastic V12 engine; it handles superbly, like the thoroughbred racing car it is; and it *is* a Ferrari.

1960
FERRARI DINO 246

Of all the cars I've raced and track tested over the years, the Ferrari Dino 246 must be the one with which my name is most often linked. I drove Anthony Bamford's original short chassis car on and off for four seasons in historic racing, mainly during the spell when Lloyds & Scottish sponsored the British Championship, arguably the best days of historic racing in this country. I must have competed in between 30 and 40 races in the car.

As a 1960 car, the Bamford Dino is the ultimate in the long line of front-engined Formula 1 cars, but was usually outclassed by the little rear-engined Coopers and Lotuses, which made up in lightness and agility what they lacked in power. It is no coincidence that Ferrari's only Grand Prix victory that year came for Phil Hill at Monza, where a boycott by the British works teams — they refused to race on the banked section of the track — left the Italians with little challenge on home ground.

The F1 Dino's roots go back to the 1957 1½ litre F2 Dino, whose V6 engine had been designed by Vittorio Jano with the potential to be developed for F1. This unit was progressively enlarged from its original 1,490 cc to an eventual 2,417 cc, using a bore and stroke of 85 mm × 71 mm, and in this form it powered Ferrari's new F1 Dinos for the 1958 season. Starting from a power output of 190 bhp at 9,200 rpm in 1,490 cc form, the V6 grew to develop a healthy 270 bhp at 8,300 rpm in 2,417 cc guise. Ferrari faced the new season with confidence, for its new car was all ready to go while Vanwall and BRM struggled to adapt their big four-cylinders to run on the AvGas fuel required by new rules.

The V6's two banks of three cylinders were arranged at a 65° angle, the two blocks slightly staggered in relation to each other. Twin overhead camshafts, chain-driven from the crankshaft nose, sat atop each block. There were two valves per cylinder and twin spark plugs fired by a pair of magnetos, one on the nose of each inlet camshaft. Three twin-choke Webers mounted within the vee looked after carburation. Like the Lancia-Ferrari before it, the engine was angled in the chassis so that the propshaft could pass to the driver's right (and allow a low seating position). A four-speed gearbox was mounted transversely at the rear in unit with a ZF limited slip final drive.

The Dino's first season netted Mike Hawthorn the Drivers' Championship title, although Vanwall took the inaugural Constructors' Cup. Hawthorn won only one GP (the French at Reims) to Stirling Moss's four, but the new Dino took him to five second places . . . and more points than Stirling. Undoubtedly the season's highlight came at Silverstone when Peter Collins led Hawthorn home for a Ferrari 1–2, but on the heels of that elation came Collins's death in the German GP at the Nürburgring — but he wasn't the first driver to be killed in a Dino, as Luigi Musso had lost his life at Reims.

Under Carlo Chiti's guidance, development continued on the Dino for the 1959 season, with delicious new bodywork from Fantuzzi the major change. Dunlop disc brakes and tyres were fitted, the de Dion rear end was adapted to take coil springs, the wheelbase was lengthened by 2.3 in and a five-speed gearbox fitted. The driving strength was almost completely new, Tony Brooks, Jean Behra and Cliff Allison being signed up, although Phil Hill and Olivier Gendebien remained with the team. The first race at Monaco showed that the rear-engined cars by now had an advantage on twisty circuits, but the Ferrari's brute power told on the faster circuits, Brooks winning at Avus and Reims.

For 1960, the Dino was further honed into the ultimate front-

Back in 1979 at Silverstone on one of several dozen Dino outings. Although I always loved driving the car, its determination to understeer when turning into a corner — very apparent here — was one characteristic I did not care for.

The lovely thing about the Dino is its willingness — it just wants to rev and rev. I normally took it to 8,500 rpm, but the engine's limit has to be respected.

Left A Brands Hatch start in company with Marsh Plant Aston Martin DBR4 and Lister-Jaguar. Making a good getaway in the Dino was always difficult because of the cumbersome movement across the gearbox from first to second.

Above right Leading the pack, with Richard Bond's Aston Martin DBR4 and Stirling Moss's Dino tucked in behind, through Silverstone's Copse Corner in 1980, the year of my first Lloyds & Scottish Championship title in the Dino.

Right This view of the Dino's cockpit clearly shows how the engine is angled to allow the propshaft to pass to the right of the driver's seat, while the 'back-to-front' gear-shift is on the left.

engined weapon, but it was to be a difficult twilight season, with a 1–2–3 (led by Hill) at Monza — in the absence of the British teams — the highlight in terms of pure results. The car entered its final season with revisions intended to concentrate weight within the wheelbase. Pannier fuel tanks were mounted either side of the cockpit, leaving only small fuel and oil tanks in the tail of the car. Independent rear suspension with coil spring/damper units replaced the de Dion tube at the rear, and the transaxle was turned round to fit within the wheelbase. This necessitated the engine being re-angled to provide a left-hand gearchange, the V6 also being moved nearly 10 in back in the chassis.

Not only did the drivers have to adapt to changing gear with the left hand instead of the right, but also they had to adjust to a reversed gate. By his own admission, Cliff Allison's terrifying accident at Monaco, when he was thrown out of the car after hitting the chicane, was caused by this new gear pattern: 'Going down into the chicane I got caught out by that revised gear shift, went from fifth to sixth, locked the rear wheels and glanced the barrier. No excuse, it was all my own fault . . .'

Since I had raced a Maserati 250F quite extensively before I first tried the Bamford Dino at a test session at Silverstone in the late 'seventies, I was immediately struck by how much more sophisticated and easier to drive it was. Naturally, as Ferrari's last front-engined F1 car, it felt much more modern than the 250F. Looking back on that first drive — before the car was stripped and rebuilt — it's funny that I was never able again to lap Silverstone as quickly, even though I was a bit below par, having just had my appendix out!

Just like Cliff Allison, I found that the most tricky part of driving the Dino is getting used to the strange 'back to front' gearbox. First gear is positioned conventionally enough over to the left and

Left *You need to give the Dino everything on the throttle to attempt to get the rear wheels sliding because traction is so good. As a result, my style in the car is invariably untidy.*

Right *With the rear-engined revolution in full spate by 1959, the Dino 246 was at its best on 'power' circuits — this is Tony Brooks winning the French Grand Prix at Reims that year.*

back, but for second you have to go right across the gate and forwards. Third is towards you on the right-hand side, and fourth and fifth are in the middle plane. I usually get it right, but first to second needs such a slow deliberate change that getting a good start off the grid is well nigh impossible. As the start is the only time you need first gear, there is actually never any problem during the races.

The gear-change itself is beautiful, the short lever on the left having a fairly long throw. You sit nice and low in the Dino, alongside the propshaft instead of on top of it as in the 250F, which makes you feel relatively safe. Talking of safety, I always raced the car with a leather-rimmed steering wheel, as a wooden one is potentially far more dangerous.

My best memory of the Dino is its fabulous V6 engine, which makes an absolutely glorious noise. Making the 250F comparisons again, the Dino engine is far crisper and higher revving, but it also needs to be used more. Whereas the power starts to come in at 5,000 rpm in the Maser, you need more like 6,500–7,000 in

the Dino, and I normally took it to around 8,500. I have always maintained that the Dino engine is actually less powerful than the 250F I raced, but then my 250F engine, prepared by Cyril Embrey, was a fluke, giving something like 60 bhp more than all the others. In its time, there's no doubt that the Dino was the more powerful car.

The lovely thing about the Dino is its willingness — it just wants to rev and rev. It was fairly trouble-free when I raced it, but the engine is prone to excessive valve wear. We had new valve gear made, and after that there was never any problem, but you had to respect the rev limit. The propshaft was also a little delicate.

The Dino's sophistication definitely shows in the handling, and the grip, compared with the 250F, is streets ahead. Since it understeers very strongly as you turn in — which I don't care for — my style in the car is always untidy. Once you're in the corner, you need to give it everything on the throttle to get the rear wheels sliding — the traction is superb. You can steer it beautifully with the throttle, using virtually all the power, and

as a result your exit speed from a corner is very high. This is where the Dino really scores over the opposition, and you give the impression of having far more power than the others! In the slower corners this must all look very lurid to spectators, but in the faster corners you're not piling on the power so aggressively and you can drive straight through very neutrally.

This straightforward handling character makes the Dino very forgiving, and it would be relatively easy for a driver of middle of the road ability to master, unlike a 250F. When you climb back into a Maser you think what a bag of rubbish it is: it's heavier, rougher, it rattles, shakes and rolls, and it slides all the time. But in the end I'd say that a 250F is more rewarding to drive quickly.

Now, all of this applies to the short chassis Dino which I always raced, but I've driven both of the long chassis cars as well. Neil Corner's long chassis car is more difficult to compare directly because it has the more powerful Tasman-spec 3 litre V12 engine from the GTO, but I've also driven the long chassis

car which David Clarke's Graypaul Motors built up for Albert Obrist, and which later belonged to John Foulston. That turns in much better, and you don't have to boot it so hard to break the adhesion at the rear. In fact, it feels much the same in faster corners, but the turn-in advantage makes it much easier to drive through slower ones. The V12 engine makes Neil's car heavier at the front, but its extra torque encourages the traction to break and to a degree balances out the nose-heaviness.

In terms of times on the track, the differences between the various cars are actually hardly significant. I've driven all four — 'my' Bamford car, the Bamford short chassis replica which Stirling Moss used to drive, the long chassis replica, and the Neil Corner Tasman car — round the Silverstone club circuit, and my best times are all within 0.1 sec of each other, in the 60.4 sec bracket. Mind you, the long chassis replica took a great deal of sorting by Albert Obrist to be a match for the others.

Most of my experience has been on 15 in wheels, although the car raced in its day on 16 in ones. The thinking behind the change was that the slightly larger contact patch of a smaller tyre would give us more grip, but I preferred the handling on the larger wheels as there was plenty of grip in any case. An odd result of this was that the brakes became a problem. In the end we worked out that the greater degree of offset needed for 15 in wheels caused the splined hubs to flex slightly, and a lot of vibration came through the brakes. Their efficiency was always terrific, even though I'm one of the last of the late brakers, but the car would shake like a dog getting out of a river. Oddly, this only ever happened in my regular car, but it was quite a problem as we suffered two sheared discs.

I've already described the gearbox, but this is mated to a delicious clutch. It's very important not to slip the clutch, as it's an 'organic' one with asbestos linings buried inside the 'box which cannot dissipate the heat caused by careless use. This is quite different from the 250F, which has a more forgiving small diameter multi-plate (of aluminium) clutch with better heat soak.

The steering, too, is nice — the feel is good, and it's not particularly heavy. With these old cars, though, the steering is relatively unimportant, for you guide the car through the corners with your right foot . . .

Some of my happiest racing memories have been in Anthony Bamford's Dino, and I always particularly enjoyed racing against Neil Corner and Gerry Marshall — they're the only two people I'm prepared to race within a couple of feet of. Two races stand out, back in 1981. I had an incredible dice with Gerry's Aston Martin DBR4 at the Lloyds & Scottish supporter to the British GP, but had to drop out of that one — while leading! — with the valve guide problem I mentioned earlier. A couple of months later, I was back at Silverstone for a very wet VSCC meeting, and had a terrific ding-dong with Neil until he spun his Dino.

In many ways I was very lucky in being able to drive the Dino when historic racing was arguably at its peak in Britain. Not only was the quality of the competition high, but also there was an incredible variety of great cars taking part. Let's hope those days haven't gone for ever.

1960
COOPER T53

The final Grand Prix of 1959 took place at Sebring in December, with three possible contenders for the World Championship: Stirling Moss, Tony Brooks and Jack Brabham. It was one of those complicated set-ups — if Brooks won but Brabham got fastest lap, and so on — and after 2 hr 12 min it had been settled. Young Bruce McLaren won overall — his first GP victory, just a second or so ahead of Maurice Trintignant — with Brooks third and Brabham fourth. 'Black Jack' had in fact led the vast majority of the race, but on the last lap he ran out of fuel, and literally pushed it over the line. It was enough: he had won his first World Championship, and Cooper theirs. The world of Formula 1 motor racing changed forever.

Cooper's success was for all the wrong reasons, as far as the purists were concerned. They used a commercially-available engine, their engineering was somewhat pragmatic, and they even employed drivers who got their hands dirty, even helping to design and build their own cars, for heaven's sake. Why, they even had the engines in the wrong place, behind the driver. What those purists couldn't see was that these factors gave Cooper the championship.

There are a number of distinct advantages in having the engine behind the driver. The obvious one, of course, is that there is no propshaft, resulting in two benefits. The first is that it doesn't have to find its way past the driver, so he can sit lower, which reduces frontal area quite considerably: a square foot of reduction is worth 25 bhp. Secondly, it reduces weight, simply by not being there, and a weight reduction in one area leads to another, and so on.

There is also a rather less tangible benefit, and it involves polar moment of inertia. Traditional thinking had been that a high moment, with a long chassis and the weights more or less concentrated at each end, was a 'good thing', since it took quite a lot to deflect a car from a given course — there was less likelihood of a spin. Where this missed out, of course, was in nimbleness: with a low polar moment, a car may be more twitchy, more likely to spin, but by the same token its responses are more rapid.

Coopers won because they could out-fumble the less wieldy front-engined machines on tighter circuits (they seldom shone at such places as the banked Avus, but could blow off the Ferraris *et al* at Monaco). They played a joker as well, because their low frontal area made them very quick on the straights at Spa and Reims, where Brabham was timed at 192 mph!

They also won because they were lighter than the opposition. The 1959 T51 weighed a mere 1,008 lb without driver: the front-engined BRM P25 in the same condition came in at 1,481 lb and *it* was regarded as light. The effect of lightness, of course, is that there is less load on tyres for a given cornering speed. To put it another way, for the same load the lighter car is generating a higher g-force, which means travelling faster. The 1959 racing season proved the point.

But of course others had latched on to the point, not least Cooper's arch-rival Colin Chapman. For 1960 he had a new weapon, the Lotus 18. And BRM, too, were beavering away on their mid-engined machine, the P48. They even employed both Jack and Bruce to help them — with Cooper's blessing!

The first race of the 1960 season to count for the championship was in Argentina in February. Cooper sent two of the 1959 cars for Brabham and McLaren. Young Bruce won, his second GP victory in succession, while Brabham dropped out with transmission problems. But McLaren's win was no walk-over: at the start, Ireland in the new Lotus 18 proved to be sensationally fast until he spun, to be dogged thereafter with gearchange problems. The much

Right *The Cooper T53, the 'Lowline' model of 1960, has such incredible roadholding that you can exit corners very quickly, even if the 2.5 litre Coventry-Climax engine is not the most powerful at the top end.*

Right *No matter how much I try, I cannot get very enthusiastic about the Coopers I have driven, and the T53 is no exception. It is controllable, but always feels very nervous at the rear.*

Below *I raced a T51 (the 1959 Grand Prix car) in the 1982 Lloyds & Scottish series, taking two wins in six rounds. Like Cooper's experience in the car's heyday, our problems always seemed to be with the transmission.*

more powerful BRMs and Ferraris then made the running but they too fell prey to mechanical gremlins, leaving the New Zealander to canter home.

On the way back from South America after that struggle, Jack Brabham and John Cooper decided a new car was needed. That was in mid-March, and the new car was ready in May. It was much as before, only more so.

To be honest, Cooper could never be called technically innovative — engine position apart, and that dated back to the 500 cc F3 cars, which were rear-engined so that the chain drive was a reasonable length. But Cooper did have some brilliantly intuitive people, none more so than Brabham. If he was a master of anything it was at setting up the suspension of a car — he, in effect, invented 'adjustable suspension', alternative wishbone mountings and so on, via airmail with his Australian friend Ron Tauranac. Owen Maddock, Cooper's designer, was a practical man too.

Trying to hold Albert Obrist's long-chassis Dino 246 at bay shows the T51's evil handling. It had a very wilful back end, flopping over at the rear while waggling its inside front wheel in the air.

The new car's chassis rather proved the point. Gone was the traditional curved tube spaceframe, a design that had stress engineers in hysterics — but the straight-tube replacement wasn't really much better in their eyes. Take the tubing around the rear engine bays: there were two diagonal bracing tubes between top and bottom longerons — but they met half-way along the *unsupported* bottom one. What's more, the diagonals acted as suspension and engine mounts, once again with the wishbone pivot points, for example, being sited part-way along the tube instead of at a junction of pipework. But it worked.

The whole purpose of the new chassis was to reduce frontal area, and this was achieved in a number of ways. The engine was lowered, the

steering box was moved ahead of the front axle which in turn meant the pedals could be moved forward, allowing a longer cockpit in which the driver could recline quite a bit more. This led to the new model, coded T53 at Coopers, being nicknamed the 'Lowline'. Once clothed in its aluminium bodywork which included a high-penetration nose, it indeed looked considerably sleeker.

Suspension was as before, with wishbones at each corner, but there was one major change which Charles Cooper didn't like one bit: coil springs replaced the transverse leaves at the back. The wishbones were slightly wider and those at the rear reinforced with cross-bracing. Tyres, too, were just beginning to grow in width, and for 1960 wheel widths increased from $3\frac{1}{2}$ in to $4\frac{1}{2}$ in at the front, and from $4\frac{1}{2}$ in to 6 in at the rear.

The power unit was the trusty and tried Coventry-Climax FPF twin-cam which pushed out 245 bhp, compared with the Ferraris' 275 bhp

and BRM's 272 bhp: it was not, therefore, the most poky of engines, but it was torquey, strong and reliable. Attached to it was, arguably, the most important part of the new car, Cooper's own transaxle. The Citroën-based ERSA gearbox used up until then was showing its age. As Doug Nye says in his excellent *Cooper Cars*, the new 'box was, 'Complex and tricky to make, but in this case worked brilliantly well and totally justified the trouble and care taken'. It was also wildly expensive by Cooper's standards, costing around £1,000 for each 'box, a fact which John had to hide from Charles...

The first shake-down trial of the Lowline took place on Friday 6 May, and the results were stunning. Within 10 laps Brabham was 2 sec inside the official Silverstone lap record.

The new car's competition debut came a few days later, in the International Trophy at Silverstone. Cooper's high hopes were rather shattered when Innes Ireland in the Lotus 18 walloped them, but Jack did

Jack Brabham winning the 1959 British Grand Prix on his way to that year's World Championship. In his hands, the T51 appears far tauter than the car I raced.

finish second after Moss retired. Chapman's mathematical approach, which Charles Cooper looked upon with contempt, seemed to work.

Stirling Moss won at Monaco, but Brabham proved, in the rain at least, that he and the Cooper could match the Moss/Lotus combination, only to spin and hit the wall at St Devote. Young Bruce had a fraught race, what with one thing and another, including a spin, but he eventually finished second. At only 22, he was leading the World Championship.

Then to Zandvoort only a week later for the Dutch GP, with Brabham's car being rushed back to Surbiton for a bit of intense rebuilding. Despite the rush, Brabham and Moss's Lotus blasted away from everyone else until the seventeenth lap, when the Cooper flicked a kerb-stone into the path of the

Lotus, which burst a front tyre. Moss pitted, and from then on Jack had it all his own way, giving the Lowline its first GP victory, and Jack's first of the year. Young Bruce retired with a broken UJ.

The results for the rest of the season tell it all. Belgian GP, Spa, Coopers 1-2; French GP, Reims-Gueux, Coopers 1-3 (with a private Cooper T51 second); British GP, Coopers 1-4; Portuguese GP, Coopers 1-2; United States GP, Coopers 3-4. Brabham was World Champion for the second time, and Cooper took the Constructors' Cup for the second time as well. What's more, they did it without even entering the Italian GP, whose organizers insisted on using the notorious banking. Along with the other British works teams, Cooper boycotted the event since they believed the banking to be too dangerous. To make up the numbers, the organizers allowed F2 cars to take part. The result was nine Coopers, no less, out of 16 cars on the grid (no Lowlines, though).

This Coventry-Climax engine looks a bit battered, but its power, around 245 bhp, is enough for it to push John Harper's 'Lowline' around the Silverstone Club circuit in 1 min.

This season, 1960, was Cooper's greatest year, with 'Black Jack's' five consecutive victories, and the end of an era. For 1961 the rules were changed to a 1½ litre formula.

John Harper's T53 is well-known on the historic circuits, mainly because it always seems to finish first, which I find rather selfish, particularly if I'm in the same race! It is one of three T53s made for the 1960 season, and John is 'reasonably sure' that it's FII/8/60, in other words the ex-Brabham car.

The phrase 'reasonably sure' is used with discretion since the history of the cars post-1960 is, to put it mildly, highly confused. When I asked Cooper historian Doug Nye what happened to them he simply said, 'How long have you got? It would take me three months full-time to try to sort it out — I tried, and failed.' Working on the assumption, though, that it is FII/8/60, then it had a very illustrious career in 1960, carrying 'Black Jack' to victory at Zandvoort, Spa, Reims-Gueux, Silverstone and Oporto, with further wins in lesser events such as the Silver City Trophy at Brands and the Oulton Park Gold Cup, not to mention a second in the US GP at Riverside.

John brought it out from Jersey ten years ago in what he describes as a 'totally wrecked condition'. It had been used for sand racing, and salt water and steel don't go very well together. John reckons he's saved about three-quarters of the chassis and he still has a few patches of the old bodywork, but most of the latter is new. Most of the running gear too is new, as is the engine, but he was lucky enough to save the Owen Maddock-designed gearbox.

Considering how fast he goes, John is very deprecatory about its performance. He says, for example, that it's not as quick as you might anticipate, being 'only half a second' faster than the Lotus 16. But then he diffidently adds that it was rebuilt to the *original* specification, and is totally under-developed for modern historic stuff. And then a little glint comes into his eye, and he adds that if he continues to race it and faster cars appear, he may have to do something about it, just by modernising the little things that don't show. In fact, he reckons to get another 2 sec or so out of it. I hate aiming at moving targets...

It's worth mentioning at this point that I had a fair bit of experience back in 1982 in the Lloyds & Scottish Historic Car Championship with Ken Moore's T51, a chance which came right out of the blue. I had begun to come to terms with the fact that I wouldn't be racing much that year, when Ken telephoned the Friday evening before the first race. Stirling Moss had been knocked off his motorbike, so would I like to drive one of his Coopers? Stirling, in fact, was out of action for the year, so I drove Ken's cars in all six rounds. It wasn't a bad year, and *Autosport*, in an odd fit of generosity, described my last-minute involvement as the 'saving grace of the season'.

I didn't get off to too good a start in the first round at Silverstone because the T51 suffered a gear selector problem which manifested itself by the car jumping out of gear halfway through corners. We elected to race another of Ken's cars, his 2 litre T45 in Rob Walker colours, to be on the safe side, even though this had literally been finished just the night before. It hadn't turned a wheel in anger since its Peter Denty restoration, and in the race it had a sticky gear linkage which kept me down to eighth place — actually, the smaller engine really wasn't suited to Silverstone.

Thereafter, things went rather better, and I raced the red 2½ litre T51 in the remaining five rounds. This was the last Lloyds & Scottish season, and not one of the best since some of the finest cars of previous years weren't taking part, and we only visited Brands Hatch and Silverstone. I had two wins, one each at Brands and Silverstone, a second and two thirds. The only real disappointment was at the GP supporting race at Brands, where I led off the line but dropped back to finish third when I lost third gear mid-way through. Just like Cooper's experience in the car's heyday, our problems always seemed to be with the transmission...

I'll let you into a little secret: after that season, I'm a bit wary of Coopers. They do seem to have a mind of their own when you're tramping on, perhaps a case of the tail wagging the dog, and I've never felt particularly at home in them. They are very difficult to drive well, but as a result they can be very fulfilling. Other drivers used to be quite concerned about the way it looked, the tail lurching around and the inside front wheel waving around in the air. I remember John Harper — coincidentally, he was one of my strongest rivals with his B-type Connaught in 1982 — telling me that he thought I was going to shoot off the road backwards in front of him. I was overtaking him into Abbey Curve at Silverstone, and he was so worried that he backed right off to let me through!

Having said this, the T53 was 100 per cent better in the handling stakes than the earlier T51. The T53 sits much more four-square on the road, without that flop-over, but it must be said that it carries on the Cooper tradition of being nervous at the rear. It is all very controllable, and as you know I prefer oversteer to understeer, so the only way I can really describe it is to say that it doesn't feel a very *efficient* form of tail-happiness.

And yet it is in the corners, of course, where the Cooper has it all over the opposition. Its best factor by far is its traction, both through and out of the corners. Remember what I was saying about a lighter car being able to generate higher cornering speeds, because for the same cornering speeds you're not loading the tyres so heavily — or for the same tyre loading you're travelling quicker? The T53 is an absolutely

perfect example of this. I wouldn't put the handling in the same league as the Lotus 16, which is a much more sophisticated beastie, but when it comes to roadholding the Cooper is near enough uncatchable.

The sling-shot effect down the straights which you can get by exiting corners rapidly is perhaps just as well, because the Coventry-Climax engine isn't the most powerful engine at the top end — the Ferrari Dino V6, for example, would see it off in a straight line. But it's a very strong engine, with loads of low-down torque, and really that's what you want for most British tracks. In fact I never dropped lower than third for the whole of Silverstone's Club circuit. I did contemplate second for Becketts at one point, but that was only because of a slight pick-up problem at lower revs. But it wasn't necessary, because you could use the torque instead of revs to achieve the same effect.

John was highly enthusiastic about the Cooper gearbox, and after my experiences with the earlier Citroën-ERSA device I can see why. It is really good, and you can make clean, slick changes just by a flick of the lever. We used to have fairly major problems with the older device, both with the linkage and the selectors jumping out of gear mid-corner... John rates it as better than a Hewland, and I wouldn't disagree with him there.

The cockpit is nice and roomy, and John and I are roughly the same size, so there were no problems in accommodation. Quite obviously the car has been properly sorted, so that such things as the position of the pedals and so forth are spot-on. About the only thing I noted, and it wasn't a complaint, just a fact, was that brake pedal pressures were a bit high — but then the brakes are the equal of anything else around, and drama-free.

Without doing anything foolish, and keeping well clear of the assorted Formula Silly boys who were boun-

cing off each other and the outskirts of the circuit the day I was there (Barry McGuigan, the boxer, managed to halt the proceedings for a while), I found myself lapping in 62 sec or thereabouts, which compares reasonably to John's fastest times at around 1 min dead. Thus it's an easy car to drive quickly, but I would have wanted some more practice laps, and fewer Formula Fords around, to explore the ultimate limits of the handling and claw back those couple of seconds — it's a case of diminishing returns.

It's funny, you know. Even though the T53 is capable of beating the best of them, and putting up some very, very quick lap times, I cannot find myself getting very enthusiastic about it. Sorry, John. I keep trying to think why, and there really isn't one reason. All the Coopers I've driven have been twitchy, and the T53 is no exception, but then it is controllable. If I say it feels unsophisticated, people will think I mean crude — and it's not that either. I think the best description is that it is a journeyman's car, a car built for a purpose which it achieves with the minimum of fuss, with no messing about or high-falutin' high technology. An anti-Chapman, anti-Ferrari, anti-Maserati machine, you might say. And by heaven it worked, so you can't criticize it for that! Mind you, what may not have helped was that I climbed straight into it from a Ferrari 312T3, all goggle-eyed...

One more point. I know it's something I tend to bang on about, but John has prepared and sorted the car properly. It is immaculately presented, starts instantly on the button, and shows no vices whatsoever. It's amazing how much more quickly you go when you have full confidence in a car.

Thanks for the ride, John. I will keep thinking about it, and maybe one day I will get it all straight in my mind and become a Cooper convert!

1960
MASERATI BIRDCAGE

Long after it should have been retired, the Birdcage Maserati was winning races and championships. One was particularly memorable. As late as 1972, a Birdcage won the JCB Championship for historic racers, the clincher coming at the last race ever to be held at the Crystal Palace. The winning car was a spaceframe Lister Jaguar driven by a gentleman usually described as 'burly' and called Marshall or something like that, but, by coming second, the Maserati's driver became the JCB Champion for 1972. That was me...

I also remember the first time I drove a Birdcage — it was on the road, to Silverstone. As if that wasn't bad enough (there was 'an episode' which I'd sooner forget), the owner of the car, Anthony Bamford, was standing at Woodcote when I spun it in the wet three times on the grass after crossing the 'Woodcote river', without hitting a single thing...

There was some great racing in those days. One of my closest rivals was Nick Faure in another Birdcage the one with the long windscreen. He was just as quick as me but very much a gentleman. If you came up beside him, and waggled your arms around, he would back off. *Very* gentlemanly. Another, of course, was Mr Marshall, who did *not* back off!

The Birdcage really is a rather astonishing car, with one of the most complicated and sophisticated chassis ever. But then I have a theory about this. Do you remember a game we used to play at school years ago called something like 'pick-a-stick'? You let a bunch of sticks like knitting needles drop on to the floor, then try to pick them up individually without disturbing the others. My theory is that, when Giulio Alfieri came to draw up the Birdcage, his men were sitting around the factory with nothing to do except play 'pick-a-stick', and...after all, all they had to do was weld the points where the sticks crossed!

This must be the most elaborate spaceframe chassis ever made, inspired as it was by Maserati's wish to match the torsional rigidity and lightness offered by a monocoque. Jaguar had already proved the monocoque's merits with its D-type, and Maserati Chief Engineer Vittorio Bellentani had wanted to produce one of his own way back in 1954. The problem for Maserati was that it lacked the technology to produce a monocoque, since it had no craftsmen experienced in the aircraft industry. Bellentani's successor, Alfieri, therefore decided to produce a complex spaceframe, using known technology. It would reproduce the stress-sharing characteristics of a monocoque, yet be easier to build and repair.

It was in late 1958 that a prototype chassis was welded up, 'pick-a-stick' style, from 200 lengths of 10 mm, 12 mm and 15 mm thin-wall steel tube. A degree of elasticity was built into the lattice structure to prevent the welds from cracking. The finished spaceframe weighed a mere 66 lb, and it far exceeded the torsional rigidity of any previous Maserati chassis. With this groundwork done, design of the new *Tipo* 60, which would earn the nickname 'Birdcage', began in earnest.

These were bad times for Maserati — the company was close to bankruptcy. Despite Fangio's 1957 Formula 1 World Championship title in a 250F, and the fearsome 450S's near-miss in the World Sports Car Championship, cash flow problems for the Orsi empire resulted in the Italian Government stepping in to manage the finances. Without question, this meant the end of factory racing programmes, although Maserati was permitted to continue building customer racing cars.

Once some money had been paid by creditors, Alfieri was able to set to on the *Tipo* 60's design in late 1958. In order to appeal to customers in Italian national racing, it would be

Although the Maserati Birdcage is often considered a hairy machine, the sort you throw around, it is a light car to drive, almost a fingertip racer.

The Birdcage's steering is light and quick, but not very exciting — it feels as it if has negative offset, being rather vague and having little self-centring effect.

an uncomplicated 2 litre car. Maserati's existing 200SI four-cylinder was redesigned so that it could be angled at 45° below the *Tipo* 60's low bonnet line, and the original 92 mm × 75 mm bore/stroke dimensions were altered to a more oversquare 93.8 mm × 72 mm to allow extra revs, producing a capacity of 1,989 cc. Revised valve gear and larger ports were added, the inlet and exhaust manifolds were transposed to suit the 'lay-down' mounting, and a coil and distributor fired twin plugs per cylinder. After some bench work, an encouraging power output of 195 bhp at 7,800 rpm was achieved.

Power was transmitted through an improved version of Maserati's five-speed transaxle, and suspension followed 250F practice in having double wishbones and coil springs at the front, and a de Dion layout at the rear.

Stirling Moss enthused greatly after testing the prototype at Modena and the Nürburgring, but all the orders for the initial batch of six cars came unexpectedly from the USA, where customers, led by Joe Lubin, asked for a 3 litre derivative. By mid-1959, therefore, the *Tipo* 61 had evolved, with a 100 mm × 92 mm 2,890 cc four-cylinder engine delivering 250 bhp at 6,500 rpm. This fell short of the 300 bhp or so of the rival Ferrari Testa Rossas and Aston

Martin DBR1s, but the Maserati had a crucial weight advantage of nearly 400 lb, as well as better roadholding, handling, braking and traction.

A total of 22 Birdcages were eventually built, six of them (including the prototype) being 2 litre cars, the other 16 3 litre cars. All the larger-engined cars went to American customers, the most significant being 'Lucky' Casner's Camoradi team. The Birdcage enjoyed immense success in SCCA racing, but Camoradi, with a little works support and sometimes precarious financial backing, established the Birdcage's importance in the World Sports Car Championship.

Camoradi's early World Cham-

pionship races in 1960 followed a familiar Maserati pattern — the *Tipo* 61 proved to be fast, but fragile and unlucky. At Buenos Aires, a single Birdcage for Masten Gregory/Dan Gurney left the Ferraris in its wake until a rear damper mounting broke. At Sebring, Camoradi entered three cars, but one didn't make the race after its engine destroyed itself. Moss/Gurney led comfortably until final drive failure, while the other car, driven by Gregory/Carroll Shelby, succumbed to an oil pipe breakage on the third lap, apparently caused because the car had been insufficiently warmed up.

Alfieri responded to these disappointments by strengthening the transaxle, but those promising runs teased enough money out of Orsi to allow Camoradi to enter one car in the Targa Florio for Nino Vaccarella/Umberto Maglioli. They led by 5 min, but Vaccarella crashed after his engine cut out in the middle of a corner. At the Nürburgring 1,000 km, however, a Birdcage finally held together long enough for Moss/Gurney to win after an exciting race, while a second entry for Gregory/Gino Munaron finished fifth. This was the peak of its career.

Three cars went to Le Mans, and there were three body styles for this fast race: a 'streamliner' with a long

tail and big-windscreen bodywork, a long-tail car with a conventional front half, and a regular car. Clocking 169 mph down the Mulsanne Straight, Gregory built up a huge lead in the 'streamliner' until it dropped back with starter motor trouble, eventually retiring with a blown engine during the night. The other two cars also retired, Munaron/Giorgio Scarlatti with starter motor failure and Casner/Jim Jeffords after a visit to a sandtrap. It was the same old story — the Birdcage was fast and handled well, but unreliability (as well as poor preparation and suspect team management) invariably ruined every-

Right *The Tipo 61 Birdcage's 3 litre four-cylinder engine is not one to set the pulse racing, but it thumps out plenty of power and torque throughout its range with relatively little vibration.*

Right *The facia comprises a chunk of flat aluminium sheet on which minimal instrumentation is scattered. The tachometer is red-lined at 7,000 rpm.*

thing in the races.

With lessons learned, the Birdcage should have swept all before it in 1961, even though Alfieri was drawing up a new rear-engined *Tipo* 63, but Maserati was still unable to afford a works team, and its number one customer, Camoradi, was having trouble paying the previous year's bills. Various customers, like Cunningham and Serenissima, kept the Birdcage in the picture as a second string to their *Tipo* 63s, but the best Birdcage performance of the year came when Casner managed to get the money together for a Camoradi entry at the Nürburgring. Sharing with Gregory, he won against all the odds on a circuit where the

Birdcage's superb handling was worth a lot.

Like so many other glorious Maserati sports racers, the Birdcage was far more bark than bite, and you have to wonder what a proper works team might have achieved with it in 1960. Yet its flashes of brilliance, most notably its two wins at the Nürburgring, showed that it was *the* sports racing machine of its time.

The opportunity to relive my enthusiasm for the Birdcage came when Nick Mason invited me to try his newly-acquired 3 litre *Tipo* 61 at Mallory Park in 1984. I jumped at the chance, because this isn't any old Birdcage — it is the one that gave me that JCB Championship.

Settling into the Birdcage, you might expect to be surrounded — or even trapped! — by a network of tiny tubes, but actually you aren't too aware of the spaceframe around you. Of course you can see it on the floor, and the sides, and on top of the facia, but what dominates the interior is the big, wood-rimmed steering wheel and the facia itself, an absolutely flat chunk of alloy containing four instruments.

Dare I say that the engine is rather boring? Being just a big four-cylinder, it isn't particularly pleasant, especially at idle — but, surprisingly, it doesn't vibrate as much as you might expect when running at peak revs. It runs up to

7,000 rpm, but in deference to Nick I didn't take it over 6,500 rpm. Not, I think, that you need to rev it much over that anyway — I only used the 7,000 rpm red-line in top during a race — since, being a bit of a thumper, there's plenty of power and torque at almost any revs.

Many people seem to think that the Birdcage was a hairy machine, the sort you throw around, with plenty of opposite lock. You can if you want to, but if you do you're losing time. It's a light car, much more of a fingertip machine like, for example, the Lotus 16, although the handling is neutral with a slight tendency to oversteer. The steering is slightly odd, too: it feels rather as if it has negative offset, being rather vague, and there isn't much self-centring. It's light and quick, but not very exciting — you simply turn into a corner and the car goes round. In fact, I'd go so far as to say it's not a greatly entertaining car to drive, just quick and competent.

You are not really aware of the complex lattice structure of the space-frame chassis when you sit in the Birdcage, but this view through the windscreen gives some idea of why the car gained its nickname.

Since I drove the car back in the early 1970s it has been fitted with wider wheels, and I don't think this has improved it at all — in fact I'd say the opposite. I don't think the chassis can take the increased offset this provides, and this may explain the steering vibration and raggedness that I experienced around Gerards. Whatever it is, Nick planned to cure it before undertaking serious competition work.

One of the better features of the car is the gearbox, which is a lighter, more compact version of that in the 250F — and the 250F's is one of the best in the world. That of the Birdcage isn't far behind. Quick, light, easy, clean, precise — what more could you ask for?

But probably the most sensational feature of the car is the braking. With those all-round discs you could — and I did — outbrake almost anything else on the track. In fact, they would stop the wheels going round if you let them. This didn't necessarily *stop* the car...

Going back to the racing days, I remember one occasion when we wanted to check the gearbox. Getting it out was easy enough, but when we came to put it back — no way! It was like one of those bent wire puzzles! It took us three days to get it back, and we eventually had to cut through some tubes and weld them back afterwards.

I'm also reminded of something Stirling Moss once said: 'If there's one thing you can rely on with a Maserati, it is that somehow or other it will pump out oil.'

Guess what happened at Mallory Park. Fortunately it was only a little leak, and easily curable, but times don't change...

1962
FERRARI 196SP

When John Godfrey, the owner of this fabulous little Ferrari 196SP, told me that its finest hour was finishing second in its first race, the 1962 Targa Florio, I imagined that it would be a pretty nimble car to drive. After all, the Targa Florio was an endless series of twists and turns over the 44-mile Little Madonie circuit, with a reputed 710 corners and 400 gearshifts on every lap. Only the most agile of sports racing cars were in their element here.

John then went on to tell me that the car's other significant achievement was winning the 1962 European Mountain Championship in the hands of Ludovico Scarfiotti. The sinuous hillclimbs of those days were not terribly much like our Shelsley Walsh or Prescott, being more like Alpine passes in their proportions, so superb handling was the most important quality for the successful cars in this forgotten branch of international motor sport.

After that little bit of introduction from John, I jumped into the 196SP raring to go. I felt immediately at home in the spacious cockpit, sitting very snugly in a little cloth-trimmed bucket seat, legs outstretched and arms slightly bent for a relaxed stance behind the alloy-spoked, wooden-rimmed steering wheel. In

front is a very large tachometer red-lined at 7,500 rpm, flanked by two smaller dials on the left marked 'olio' (oil for non-linguists) indicating temperature and pressure, and two on the right saying 'acqua' and 'benzina' (yes, you've guessed … water and fuel). There's a small seat to my left for the passenger which the rules assume needs to be carried, and alongside my right thigh is the chromed gate of the five-speed gearbox. First is a dog-leg to the left, and reverse ahead of it is protected by a small hinge which has to be flicked away to allow the gear to be engaged. All of this, in fact, is typically Ferrari, and completely familiar.

Having expected so much of the handling, it was that aspect of the car which made the most impact on me. Like any Ferrari, the 196SP really has to be told who's boss. You have to grab hold of the car and power it round the corners, otherwise it'll just be a handful. All the sports cars were like that up to the famous 512 of 1970 and 1971, but with the 312 which came next they suddenly changed overnight into Formula 1 cars.

That said, though, there was something rather odd about the 196SP's handling that I found hard to put my finger on. As you would

expect, it took a wide line when I was off the power, but it wasn't actually understeer. It felt as if the car was being pushed wide rather than doing it because the wheels were losing grip at the front. Give it some power, and the car would take a tighter line relative to the amount of pressure applied by the right foot. Remove the power, and it would start to run wide again.

Now, far be it from me to suggest that anything learned in my truck racing exploits can be applied to historic racing cars (most of them aren't as powerful for a start), but this running wide with lift-off feels just like the ERF I've driven! It's caused by a locking differential on the truck, so I reckon the characteristic on John's car could be the result of a tight limited slip differential.

You can slide the car very easily on the power, but it has this feeling of rolling a little at the back as if the suspension is too soft to try to compensate for the locking diff. The suspension is a double wishbone arrangement with coil springs and Koni dampers at front and rear, but having an anti-roll bar only at the front strikes me as odd. I would say that an anti-roll bar would be necessary at the rear, and John showed me the mounting points on the chassis frame where Ferrari had

experimented with one. It would be interesting to know why they rejected it.

The engine feels so good that I thought at first it must be larger than 2 litres. The 60° V6 has a single overhead camshaft on each bank in contrast with the twin cams on the 2.4 litre V6 of the front-engined Formula 1 Dino which I've driven so frequently, but it makes the same

gloriously crisp and throaty noise. John is very gentle with it these days because spare parts don't exist, so I stuck to 7,000 rpm. Judging by how smooth it is, I would imagine that Lorenzo Bandini, Giancarlo Baghetti and Ludovico Scarfiotti could have taken it comfortably over 8,000 rpm, and John says that when he once took it to 8,500 rpm he was just beginning to get valve

bounce — so there's lots in hand.

Its eagerness to rev is lovely, the power starting to come in at 4,500 rpm. By 5,000 rpm it's all there, which gives a usefully wide spread of power up to the quoted peak of 210 bhp at 7,500 rpm. Oil pressure of 4 kg per sq cm on the metric gauge seemed to me a little on the low side, but John says that's normal, while oil temperature was

Above *The 196SP, like any Ferrari, has to be driven confidently and powered round corners. One of its best features is the brakes, which allow you to run very deep into corners.*

Left *Developing around 210 bhp at 7,500 rpm, the little 2 litre V6 engine, with a single overhead camshaft for each cylinder bank, makes the same crisp and throaty noise as the twin-cam 2.4 litre V6 which I know so well from the Formula 1 Dino.*

hitting 100° in surges. Throttle response is instant, although John reckoned that the carburettors — three double choke 42DCN Webers mounted on a single manifold within the vee — were not quite on song, taking just a little crispness off the engine note.

The gearbox is very pleasant to use, with a short throw and smooth action. I found that it baulked a lit-tle going across the gate from third to fourth, but that's a standard Ferrari trait caused by everything flex-ing slightly and stiffening the linkage. Coming down through the gears, the change from third to se-cond is also a little clunky, and you have to get used to keeping the revs well up on down changes. The flywheel is so light that the revs die quickly.

Above *The facia, finished in black crackle paint, is dominated by a rev counter (red-lined at 7,500 rpm) flank-ed by two pairs of gauges, with oil pressure and temperature on the left and water temperature and fuel pressure on the right.*

The 196SP is a little over-geared for Donington, especially as I was experiencing the slow and 'Mickey Mouse' new loop for the first time when I drove this car in 1986, but I could go up to 7,000 rpm in top down the Craner Curves. I reckon that the car could go flat through the last left-hander before the hairpin, but I wouldn't be happy because of the way it runs wide. Besides, you

Right *Although the cockpit is comfor-table, I stick out into the airstream so much that buffeting is quite severe at speed — a small perspex fairing on top of the 'screen would help.*

Although six cars from the SP family (with V6 or V8 engines in capacities from 2 litres to 2.8 litres) survive today, John Godfrey's 196SP is the only one in completely original condition.

Apart from winning the 1962 European Mountain Championship in the hands of Ludovico Scarfiotti, the greatest moment for John Godfrey's 196SP was second place in the same year's Targa Florio, driven by Lorenzo Bandini and Giancarlo Baghetti.

don't do things like that in someone else's car. Let's say that if it was mine I might have a go!

The brakes are so good that you can go very deep into corners. I wouldn't want to frighten John, but there aren't many cars which you can take beyond the 100 yards mark into Redgate. The brake pedal has very little movement, with a reassuringly solid feel. All the controls, in fact, are easy and light. The steering is gorgeous and the clutch comfortable to use, although I would appreciate a plate to rest my left foot on. The car is so nimble and relaxing to drive — as well as feeling strongly constructed — that it would be perfect for the Targa Florio.

If I have any other reservation, it is the buffeting in the cockpit at speed. As I'm taller than John I probably feel it more, and would want to attach a small perspex fairing to the top of the 'screen. There are two small holes drilled there showing that in the past someone else has done exactly that.

Having enjoyed driving the 196SP so much, I was particularly interested to find out more about its history, as so little has been written about it. John Godfrey, in fact, is so fascinated by the SP series that he has written a book, and dug out hundreds of photographs — all he needs is a publisher! Naturally, he gave me chapter and verse.

The first of the SP series actually appeared in 1961, a year before John's car was built. This was the 246SP, which was significant for being Ferrari's first rear-engined sports car, using the same Vittorio Jano designed 2.4 litre V6 that powered the Formula 1 Dinos between 1957-60. Two 246SPs were built for the 1961 World Championship season, and were run with great success alongside the front-engined 3 litre Testa Rossas to give Ferrari the championship title.

The new 246SP was first raced at the opening round at Sebring by Wolfgang von Trips and Richie Ginther, but it retired from the lead when it went off the road with broken steering. This promising debut was fulfilled at the next race, the Targa Florio, when von Trips drove brilliantly to a slightly fortuitous victory, for Stirling Moss's leading factory Porsche broke its transmission with just four miles to go. At the Nürburgring 1,000 km one of the two 246SPs entered finished third in the hands of four drivers, Phil Hill and Olivier Gendebien joining von Trips and Ginther.

Le Mans saw a Testa Rossa swansong as the old front-engined cars took the first two places, Hill and Gendebien the victorious drivers, but the singleton 246SP of von Trips/Ginther acquitted itself well. It was lying second at half distance when a miscalculation by the team management allowed it to run out of fuel on the circuit. By this stage of the season, Ferrari's two-pronged effort had yielded the championship, so just one 246SP was entered for the final round at Pescara, Baghetti and Ginther leading in the early stages until the steering broke, the second such failure that season.

Four more SP cars were built for the 1962 season, and the two 1961 cars were rebodied so that all six cars were outwardly identical. There was, however, only one car with the 2 litre engine, and this is the one that John Godfrey owns today. Besides the two existing 246 cars, there were also two 248SPs with 2.4 litre sohc V8 engines, and a 286SP with a 2.8 litre version of the 196SP's V6 engine. It all became even more confusing in April of that year when the V8 engines were increased in capacity to 2.6 litres and the large V6 dropped, so that all three of the larger engined new cars became 268SPs.

This numbers game became yet more impossible in 1963, when two of the cars — one of the original 246SPs and a 268SP — were installed with the 2 litre V6 to become 196SPs. In one form or another all six SPs exist today (although one consists only of a V8 engine and transmission and part of a chassis frame), but John's car is the only one that has not been partially or wholly rebodied, re-engined, or converted into coupé form and back to SP spec again.

What all this boils down to is that John's car is the one and only original 196SP, and it remains in exactly the form in which it was raced by the factory in 1962. It is the only team car still with the twin nostril nose, and the only departures from originality are the installation of an ammeter and the replacement of the dynamo with an alternator. There can't be many cars of such pure originality around today — even the wheels and dampers are date-stamped '1961'...

Apart from the Targa Florio and European Mountain Championship successes mentioned at the beginning, this 196SP's only other 1962 race appearance was in the Nürburgring 1,000 km, from which Bandini and Baghetti retired with a cracked sump plate when lying fourth. It is worth pointing out, though, that second place on the Targa Florio (and first in the 2 litre class) was a remarkable achievement from a car that was aimed at class, not overall, honours.

Ferrari sold the car at the end of the season to NART (North American Racing Team), and they raced it only at the 1962 Nassau Speed Week in the Bahamas. It then passed into private hands, and John Godfrey bought it in 1969. He competed in post-historic events in England between 1970-74, and now just brings it out occasionally for 'fun days', such as the Graypaul test day at which I tried it.

The 196SP is a gorgeous little car which has a small but important part in Ferrari racing history. I'm really grateful to John Godfrey for letting me have a go in it.

1962
TURTLE
DRILLING SPECIAL

Like the Moon, the Indianapolis 500 is unique. And, as the Moon is to the Earth, so Indy 500 is to motor racing: remote, spectacular, a place for heroes, but always on the periphery of the scene, with its own rules and regulations. It is truly one of the great races of the world, and, to many millions of Americans, the greatest.

What makes Indy so special? For a start, it is the oldest race in the world still run at its original location, on what is essentially the same circuit. Secondly, prize money has

always been considerable. Thirdly, it has consistently been one of the fastest races ever run.

Indy has always seen a unique evolution of cars, and the early 1950s were the years of the classic sprint car, upright machines with the engine in the front driving the rear axle — which meant that the driver sat high, on top of the propshaft. Lee Wallard won with just such a machine in 1951, and Troy Ruttman in 1952, but these were the sprint cars' high years, because by this time the classic roadster had ar-

rived. The roadster would be the archetypal Indycar until the rear-engined revolution in the 1960s.

Indy technology has always been a strange mixture of the advanced and the primitive. There had been successful front-wheel drive cars, but the other ideas hadn't worked. They had tried mid-engined, four-wheel drive, twin-engined four-wheel drive, and the good ol' front-engined rear-wheel drive configurations. You name it, Indycar designers have tried it.

Light alloy wheels were introduc-

Below left *My lasting impression of the Turtle Drilling Special Indycar is of never-ending, shattering acceleration, like being tied to a rocket. Its Offerhauser four-cylinder engine has an incredible torque curve.*

Right *Like all Indycar 'roadsters', the Turtle has an off-set driving position, with high bodywork to the left and a deep cutaway to the right. Notice the nudge bar at the rear and the crude steering arm poking through the body.*

Right *Vivid paint schemes, wonderful names and colourful decals are all part of a 'sixties Indycar's charisma — this was a world away from European racing.*

ed by Ted Halibrand, long before European racing cars adopted them; fuel injection was widely used years before such systems were standard wear in Europe; disc brakes were seen at Indy for the first time in 1951; designers flirted with independent front suspension in the late 1940s. Despite all this, the typical Indycar of the early 1950s was, by European standards, old-fashioned.

So where did the roadster break new ground? It sounds obvious now, but it wasn't then. The trick which Frank Kurtis initiated was to off-set the drivetrain to the left and put the driver on the right, an innovation which had two advantages. First, the propshaft bypassed the driver, allowing him to sit lower, thereby reducing frontal area and lowering the centre of gravity. Secondly, and possibly more importantly, it gave the car a left-hand weight bias, which meant that in the corners — all of them left-handers, remember — weight transfer was lower than with a standard configuration. There was a more even balance, leading to higher cornering speeds, and less strain was put on the outer tyres. It worked.

The first roadster — so named, incidentally, because the driver sat lower, rather like an open passenger car, or 'roadster' in American parlance — was the Kurtis-Kraft 500A. Apart from its off-set drivetrain and lower seating position, it featured the ubiquitous Offenhauser engine. The famous four-cylinder Offy had won its first Indy 500 in 1935, yet its roots go back to Leo Goossen's Miller design of 1931. In Kurtis's machine, the Offy was conventionally angled over to the right to minimise frontal area. There was a spaceframe chassis, tubular axles front and rear with transverse torsion bar springing, and disc brakes. And this description fits virtually every roadster you could name.

It would be nice to say that a roadster won first time out in 1952, but it didn't. However, Bill Vukovich was leading easily in the

Kurtis-Kraft when a suspension part broke and he crashed with only 22 laps to go. No such thing happened in 1953 and 1954, Vukovich winning at a canter in both years to take home prize purses of $246,300 and $269,375 respectively. That's about 10 times more than I've won in 22 years of racing...

Kurtis-Kraft roadsters accounted for over half of the entry list by 1955, and Bob Sweikert's won. A variation on the Kurtis theme won again in 1956, but this time the chassis was from a name famous at Indy, that of A.J. Watson. He took the off-set idea still further, pushing the drivetrain even more to the left, but kept the engine vertical. His car was good enough for Pat Flaherty to win. The next two years, 1957 and 1958, saw wins for Sam Hanks and Jimmy Bryan respectively, in the 'Belond Special'. Built by Quinn Epperley for owner George Salih, this chassis put the Offy at 72°, almost over on its side.

And so it went on, small change following small change, a refinement here, a tweak there. All the time the Offy engine was gradually developed by Louis Meyer and Dale Drake, but the basic design soldiered on in 4.2 litre capacity after 1957.

Between 1959–64 the combination to run was a Watson chassis with an Offy engine, this equipment giving A.J. Foyt and Rodger Ward two wins apiece, and Jim Rathmann and Parnelli Jones one each. By 1964, Foyt was lapping the Brickyard at 147.35 mph (compared with Vukovich's 128.74 mph in 1953) and taking home more than $500,000 in prize money. These were the great years of the roadster, with many highlights.

In 1959, Ward won by 23 sec from Rathmann, who in turn was only 30 sec in front of Johnny Thompson, after a race in which the lead changed constantly. It was the same story in 1960, *Autosport* recording, 'From start to finish it was a beautifully-driven, hotly-contested race. Never has the contest been closer or the issue more in doubt right up to the last minute. In how many races, long or short, have you seen the lead change hands 29 times?'

The story of 1961 was really that of the ninth-placed car — Jack Brabham in the under-powered, rear-engined Cooper Climax. Were it not for tyre problems he might have finished higher, surrounded by the thundering roadsters. Nevertheless, there was another close

finish, Foyt just grabbing victory from fighting little Eddie Sachs. But the rear-engined revolution was still some way off in 1962, when Watson cars not only set a new lap record and won the race, but also filled five of the top six places. Now that's domination.

While the 1962 race saw a couple of rear-engined cars which failed to make any impression, Lotus's visit in 1963 changed all that. Jim Clark was a very close second to Parnelli Jones' Watson-Offy, and suddenly the roadster's days looked numbered. Foyt gave a Watson–Offy its last win in 1964, but by now the grid was crawling with rear-engined cars and the media was beginning to refer to the roadsters as 'dinosaurs'. It was a shame, in a way, because the rear-engined cars were never as aggressive or thrilling as the roadsters, which deserve a better epitaph than the word 'dinosaur'.

In case you're wondering where the Turtle Drilling Special comes into this story, we're getting close! Go back again to 1960, when the Indy 500 entry list contained at least two cars which weren't Watsons: the Schmidt Special and the Bill Forbes Special. They were the handiwork of long-time constructor and mechanic Wally Meskowski.

If you trickle through a bend the Turtle will plough straight on, but if you power it round, with the tail sliding, it will corner quite well, even through the right-handers which it was never designed to tackle.

The gearbox has only two speeds, and I was told to use top for starting! We used a rope the first time, but here Ludovic Lindsay, Patrick's son, lends a hand.

Wally had been chief mechanic for the first time at Indy in 1953 with Rathmann. He was most famous for his sprint cars — at one time Foyt had several cars by Meskowski, and in 1965 he was builder and entrant of the car which won the Sprint Car Championship, driven by Johnny Rutherford. His team in 1966 included both Rutherford (injured, unfortunately, at the beginning of the year) and Mario Andretti, while other names associated with him are Eddie Sachs and Ronnie Bucknum. He was paralysed in the late 1970s in a car crash while towing a racing car, and died soon after.

The car Meskowski designed followed state-of-the-art lines closely. There was, of course, that 4.2 litre, four-cylinder Offy engine, off-set to the left and placed vertically, in line with the off-set transmission. There was a tubular spaceframe carrying beam axles at both ends, with transverse torsion bars operated by trailing arms at the front and leading arms at the rear. There were — naturally — disc brakes all round, Halibrand wheels, and push-me-pull-you steering via a long drag arm and a steering box under the steeply raked dashboard. The bodywork was typical of the period, right down to a bumper at the back.

To drive the first car, Pete Schmidt, the owner, called upon the services of Bob Veith. He'd had his first race — and best finish — at Indy in 1956, coming home seventh in the Federal Engineering Special: he would continue racing until 1970. Veith qualified the Schmidt Special, number 44, at 143.363 mph. During the race itself Veith was rather overshadowed by the battles in front of him, particularly that for first between Rathmann and Ward. True to the *Autosport* description I quoted earlier, these two were never far apart, even pitting together at one point with Ward back out again in 21 sec, Rathmann in 22! At no point during the last 100 miles was there more than a car's length between the two of them: then, on the 197th lap, Rathmann passed Ward and held the lead to the finish. After the race Ward's right front tyre had worn through two plies of cord, Rathmann's right rear the first ply. Neither could have lasted another lap. Veith finished eighth, the car's best result as it turned out, averaging 135.432 mph to Rathmann's 138.768 mph.

'There's nowt so old as last year's car' proved a true adage in 1961. Veith was back with the Schmidt Special, but after an unsuccessful qualifying attempt looked for a drive elsewhere. Jack Rounds practised but did not make a qualifying attempt as he put a rod through the side of the engine and spun.

The car was back yet again in 1962, this time owned by Ray Howard, called the Turtle Drilling Special, and driven by Leon Clum: alas he had no more success, and didn't qualify. The car did, however, have a moment of glory when it was used as a camera car by Jim Hurtubise!

It was then retired and stored in a St Louis warehouse. In the late 1970s it was shipped to Los Angeles where engine and running gear were checked over, vital components magnafluxed, and then reassembled with new hoses, bolts and wiring. It was run in a four-lap exhibition tour at the Ontario Motor Speedway in 1979, driven by Sam Hanks, and then early in 1984 the Hon Patrick Lindsay brought it over to this country.

I first saw it at a private test day at Silverstone that same year, and fell in love with it. Who wouldn't? With its gold and orange colour scheme, decals, and sheer impression of brute force, it looked sensational. By making a nuisance of myself, Pat let

me out in it for a few laps. I believe I yelled 'Hallelujah' when, eventually, I brought the car in — and that was a fairly accurate description of how I felt. It really is an incredible machine.

The seating position is slightly, but not awkwardly, different. There's high bodywork on your left, but a cutaway cockpit on your right. Your legs are down in a tunnel alongside the engine, in what became nicknamed the 'luggage compartment'. There's an enormous, nearly flat steering wheel with a big padded boss in the middle in front of you, and a two-speed gearbox on your left — you could describe its ratios as ultra-high and Mount Everest. The pedals were fine for me, including the massive brake.

We started the car at the end of a rope. 'Do I start in first?' I asked innocently. 'No, top,' came the answer. Hmmm. However, a quick tow down the pit lane and that big four-cylinder engine thumped instantly into life.

And what a piece of machinery! It has to be one of the most torquey and flexible engines ever. It is astonishingly smooth, even at idle, and pulls cleanly and incredibly powerfully at any speed. It has a torque curve that starts at zero revs and just climbs to infinity. With so much torque and power you don't need the gearbox really — at whatever speed you put your foot down there is an instant response, and a very lively kick in the back, with no flat spots. It's a glorious engine, and nothing like the antiquated lump of iron that I expected.

Jim Fitzgerald, who looks after the car, wasn't quite sure what peak revs were, so we stuck to 6,000 rpm — but even so, the acceleration is such that you're only half way down Club Straight at Silverstone before

you have to feather the throttle to prevent over-revving. Certainly the lack of gears is no hindrance to one's forward progress!

With a locked rear differential, cornering techniques require special attention. If you try to pussy-foot through it will have you straight off, nose-first, so you have to boot it to get the tail round, but if you treat it like that it corners remarkably well — even on right handers, which it isn't supposed to do! I reckon you need a lot of bottle to throw it around, and if you do it behaves magnificently, like a big go-kart. But to keep it up for 500 miles — those boys really were heroes!

Lifting off causes tail wiggles from all the reverse torque and the locked diff, and I was getting additional wiggling from the back under braking at first, too, while the pads bedded in — you would need a wide track if you had two of these cars side by side! Nevertheless, the brakes worked very well once they were bedded in.

But the overriding impression is one of shattering, never-ending acceleration: it's like being tied to the tail of a rocket. Without trying too hard I recorded 1 min 6 sec around the Silverstone Club circuit. I expected that 1 min 3 sec would be on the cards with the way the car was then set-up, straight from the box, and sure enough Neil Corner recorded just those times some time later after a few more laps.

For a car designed to lap a fast circuit with nothing but long, left-hand curves, the Turtle Drilling Special has the most amazing low-down punch and cornering powers in any direction. On the rare occasions that Pat Lindsay drove it, his regular opposition had a thing or two to think about. With a proper gearbox and attention to the brakes, it would win races at Silverstone very easily.

1962
LOTUS 25

It's small and beautifully formed. Take off the cockpit and engine covers and it looks like a scale model, but two-thirds full size, a toy for a very spoilt boy. The steering wheel is about the size of a side plate, the space between the long, aluminium-panelled cockpit sides barely wide enough to take a set of sub-teenaged limbs. The suspension components — wishbones, trailing and transverse arms, steering links — look wispy thin, like the legs of a spider. The engine, too, might be something from a large model aircraft, the eight exhaust pipes metal snakes writhing and twisting together. It is more than just neat and compact, it is a perfect miniature. It doesn't seem possible that this could be a genuine racer...

Over the years, I have track tested a considerable number of racing cars. Some, in the great scheme of things, have been important, some famous, but few have been quite as significant as the Lotus 25. To put it simply, every single modern Formula 1 racing car can trace its heritage back to the little green projectile that first appeared in public in practice for the Dutch Grand Prix at Zandvoort in 1962.

The 25's breakthrough came in what has come to be known as its monocoque chassis. Until the advent of the 25, most racing cars depended on a space-frame structure to hold driver, drivetrain and suspension together: to act as the chassis in fact. Some of these devices were remarkably sophisticated — not least those of Colin Chapman — and served their purpose well. Most designers accepted the old dictum of leaving well enough alone, but not Chapman.

The idea for the monocoque chassis came to Chapman after it became apparent just how stiff for its weight the backbone chassis of the Elan was. He realised that the sides of the backbone could be spaced far enough apart to allow a driver to sit between them, and that an old problem with aluminium fuel tanks chafing through against tubular spaceframes could be eliminated by rubber bag fuel tanks within box sections at the sides of the backbone.

To be pedantic, the 25's chassis is not a true monocoque: it would be more accurate to call it a stressed-skin structure. To be a genuine monocoque, the skins on the side would have had to wrap up and over the driver as well. Everyone, in fact, is familiar with a true monocoque, an aircraft fuselage, which is basically a large diameter, thin-skinned tube.

What is so special about a monocoque? The late John Bolster put it very succinctly, as only he could, back in *Autosport* in 1962: 'I have often repeated the undoubted truth that the strongest and most rigid car chassis is a tubular backbone of very great diameter and the minimum wall thickness... Chapman has adapted it to the single-seater racing car. The tube has become a much more complex structure because it has to be pierced to admit Jimmy Clark and a Coventry Climax engine. The rigidly mounted power unit is a stressed member, but Jimmy isn't. Perhaps he will be welded into next year's model.'

There had been monocoque (or semi-monocoque) racers before. There was the unheralded Killeen Special, the D-type Jaguar had a monocoque centre section, and even some of the spaceframe cars had some form of external skinning rivetted on. And, by 1962, almost every mass-produced road car was to all intents and purposes a monocoque. Chapman's genius was in seeing the advantage of this form of construction, then designing a chassis of the utmost simplicity and strength but with minimal weight.

It consisted, basically, of twin D-shaped tubes running fore and aft, of large diameter and therefore great torsional strength, joined together by the undertray, front and rear suspension bulkheads, another behind the

Neatness is all in driving the Lotus 25. Contemporary rivals, like Coopers, feel like trucks against the 25's delicate and light character — it was so advanced.

The little 1½ litre Coventry Climax V8 has astonishing torque and immediate response; during my 'running-in' session, I took it to 7,500 rpm, but 9,500 rpm was the peak in its day.

driver, and the instrument panel structure. It weighed 65 lb bare, and gave a torsional rigidity of 1000 lb ft/deg, which rose to 2400 lb ft/deg when the engine was attached. This compares to about 700 lb ft/deg for the spaceframe 24...

The dimensions of the revolutionary chassis were such that it picked up the suspension points of the proven spaceframe 24. Like the 24, the front suspension was by wishbones and coil springs, and in typical Chapman fashion the coils were tucked inside the chassis and the steering arms were on the same level as the upper wishbones — there was little to interrupt clean air-flow. At the back there were lower wishbones, upper transverse links and twin radius arms each side, and outboard

coil springs and dampers.

Powering the 25 — and its predecessor and successor, the 24 and 33 — was a truly magnificent engine, the Coventry Climax FWMV V8. It started life with a bore and stroke of 63 × 60 mm, for a capacity of 1495 cc. With a 10.4:1 CR and four Weber 38DCNL carbs it gave 181 bhp at 8,500 rpm. Over the years between 1961 and 1966 it was extensively modified, with bigger valves, higher compression ratios and, importantly, Lucas fuel injection and a shorter stroke, which dropped to 51.56 mm and eventually to 45.47 mm, the bore rising to 67.94 mm and 72.39 mm respectively. Towards the end four-valve heads appeared, and in 1966 the capacity was increased to 1974 cc as

an interim measure before the 3 litre engines became available. There was a 'flat crank' version too, developed to give a simpler exhaust pipe pattern for a possible front-engined Ferguson racer. In 1½ litre form, the ultimate power was 213 bhp at 10,500 rpm. In comparison with recent F1 cars, with blown engines of the same capacity giving 1,000 bhp and more, this may not seem much, but back in the mid-sixties it was highly impressive.

Couple Chapman's advanced chassis, the jewel-like Climax V8 and Jimmy Clark, and you had a combination that has gone down in history. In 1963 they won seven out of ten qualifying World Championship GPs, and in all 25s won no fewer than 14 such events. Clark took most

Above *The quality of Cedric Selzer's workmanship on this 25, which began as the wrecked remains of chassis R5, crashed by Trevor Taylor at Spa in 1963, is absolutely first class.*

Right *The engine acts as a bracing member above extensions to the monocoque chassis: in this capacity, 1,495 cc, the Coventry Climax produces around 180 bhp.*

Left *Just look at the economy of the 25's design. You can see the two monocoque sections (containing rubber bag fuel tanks) on either side of the driver, the snug cockpit, all the ancillaries up at the front and the skimpy suspension.*

Below *Ready to fire, with Cedric Selzer at the rear wheel: the 25 is as perfectly prepared as you would expect from the man who tended Jim Clark's cars for four years.*

of the important victories, and it must be said that the team's number twos didn't seem to have either as much luck or flair as the little Scot — but Trevor Taylor, Mike Spence and Peter Arundel did add to the catalogue of places and victories that made the 25 one of the most suc-

cessful racers ever.

Only seven 25s were made, numbered 25/R1 to R7. Of these R2, R4 and R6 were the most successful. R1 was written off in the finish line collision at the 1962 French GP after six races, and R5 in Trevor Taylor's 1963 Belgian GP accident in practice

after six races as well. R5 had been built especially for the 1962 South African GP, an event on which everything hinged — both Clark and Graham Hill (in a BRM) were in with a chance of the World Championship. From the start Jimmy ran away and hid and there was nothing

Graham could do about it, but then the gods frowned: on lap 59 the 25 came past trailing a thin plume of smoke. The next lap it was worse, and worse still on the next. On the 62nd lap Jimmy cruised into the pits and out of the race. A bolt had loosened in the block, and all the oil had drained out. Hill won the title.

Into 1963 Clark took R5 to wins in the non-championship races at Pau and Imola, and back in England won the International Trophy and took over R5 from Taylor to finish seventh in the Aintree 200. Then, during practice for the Belgian GP at Spa, Trevor found himself with deranged rear suspension half-way through the banked curve called Stavelot — an inboard rear wishbone mounting had come loose. The car scraped along the stone wall and smashed into an observer's hut. Taylor survived, but the car didn't.

Well, not all of it. Cedric Selzer, the South African mechanic who looked after Jimmy's car in his first World Championship year, 1963,

and stayed with Team Lotus for four years, takes up the story.

'In the accident, the car was effectively broken in half — when we went to rescue it the only thing that was holding it together was the bag tanks. When we dragged it out it was like pulling on an elastic band! It was brought back to the factory, what was left of it, as scrap, and thrown out on to the heap. I asked permission to take some of the bits as souvenirs, which was granted, so I took the front and rear bulkheads, the engine mountings, the inner skins on the back, the radius arm pickups, the uprights and sundry bits and pieces.

'Then, about four years ago, I decided to see if I could put the car together. I'd heard that there was an engine-and-a-half lying in Detroit,

One of the great combinations in motor racing history: Jim Clark and Lotus 25, World Champions in 1963 after an amazing season of seven Grand Prix victories. This is Clark winning in Mexico in 1962.

but no-one actually knew who owned them. Then a friend 'phoned and said that he'd traced them and the owner was willing to sell — but he wanted £30,000! They were offered to me and about four other people. I thought the best thing to do was go out there, so I jumped on the next aeroplane. I left on the Friday morning, by Friday afternoon I was in Detroit, negotiations took place on the Saturday, by Monday the money was in his bank, and by the following Friday the engine-and-a-half was at Heathrow.

'They were originally Rob Walker's engines, and the bloke in Detroit had them in a 23. When I first saw them they were laid out in bits on a huge table in his basement. Both had blown up at some time, and I had to weld the crankcases, for example. I also had the fuel metering units redone and so on.

'So I then had an engine, and started putting the car together — without any help from Lotus at all, incidentally. No drawings, nothing.

The front bulkhead was so bad I had to take it apart to see how it was made. Fortunately the suspension pick-up points were the same as on the 24, so I rebuilt it. The rear bulkhead was very twisted but we managed to straighten it and re-use it. The rest I had to redraw and make up. I bought new wheels for it, but couldn't get a proper ZF gearbox — I've been trying for six years — so I put in a Hewland: 25s did run with Hewlands, so that's reasonable.

'I've been rebuilding it, in the evenings, over a period of years. It's taken a bit longer than it used to back in 1963! I'm not going to claim it's original, just that it's rebuilt from a wreck.

'It sure takes me back...'

And Cedric isn't the only one it takes back — me too. Who could forget Jimmy and the 25? I had known for some time that Cedric was rebuilding R5, and must confess I had chivvied him on and off since he started, to get him to finish and let me drive it. It was very much a sorting session: no heroics, and some slow laps to warm it up first.

It is, in my opinion, the first truly sophisticated rear-engined F1 car. It's beautifully proportioned, and it's the old story — if it looks right it *is* right. Cedric has done a brilliant restoration job.

The cockpit looks incredibly thin and narrow, but in fact is surprisingly roomy, and is more difficult to exit than enter! The only thing is, Jim Clark had shorter legs than me, and I could have done with another inch in length. The instruments are easily visible in front of you, with the ammeter on the left, then a water temperature gauge (running at 65-70°), then oil pressure (85-90°), the tacho red-lined at 8000 rpm for test purposes, then oil temperature — barely registering — and fuel pressure, about 100 psi. There's a conventional H-pattern gear change, with first towards you and back, and — apart from that inch too little legroom — there are no pedal problems, although I could have done with a left foot rest. There's a really tiny little steering wheel, the equally tiny gear lever (with a knob that's too big) is within a hand-span reach, both perfectly placed, and the seat back feels comfortable and nicely supportive. Jim Clark at first found the very reclined driving position a problem, but he gradually got used to it.

The engine is a twin-plane crank unit, with cross-over exhausts, and sounds absolutely *fantastic* — the noise is just delightful. The response too is immediate, and for a 1½ litre V8 pull from 5,500 rpm, but is perfectly tractable from even lower revs. I started using 5,000 rpm at first, to run it in, and eventually took it up to 7,500 rpm — I believe peak revs were around the 9,500 rpm mark in its day, at which point I should think it

was really *flying*. The gearbox as set up at the moment is too low-geared in fourth.

When it comes to the handling, you really need power to hang the tail out, and when you're running it in you don't have much. But hanging the tail out is *not* the way to drive this car. Neatness is all. It's delicate and light to drive, like so many modern cars — in fact you tend to forget that it's more than 25 years old. There's just no comparison with the contemporary Coopers, which are like trucks next to the 25.

Cedric has set up the suspension from experience and memory. The modern tyres are slightly stickier, so he has reduced the camber by 50 per cent all round, and rear toe-in by the same proportion, from $\frac{1}{4}$ in to $\frac{1}{8}$ in! He reckons the ride height at the moment is a bit too low, due to the springs settling, but I'll take his word for it. All I will say is that, straight out of the box, it's one of the best handling cars I've ever driven.

And to drive the 25 really is emotional. There's all that history behind it, its innovation, its fame in the hands of Jimmy Clark. It is, simply, one of the major highlights of my track testing career, and for that I am grateful to Cedric, and his partner Michael Strauss, for allowing me out in it. So tiny, so perfect, so beautiful, so sophisticated, so *important*. What more is there to say?

1964
BRM P61

This is one of the most difficult track tests I have had to write, not because we had major problems with the car, nor even that inclement weather spoiled the testing. No, it is difficult simply because the BRM P61 is so undramatic. It does everything so well that it's actually quite tricky to describe how it drives!

Before I have a go, however, let me put the car into its context, for the P61 marks a rare zenith in

BRM's sorry tale of disappointment. The team from Bourne struggled to make its mark in Grand Prix racing for 25 years, yet only for the next four years between 1962 and 1965, during the 1½ litre formula

BRM P61/5 looks beautiful but discreet, and the same could be said of its handling. It corners with absolutely no drama — predictably, neutrally and controllably.

era, was it really in the top bracket.

Those four years saw 11 GP victories and Graham Hill's 1962 World Championship title. Hill came within a whisker of the 1964 title as well, with more points than any other driver, but he had scored in too many races. BRM took the FIA Constructors' Cup in 1962, and finished runner-up in the next three years. The success was sustained, with four wins in 1962, two in 1963,

After curing slight skittishness by adjusting the rear anti-roll bar, I found the BRM a joy through corners. It can be made to oversteer, but the smoothest approach is the best.

Along with its impeccable handling, the BRM has light and responsive steering and utterly dependable brakes — it is hard to fault.

Left *The P61 will always be associated with Graham Hill, who came within a whisker of the 1964 World Championship in the car. Here he is at Monaco in 1965 scoring one of his five victories at the street circuit.*

Right *The cockpit is snug, with left-hand gearchange, leather-rim steering wheel and instruments all perfectly placed — the car's owner back in 1982, Mike Harrison, cut away the side screens to give himself shoulder room.*

two in 1964 and three in 1965.

Just how heart-warming this was for BRM can be measured by the paltry rewards it earned in the other 20 or so seasons, with just six GP victories notched up outside this period. BRM took nine years to win its first GP with the P25 in 1959, there was one more in 1966, and four came in another little flurry of promise between 1970 and 1972. The total of 17 is today hugely exceeded by similarly long-standing teams like Ferrari, Lotus, McLaren and Brabham, and even Williams — whose first win came only in 1979 — is comfortably ahead. Yes, there are many more GPs in a season nowadays, but by any standards the BRM record is one of almost unmitigated failure.

But back to the 1½ litre cars, the ones that broke the mould. The car which won the 1962 World Championship, the P57, used a spaceframe mated to BRM's V8 engine and transmission. But this was the year when Colin Chapman introduced the monocoque chassis to Formula 1 with his Lotus 25, and BRM had to follow, although Raymond Mays agonized about abandoning the super-successful spaceframe car too readily. He decided that BRM should build an experimental monocoque chassis,

designated the P61, and develop it during the 1963 season. This was a 'partial monocoque', comprising a double-skinned alloy structure shaped like a cigar tube, with a hole at the top where the driver sat. Aft of the driver, the engine, transmission and rear suspension were supported by a tubular frame which could be quickly unbolted for major work.

The P61's engine was the high-revving 1,498 cc 90° four-cam V8 which Peter Berthon had designed back at the beginning of the 1½ litre formula. In its early form it developed 184 bhp at 10,000 rpm, but by the time the P61 was current more than 200 bhp was available. Power was transmitted through a six-speed BRM-designed transaxle.

Double wishbones for the development P61 followed the P57's suspension layout at the rear, although the coil spring/damper units were moved inwards out of the air stream, being actuated at their lower ends by long pushrods attached to the bottom wishbones. The front suspension was completely new, following Lotus practice in using slim top rocker arms connecting to inboard coil spring/damper units. To minimize frontal area, the rocker arm entered the body below the top of the spring, using a complex linkage to mate to it. Wide-based wishbones formed the lower links at the front.

Hill practised the car for the first time at Zandvoort, but locking brakes and 'wandering' on the straights dictated that he raced his regular P57 instead. At Reims, however, Graham put the new car on the front row of the grid, and in the race gave it a debut third place despite being penalized one minute for a push-start. This development car had only one more race, at Monza, where Graham qualified second and ran with the slipstreaming lead bunch, with spells at the front, until stopped by clutch failure.

Lessons learned that season went into the Mark 2 version of the P61 raced throughout 1964 and 1965. Labelled the P261, this car differed from the prototype in having monocoque spars extending rearwards to cradle the engine, allowing the old tubular frame to be discarded. The only other major difference was to the rear suspension, where the spring/damper units were moved outboard again. Chief Engineer Tony Rudd had hoped to clean up the airflow around the rear with a new 'in-vee' exhaust system, but the modified heads required by this compact arrangement could not be developed until later in the

Left *The 1½ litre era generated some wonderfully svelte Formula 1 shapes, and the P61 is among the finest; it is like a cigar tube with a hole cut in the top for the driver.*

Right *That little 1½ litre V8 is a jewel. It revs smoothly and sweetly, delivering its biggest punch between 7,000 and 9,000 rpm, a tight band which caused BRM to use a six-speed gearbox.*

season, leaving no option but to route the exhaust through tunnels in those monocoque extensions.

Hill's first race of 1964 in the P261 was in pouring rain at Snetterton, where he led for seven laps until aquaplaning into an accident that resulted in an amazingly spectacular racing photograph, a shot taken by a *Daily Mirror* photographer as the car cannoned over his head. A British preamble to the GP season saw three more races, Hill leading at Goodwood until two laps from home and taking second places in the Aintree 200 and Silverstone International Trophy.

The P261's first GP was at Monaco, and what a debut it was, Hill leading team-mate Richie Gin-

ther home to a tremendous 1–2. How many cars have managed that in their first GP? Apart from being highly competitive, the P261s were also quite reliable, and through that season Graham accumulated points with his consistent finishing record. He was fourth at Zandvoort, fifth at Spa, and second at Rouen, Brands Hatch and the Nürburgring. Winning again at Watkins Glen put him top of the table with 39 points to the 34 of John Surtees and 30 of Jim Clark. He was clear favourite in the three-way struggle that would make the Mexican GP the most tense season finale ever.

Graham worked his way up to third place in the race, content that finishing in this position would

assure him of the title. Behind him, though, Lorenzo Bandini began to pile on the pressure a little too enthusiastically, trying in vain to nose his Ferrari ahead at the hairpin bend. Graham shook his fist, but Bandini continued the harassment with a second ill-judged overtaking move. The two cars collided, and one of the Ferrari's wheels buckled the BRM's exhaust. Hill had to make two pit-stops for repairs and finished eleventh, leaving second-placed Surtees one point ahead. Surtees was a worthy champion, but I've always felt that Graham Hill and BRM were the real winners in 1964.

BRM showed well in 1965 too, Jackie Stewart helping to keep the impetus going with a superb first season. Hill won at Monaco and Watkins Glen, Stewart at Monza, and each driver finished runner-up three times to give BRM six second places. Had Clark not enjoyed an exceptional season with his Lotus 33 to win all bar one of the other GPs, BRM would have had another World Championship. For 1966, F1 was run to new 3 litre rules, but Stewart and Hill gave the P61 a fitting swansong by finishing first and third at Monaco, powered by 2 litre versions of the V8.

The car which I drove is chassis number P61/5, first raced at Spa in 1964, Hill taking fifth place. It achieved its best finish a few weeks later at Rouen when Hill finished second, but was used only in practice by Graham at Brands Hatch. He crashed it at Solitude, retired at Zeltweg and drove it only in practice at Monza. Ginther took it over for the last two GPs of the season, finishing fourth at Watkins Glen and eighth in Mexico.

Hill used P61/5 usually as a practice car for 1965, at Brands in March, Goodwood in April, Silverstone in May (when Jackie Stewart practised in it too), and at Monaco at the end of the same month. At Spa (held, one suspects, rather worryingly for superstitious drivers on the 13th) Graham finished fifth. Finally, P61/5 was comprehensively crashed during practice by Graham at Clermont-Ferrand, and honourably retired from the team. It seems that the damaged chassis was quickly replaced by a spare which assumed the old chassis number and documentation. The distorted tub was subsequently rescued and then rebuilt as a complete car: evidence for this story includes holes drilled in the outer skin on each side where little wing-shaped pods were tried in testing during 1965.

The car was sold to BRM collector John McCartney, and thence to Mike Harrison. When I drove it in 1982, the car had competed in only one race after a major rebuild by Hall & Fowler, Mike Littlewood

having taken it to a win at Donington in an HSCC Pre-65 single-seater race. With relatively little mileage under its belt, it still needed a bit of sorting when I drove it — but only a little. A day's track work, which could have included setting it up for driver preferences, was all that would have been needed.

But to the car itself. You have to admit that it is one of the most beautiful racing cars ever built. Slim, clean-lined, it indeed looks like a cigar tube on wheels. In action, it's more like a bullet on wheels!

In general the cockpit is a snug fit but the controls are perfectly laid out. The seat is very comfortable but personally I would have preferred a more upright stance: a bit of foam padding behind my head cured that. Part of the side screens had been removed by Mike Harrison to suit his build, but were I to drive the car in a race I would have them replaced, since on the faster straights my head was being buffeted, which is tiring.

It's more years than I prefer to remember now since I first sat in front of a 1½ litre BRM engine, and that was in a Chevron B8. Every time I experience this V8 again, I'm reminded of what a perfect little jewel it is. Once we had cleared a plug problem, it just sang along. It's as smooth and as sweet as you could wish for. It starts instantly, idles without lumpiness, and is untemperamental at low speeds. It begins to pull strongly from about 6,000 rpm, and is 'on song' by 6,500–7,000 rpm, screaming powerfully up to 9,000 rpm, which is what I was pulling on Hangar Straight and up through Abbey on Silverstone's full GP circuit.

A 2,000 rpm rev band may not sound like a wide power spread, but you have a six-speed gearbox as well, so it's not too difficult to keep it on full power. The change for the BRM 'box is a bit stiff, and you have to be deliberate about the movement. It's not an electric switch type of change, but it is quick and positive. I cannot remember

anything about the foot controls, which is always a good sign — it means that they are working properly.

When I said the car was undramatic I was really talking about the handling. The period between 1959, when the Ferrari Dino was competitive, and 1964, when this BRM appeared, saw some significant changes. There was the reduction in engine size to 1½ litres for a start, but much more important was the wholesale change-over to mid-engined designs and — possibly of equal importance — the rapid growth in tyre widths.

If I've done my sums correctly, this means that tyre widths were up by 30 per cent, weight down by roughly the same amount. This in turn led to cornering forces up by 50 per cent and therefore speeds up by 20 per cent. Thus, even with only 1½ litres, and around 200 bhp, the BRM corners very rapidly indeed.

At the start of the test the car was a bit skittish, but a slight adjustment to the rear roll bar cured that. I know I like oversteer, but with something like the BRM tidy driving is the quickest way.

You *can* make it oversteer, but lifting off scrubs off the speed and brings you back on line again — it's very easy to catch. The P61 slides beautifully, predictably, neutrally, and without drama. The steering is light and responsive, and the combination of all these factors makes it one of the best handling cars I've ever driven. The brakes, too, are fantastic, again displaying no quirks.

That superb engine, the predictable controllability, the sheer lack of fuss about the P61, add up to a car that is sheer magic. It's a pity, though, that Mike Harrison didn't find it so. He's a bit bigger than me and could barely sit in it. He confesses that it was a mistake to buy the P61 without trying it first, and he only ever drove it for one lap! John Foulston bought it from him, and now it lives with a BRM-mad collector in Switzerland. I hope he's enjoying it as much as I did.

1965

ROVER-BRM GAS TURBINE

To say I've always wanted to drive the gas turbine Rover-BRM is stating the obvious, for plenty of other drivers must have shared this ambition. The history of motor racing is peppered with oddball innovations, and this must be one of the oddest cars to have raced at Le Mans. As such, it deserves a good introduction.

The car made its public bow at Le Mans in 1963 in an unusual way. Promptly, traditionally, at 4.00 pm the majority of the field howled, screamed, barked and roared its way off. Then, after a 30 second pause, there came a sound quite unfamiliar on a race track, a whoosh, a whistle and a whine, not particularly loud. From the back of the grid, an ugly, hump-backed dark green car, numbered 00, crept off down the start straight and into the history books. For the first time a gas turbine car had taken to the track in serious competition.

The story of the Rover-BRM really starts in the depths of the Second World War when Rover was commissioned by the government to develop and build Frank Whittle's invention, the jet engine. Rolls-Royce later took over the work, but Rover kept a small team to develop the jet for possible road use or as a portable power pack. Throughout

the 'fifties work continued on gas turbines, with occasional glimpses of the results. There was the famous JET 1, the first car powered by gas turbine in the world which now lives in the Science Museum in London. Based on a decapitated Rover P4, it had its 100 bhp engine placed amidships. Later, with a 230 bhp unit, it set the first gas turbine speed records with a flying kilometre of 151.96 mph.

This was followed by T2, T2A (both based on standard P4s), T3 (a remarkable machine with four-wheel drive and its gas turbine mounted in the tail) and T4 (which used a P6 bodyshell years before the P6 appeared). But however hard the Rover team tried, they faced two major gas turbine disadvantages — primary cost and fuel consumption.

The quantum leap in thinking which led to a Le Mans project came when William Martin-Hurst, a competition-oriented man, became Managing Director in 1962. He instigated Rover's brief period of rallying in the early 'sixties, first with the heavy P5 and then the elegant P6, and saw in gas turbine technology the potential for a real racing standard-bearer for the company. His ideas for a Le Mans car fell on deaf ears at first, but gradually he won round his staff, and par-

ticularly Maurice Wilks. There was, in fact, a reason for choosing Le Mans: l'Automobile Club de l'Ouest was very keen to have a gas turbine car competing, and had posted a 25,000 francs prize for the first such car to complete 3,600 km (or 2,237 miles) in the race.

With no experience of designing and building a sports racer, Rover cast around for a suitable partner, and reached an agreement with Sir Alfred Owen of BRM. 'Wilkie' Wilkinson was working at BRM by then, and he had vast knowledge of Le Mans. Tony Rudd, now with Lotus but then at BRM, recalls the rush with which work got under way: 'A "Big Strategic Plan" was drawn up, working back from Le Mans — x weeks for the body, y weeks for the chassis and so on. Unfortunately, nobody told Wilkie or myself: when I first heard about it we were left with just 10 working days to design and build the thing for the Le Mans test weekend in April. We took a 1961 Climax-engined car, and a very large hacksaw, and made it longer and wider...

'When the Rover people sent us the engine it weighed 150 lb, ready to run! There were no radiators, no water, no extras — we fell in love with it on the spot. When we did our

Above *You have to rethink completely how to drive when you step into the Rover-BRM. Everything seems to happen in delayed action, and with only 140 bhp carrying 15 cwt, the performance is as modest as you would expect.*

Left *Left-foot braking is essential. When you approach a corner, the throttle delay gives the impression that the power is still on while you brake, and then you must apply the power again a few seconds before you want it, while you are still braking.*

Above *There are hints of Lotus Plus 2 and Ferrari 250LM in the beautiful shape drawn by William Towns after Rover designers objected to the ugliness of the first prototype.*

Right *I could see why the Rover-BRM would have worked well at Le Mans, with its long straights and relatively few corners, but around Donington it was hopeless — there is little time to build up speed between corners!*

Right *The rev counter looks a bit fee-ble with markings up to only 7,000, but an extra '0' has to be added — take anything else to 65,000 rpm and bits of engine would appear on the track behind you.*

Rover's gas turbine, with heat exchangers on each side, sits ahead of what looks like a conventional gearbox, but in fact the car has no gears. Disc brakes are very large to compensate for the lack of engine braking.

After its hurried construction, the ungainly first prototype looked unfinished when it appeared at the Le Mans test day in 1963, but it performed in the race — as a 'demonstration' entry — with distinction, completing a distance which would have placed it eighth.

The restyled car, which arrived at the 1964 Le Mans test sessions, looked gorgeous, but unfortunately its race appearance had to wait a year after it was wrapped around a tree on the journey home.

sums we ended up with a car 150 lb under weight. So the bottom frame tubes were opened up, and lead poured down them to act as ballast!'

Mark Barnard was an engineer in the gas turbine section of Rover at the time, and his team prepared the engines while BRM worked on the chassis. 'We had a 140 bhp unit with heat exchangers, but chose a slightly more powerful light industrial engine without exchangers for the race. We had two, actually, one giving 145 bhp, the other 148 bhp, and we built a test-bed to simulate Le Mans, putting them through a number of "runs".

'Our first proper run was at MIRA with Graham Hill driving. The car was very low, with minimal ground clearance, and Graham was grounding it on the banking at 110 mph, but he just kept going. On another occasion, with Ginther at the wheel, we were checking top end performance. We found an aerodrome with a two mile straight, and Ginther climbed in and set off. He came back almost immediately, and made me get into the passenger seat! At about 80 mph there was this blast of very hot air over our necks! There was a colossal recirculation of hot exhaust gases back into the cockpit because of some aerodynamic quirk. That's why the early car sprouted a large stub exhaust.'

BRM's part of the car was bang up to date, with a tubular steel spaceframe chassis, wishbone and coil spring suspension and huge disc brakes to cope with the lack of engine braking. The test weekend revealed severe lift at speed, but this was cured in time for the race itself.

The Rover-BRM behaved impeccably at Le Mans apart from fuel pick-up problems and heavy oil consumption, and with 3¼ hours to go it had already exceeded the 3,600 km target. By the end of 24 hours it had covered 4,173 km (2,593 miles) at an average speed of 107.8 mph. Although the car was officially giving a demonstration run, it would have been eighth overall had it been classified in the results. The one snag was severe fuel consumption,

the gas turbine guzzling a gallon of paraffin every seven miles.

For 1964 the ACO allowed gas turbine cars to compete properly, so the Rover-BRM was entered again, with two major differences. The first was an all-new coupé body, as beautiful as the previous one had been ugly. The Rover styling studio, appalled by the car's hideous looks, demanded permission to draw up a new shape, and this was granted. Under the direction of David Bache, William Towns designed the sleek lines which worked as well as they looked, giving a Cd of about 0.32. The other major change was to incorporate heat exchangers, consisting of large ceramic glass discs which rotated slowly on either side of the engine.

The revised car practised at the 1964 test weekend with an old engine installed, but it didn't appear for the race, the reason given being that the new engine, with heat exchangers, would not be ready in time. This wasn't exactly true, as Tony Rudd recalls: 'Driving back from the test weekend, the car was put on this fancy articulated Land Rover they had. Somewhere on the way back the outfit started to snake, and the car fell off the trailer and wrapped itself around a tree! It could have been repaired, but Bourne was very, very busy — it was a neck and neck Formula 1 season, and our drivers were stuffing cars at a fair rate!'

This allowed much more time to prepare for the 1965 race, and the rear suspension was uprated by grafting on parts from the 1964 F1 BRM. Graham Hill and Jackie Stewart, neither of whom cared for the Sarthe circuit but adopted their usual professional attitude, drove for this second Le Mans appearance, but this outing wasn't quite as spectacular as the first. Early in the race the engine ingested a 'foreign body' (Tony Rudd: 'Somebody's overall button fell into a heat exchanger!') which caused some internal damage and a dangerously high exhaust temperature. To overcome this, fuel

delivery was reduced despite the loss of performance, and the car whistled on to complete the 24 hours in tenth position at an average of 98.8 mph, covering 3,816 km (2,371 miles). ACO rules placed the car in the 2 litre class, in which it finished third. Interestingly, fuel consumption was vastly improved, its 13.5 mpg being the second best figure among those which finished.

And that, effectively, was the end of the Rover-BRM saga, William Martin-Hurst calling a halt to the programme after the race. The idea had been to show that the gas turbine was an effective alternative for a road car, and this was patently not the case.

The car now belongs to British Motor Heritage, the independently-controlled trust which was set up to preserve the heritage of the companies in the British motor industry. The total number of vehicles in the collection exceeds 300, of which around 100 are permanently on display at BMH's museum in Syon Park, Middlesex. After much negotiation with BMH's Peter Mitchell and David Bishop, the opportunity eventually arose for me to drive the Rover-BRM at Donington on a glorious sunny day.

It is a very, very pretty car, with touches of the Ferrari 250LM and Lotus Plus 2 about it. Getting into it is slightly more difficult than, say, a GT40, because the doors are narrow and the front wheel well intrudes into the entrance space. Once in the cockpit, which is small but adequate, I found the driving position very comfortable but short in the arm for me — apparently it was tailored for Graham Hill, who liked it that way.

You're surrounded by a totally different array of instruments, with 'Jet Temperature' and all sorts of other peculiar things that you don't understand written on them. Mind you, the 7,000 rpm tacho looks unexciting until you realize that you have to add a zero to all the markings — it actually reads to 70,000 rpm! I have never actually, and intentionally, revved anything to 65,000 rpm (the 'red line') without everything appearing on the road behind me. Then there's a temperature gauge which reads to 700°C...

At this point it might be as well to explain how a gas turbine works. If you know how a turbocharger operates, you know how a gas turbine does as well. A compressor at the inlet feeds air to the combustion chamber where fuel is added and ignited. The hot gases then feed a turbine which drives the compressor (consider a petrol engine as purely a combustion chamber and you get the drift).

With a pure jet engine, the enormous amount of exhaust energy is expelled from the back as thrust — the compressor takes only a fraction of the force. With a gas turbine, a second power turbine is added, unconnected to the first, but running on a transmission shaft, the energy thus becoming shaft horsepower rather than thrust.

Although simple in theory, the gas turbine is rather more complex in practice. To obtain its power and efficiency, it must run at high speeds and temperatures, which means using exotic materials in its construction. High fuel consumption, particularly when not running at full power, is another problem, and this is overcome by a heat exchanger. The reason for one is simple: the greater the temperature to which the incoming air is heated, the greater the expansion. Any heat which escapes represents wasted fuel, so if some of this lost heat can be used to warm up the incoming air, less fuel is required to heat it up to maximum.

The starting procedure couldn't be simpler. You throw a big switch then press a button, and it all happens automatically from then on. The starter motor gradually builds up the revs to about 25,000 rpm, when a growing rumble, accompanied by a rising whine, is heard: the engine has fired. The tacho swings around to 40,000 rpm, the 'set ground idle speed' as it is called. To

prevent the power turbine running away and damaging itself, you have to hold it on the brakes — the turbine acts as its own torque convertor, like that of an automatic transmission car. Which is why you can't go from forward to reverse in the simple gearbox — if you hit neutral, bang!

If you lift your foot off the brakes, the car will take itself off, up to about 30 to 40 mph, without you touching the accelerator pedal. If you do floor the accelerator, the effect is just like taking off in a jet plane. The engine note rises, the tacho swings round to 65,000 rpm, and there is a gradually increasing shove from the tail, growing stronger the faster you go. The Rover-BRM won't wheelspin away from a standing start, and up to about 60 mph feels distinctly sluggish, but from then on it begins to build up speed at a faster and faster rate, the whistle from behind growing to an impressive roar — yet even on full throttle it's not particularly noisy, and the noises are all pleasant ones. Everything seems to happen in delayed action, a sort of slow motion, you might say, but with only 140 bhp on tap, in a gearless car weighing about 15 cwt, set up for Le Mans, the performance is as unsparkling as you might expect.

The driving technique is, of course, totally different, and very dependent on engine characteristics. It's rather like a combination of a tiny engine and a turbocharger with enormous rotors — it takes time both to build up speed and to die down. Going into a corner, it is essential to anticipate the inertial effect (if I can call it that) which means that there is not only no engine braking but in fact a feeling that power is still on, and the need to build up speed and power again for when they will be required. Thus you have to left foot brake — no problem in a two-pedal car — and, what's more, balance brake against accelerator so that you're braking at the right time

and accelerating at the right time.

My technique, like those who raced it, was to brake hard before a corner with the foot off the loud pedal, then at about the 50 yard mark (depending on the corner) accelerate hard while still braking. Coming up to the Mulsanne Corner, Graham Hill used to plant both feet firmly on the brake pedal, and then about 150 yards before he arrived at the corner transfer his right foot hard on the loud pedal. Using my left foot braking or Graham's two feet technique, you have power and speed building up as you come off the brakes, and the car accelerates through. If you've knocked enough speed off, you get around — if you haven't, you've had it! It'll just push you straight on as if you've tried to go through without lifting, which would be puzzling to on-lookers.

The handling is rather disguised by the 'straight on' engine effect, which gives the impression that it understeers mildly. Of course, you can't steer it on the throttle like you can with a piston-engined car — there just isn't the instant response. Nevertheless there is plenty of grip, and it's an undemanding car to drive at something less than the limit.

The over-riding impression of the car, then, is that you're totally dependent on the brakes, and, as they survived Le Mans without a problem, I'm happy with this. Obviously it's ideal for Le Mans, with its long straights and relatively few corners, and around Donington it's pretty hopeless — there's relatively little time to build up speed between corners. On the other hand, there can't be an easier racing car to drive in traffic: at one point we found ourselves as part of a demonstration, and under those conditions you treat it like an automatic, foot off the accelerator and use the brake to slow down or, by lifting off, speed up. It's even quiet enough to carry on a normal conversation ...

The Rover-BRM is one car I most certainly shall *never* forget.

1965
FORD GT40

To my mind the Ford GT40 is one of the greatest cars of all time. It's stunning to look at, was fabulously successful in racing, and must be just about the most amazing car ever built for the road. Over the years I've had a lot to do with them: I ran my own road car for 25,000 miles or so, I spent two seasons racing one in Europe in the late 'sixties, and a good few have passed through my hands since then. To accompany my track test of Martin Colvill's car, it occurred to me that it would be a good idea to recall some of my experiences — good and bad, but mostly good! — in GT40s.

I fell in love with the GT40 when it first appeared, and when Ford started building production cars in 1966 I knew that I had to have one. I was running an Iso Grifo at the time, and that was without doubt the worst high performance car I have ever driven. It was a complete lemon: it had such unresponsive steering that if you got it on opposite lock you usually spun it . . . which I did. I was delighted to get rid of that, and gave a thousand quid on top to buy a GT40 through Rob Walker's garage. This was chassis '1013', the very first of the production run and the original press car, registered OVX 355D. I got it with 20,000 miles on the clock, and ran it

with the registration 69 FUH for a couple of years.

After the 'heap of Grifo' it was tremendous fun, and I suppose you could say that I drove it like a lunatic. Girls didn't like it because it was so horrifying to be driven in, especially by me! It was pretty short of creature comforts, but then it really was a racing car adapted for road use. The only concessions were solid discs instead of ventilated, Borrani wire wheels, an apology for a pair of silencers, slightly narrower tyres, heavier body panels and a couple of luggage boxes in the back. It felt just like a racing car, and eventually I fitted a race engine and BRM-type wheels.

Despite the harshness of the ride, it never shook itself apart over bumpy roads. I've driven a Lola T70 on the road, and that did itself so much damage that I thought it would need a new monocoque after just 1,000 miles. The Lola also had an unmanageable Hewland gearbox, whereas the Ford's ZF, though heavy to use, was very strong and had excellent synchromesh — racing 'boxes with synchro must be quite rare.

The GT40 was incredibly and effortlessly fast, so much so that driving it quickly was rather like lying back and watching a film. It meant

that you had to be very alert, for you came up on other cars more quickly than you expected, but the brakes were excellent. I vividly remember going to Silverstone in my car and overtaking someone at immense speed on the approach to Towcester. A copper eventually arrived at the circuit and sat by my car for three hours: I had to put on a brave face in the end, and he told me that someone had reported me for doing 100 mph more than they were! He said he couldn't book me because there were no witnesses and he didn't believe it anyway, but I got a good ticking off all the same . . .

The best high speed journey I remember was in another car owned by Kevin MacDonald. He asked me to take it to Monaco for the Grand Prix, so I decided to make the trip easier for myself by flying the car over the channel from Southend to Le Touquet. We were half way down the runway at Southend when they stopped the 'plane, saying that fuel was leaking dangerously from my car. I'd filled it to the brim because petrol was cheaper in Britain, but the rubber bag tanks moved and started spilling fuel.

We eventually cleared Le Touquet customs at 2.00 pm, and I was on the quay at Monte Carlo at 10.00 pm that evening. That's going

Above *When a GT40 is set up well, as Martin Colvill's is, it is very relaxing to race, but it must be driven smoothly as the weight of its big cast-iron engine makes the tail break away very readily.*

Left *Colvill's car is undoubtedly the best GT40 I have driven, with un-dramatic handling and an incredibly good engine. It was raced between 1965–68 by the Ford and John Wyer teams.*

some! I reckon that's a record that will never be beaten, even though we hit Paris during the Friday night rush-hour and sat for one and a half hours on the *periphérique*, and in those days the *autoroute* stopped at Valence, about 200 miles short of Monaco. I managed to put 136 miles into one hour, yet I was overtaken on the way by a 4.7 litre Maserati Indy driven, I later found out, by their chief test driver, Guerrino Bertocchi. That, apparently, was a very special car being developed by the factory. Near Paris, I decided to see just how fast the GT40 (this one had a steel crank engine) would go: it went up to 7,000 rpm in top, which was near 190 mph, and held it for 10 miles!

Running a GT40 had its drawbacks, mind you. The only place for luggage was those two little boxes in the back, and since they sat right by the exhaust everything inside got cooked — your toothpaste melted and shampoo bottles burst! You also got soaked when it rained

because it leaked like a sieve, but at least it was fairly reliable if you looked after it properly. The gear linkage needed lubricating regularly, but the most important thing was to take the car to bits and dry everything off if it rained. So many GT40s, sad to say, have rotted because there was insufficient rust-proofing in the steel monocoque's side sections.

I had very few problems with my road car: the only two I can remember were a burst water hose and a worn camshaft lobe. Another GT40 I drove let me down at Luton with a cracked distributor cap, which was a common problem because of the carbon deposits caused by poor sealing where the exhaust goes from four into one. Everything got covered in carbon, including the distributor, and a drop of water would crack its cap. The police were very kind to me that time and towed me to a garage, not saying a word about all the noise I'd been making. That car, registered MRC 741K, had

been owned by Paul Hawkins and is now in the Midlands Motor Museum.

It's fair to say that the GT40 is probably the quickest road car there's ever been. One did a standing ¼-mile at Santa Pod in 12.3 secs, while *Motor*'s Roger Bell said that the car would rocket up to 120 mph and beyond faster than any car the magazine had ever tested. John Woolfe's 7 litre Cobra had been fractionally quicker to 100 mph, but after that the Ford's aerodynamics came into play and left it far behind. *Motor* later tested the MacDonald car, and found it even quicker: 0–60 mph in 4 sec, 0–100 mph in 9 sec!

I also spent two very happy years racing GT40s, which all came about because my friend Peter Sadler invited me to race his car (chassis '1010') on a 'he who bends it mends it' basis. I was very excited about that, because I hadn't been racing for that long, and had only been really successful in a Ginetta G12.

The GT40 was such a strong car

This car started life with a 7 litre V8 engine, but the rules change in World Championship sports car racing for 1968 led to a 4.7 litre being fitted.

that we rarely had any trouble with it, though in my first race at Barcelona in 1968 an engine main bearing failed. It was already gone when we started the race, but we finished fifth (just missing the prize money!) by sticking to 4,000 rpm, which just proves that you don't have to rev GT40s. I remember that race well, unfortunately, because it was announced just before it started that Jim Clark had been killed at Hockenheim.

From there we went to the Nürburgring and Spa on consecutive weekends. That was my first visit to the 'Ring, and my first lap took 25 minutes because it snowed! There I was, exploring the track, and suddenly I was stuck on the hill up from Adenau, in first gear in an inch of slush going nowhere! They all thought I'd had an accident. I think we would have finished fifth at Spa, but Peter managed to put in too much fuel — it spilled inside the car and we had to drill holes in the floor to drain it out!

I had a break through the summer before driving the car again in a small GT race at Oulton Park in September. John Bridges in his Chevron and I had a terrific scrap, I broke the lap record by 2 sec, and at the finish damned nearly hit the poor man with the chequered flag. As Ian Titchmarsh wrote in *Autosport*: 'The GT40 just scraped in front, missing the man with the chequered flag by inches.'

My best GT40 result came at the end of the year in the Montlhéry 1,000 km, where we finished in third place six laps down on two Porsche 908s, and won the Group 4 class. That race showed how strong the GT40 is: at the end of the straight, approaching at 180 mph or so, the road falls away into a dip which is notoriously hard on suspensions. Everybody else was having to brake before it, but I would just fly over — it certainly felt like flying — and land with a crash on the other side. The only suspension breakage, by the way, that I've ever experienced on a GT40 came years later in the JCB car when a rear upright frac-

tured after I'd hit something. In fact, when we took the upright to bits we found that the drain hole at the bottom was blocked, and water had frozen inside and burst it. I recall that *Autosport* quoted me as saying about Montlhéry that, 'I spent most of my time just trying to see how much quicker than Sadler I was' . . . which upset Peter a bit, especially as he'd let me do two stints!

Sadler went off to race with Paul Vestey in '69, so I was left without a regular drive, pacing around wearing out the carpet. The only thing for it was to race my road car, so off I went with Johnny Blades to Vila Real in Portugal in July. We didn't do much to the car — it still had its radio! — and we had a terrible time with overheating in the hottest weather I've ever known. The brakes also failed at one point, but we finished after a long stop.

I remember the race well because I nearly killed Johnny afterwards. We had to push the car into *parc fermé*, and it was so hot that it wouldn't start again. A bunch of people pushed me, I dropped the clutch sharply to clear it and it fired. I was doing 80 mph up the road when I suddenly heard banging on the roof. I looked in the mirror and there was this body lying over the rear window — Johnny had his hands stuck in the air intakes and was clinging on for dear life, having thought we were just going to potter up the road.

At this point, still wanting to race seriously in a GT40, I swapped my car for Sadler's '1010', in which he had just done Le Mans with Vestey. I did a couple of clubbies in it before tackling the Tour de France — my first and last rally, although it's really a race.

I recruited John Davenport, who was then *Autosport*'s Rallies Editor, as navigator, and we set off almost totally unprepared. For a start, I'd never stayed up all night before, not even at a party. And then compared with the French, who had been practising for weeks, our only preparation was a couple of practice hillclimbs on the drive down to the start

in Nice. I'd never been given pace notes before in any case: when someone shouts 'medium K left' or something, I don't know what they're talking about.

The format is a string of hills for the early stages before the serious stuff on the circuits later in the event, when I hoped that we would do really well. On those early hills we were normally in the top 10, which is not bad on first acquaintance. Mont Ventoux put me in a bad mood because I made the classic mistake there, arriving too fast and taking the escape road at the bottom. All the same, we did well considering that Ventoux was very bumpy and hopeless in a GT40, especially as we had to do it on racing tyres.

Davenport was relying on his Monte Carlo Rally notes, which nearly landed us in a mess coming out of Gap. He shouted, 'flat left on to kilometre straight', and I went barrelling round this bend only to find that the course had changed since the Monte and it was flat left into hairpin right. We were doing 150 mph in the dark, and bloody nearly shovelled up a crowd of people. We found out later that the organizers had changed the stage to avoid a hospital, and that's where we very nearly ended up. I was a bit dubious about those pace notes by now.

On another hill we hit a sheet of oil — a Porsche 906 Carrera's sump had been knocked off — and we swapped ends at 90 mph. Towards the end of the day, on a climb just before the night stop at Annecy, I finally had my fill of those notes. We were racing up a narrow, bumpy track, and Davenport kept elbowing me, telling me it was flat. I was flat in fourth, but not fifth, and dared not go any quicker. At the end of the stage I asked him how fast he had been up there before, and he said that the works Porsche had done about 115 mph . . . we'd been doing 140 mph plus. That was when I told him to shut up, and just tell me where to go between stages!

After the night stop — about an

One of my best memories of racing GT40s in the late 'sixties was a terrific struggle at Oulton Park with the Chevron of John Bridges. I scraped home in front by inches and nearly hit the poor man with the chequered flag.

Racing the JCB GT40 (right) on 28 May 1977 at Donington's first post-war race meeting; I won the race, but Richard Bond's Lola T70, a lighter and later car, put me under intense pressure.

hour's sleep — the alternator failed, a common GT40 problem. (The diodes used to vibrate and fracture: we noticed afterwards that the race cars always had them mounted in rubber.) There we were with no lights, and I was left tagging on to a fellow called André Wicky in a Porsche 906, racing through French villages in the dark. That was very stupid, but I'm older and wiser now.

The Tour de France ended for us on the last hill, Rainkopf, when the gearbox stripped first gear on the line. It was my fault, I suppose, since we were using Sadler's 'long' Le Mans ratios, but a real shame because we were lying around seventh and could have been leading after a few circuit races.

I did three more races that year before I ran out of money. At Barcelona I shared with one Felix Serra, but we retired with over-heating after qualifying seventh. The following weekend, at Montlhéry, mine was the fastest GT40 even though we were still running cast iron cylinder heads when most other cars had aluminium Gurney Weslake equipment. Clive Baker and I finished sixth, leading the class for most of the race before being pipped by 20 sec by Michel Martin's GT40. And finally at Hockenheim in a miserable race in thick fog around the stadium I came eighth, that weekend being memorable mainly for losing my rag when my co-driver — a gentleman who's now big in motor racing sponsorship — ruined a set of tyres in a spin and didn't own up to it.

At that point I had to sell the car, though the buyer, Trevor Graham, kindly invited me to drive it at Vila Real the following year. After that I had little to do with GT40s, apart from selling them to people, until a season in the JCB car — which I rebuilt — in 1977. It had been an early works car before being converted by JW into a Mirage in '67. It later had its roof taken off so that Steve McQueen could use it as a camera car for the filming of *Le Mans*. It had always struck me that the GT40 would make a good open car, for sun shining through that great windscreen made heat quite a problem on the road.

The GT40 is fundamentally an amazing design, and there was little you could do to modify it. The steel monocoque made it incredibly heavy but also strong, which is always reassuring. I once saw a GT40 at Spa — driven, I think, by 'Beurlys' — hit an NSU which had been parked in a previous race. The NSU was rolled up into a ball, but all he did to the GT40 was put a six

inch dent in the side of the monocoque.

The engines are also unbelievably reliable and powerful. When I got the Sadler car I bought a new engine for £300, checked it over and used it for ever. It gave 360 bhp and never went wrong, and seemed just as quick as the aluminium headed cars which were giving more than 400 bhp. GT40s were obviously out of date by '69, but mine was certainly the quickest car that year. The only real headache with them was the fact that you couldn't change ratios on the ZF 'box, so you had either to change the 'box or the cwp.

If all this makes you think I have more than a soft spot for GT40s, then you're right. That's why it was such a delight to race one again in 1984 for a *Classic and Sportscar* track test. I found myself taking part in an HSCC 40 lap historic endurance race at Donington.

I hadn't raced a GT40 since 1977, when I had a handful of races in the JCB car. One of those was at a truly historic occasion on 28 May 1977, when Donington Park was reopened for motor racing. It would have been marvellous to have won the first post-war race there, but mine — the BAT Builders Historic Sports Car Race over 10 laps — was the second on the bill. I did win it, but I remember being under quite a

bit of pressure from Richard Bond's Lola T70. That was a good showing for the GT40, for it's such a heavy car that it's never comfortable against the lighter and later T70s.

Martin Colvill's car must be one of the best around. Its preparation standard is fantastic, so good that when I looked it over I thought that there was absolutely nothing that I would have done to it. The car has an interesting history too.

It started life as chassis number '1004' in 1965, and was entered by Ford for that year's Le Mans driven by Bob Bondurant and Umberto Maglioli. They were out of the race, unfortunately, after just two hours with a blown head gasket. There's little evidence of what happened for the next two years, so Martin suspects that it just sat at Fords before being given to John Wyer for the 1968 season. With the rules change imposed for that year, the car's 7 litre engine was replaced by a 4.7 ('289') engine, and the chassis renumbered, strangely, '1084'.

Those two seasons were fabulously successful for the GT40s, culminating in that incredible Le Mans victory over Porsche in 1969. Martin's car wasn't the most successful in terms of race results, and its last documented race was the 1968 Spa 1000 km when David Hobbs/Paul Hawkins brought it home fourth.

The car then languished again before being sold in 1970 to Rodney Clarke of Connaught fame for around £5,000. It was intended to be part of his collection, and he used it very sparingly for fun on the road, having had it registered and taxed. It must have been blindingly fast as a road car, and Clarke's enthusiasm for it showed in his correspondence with Wyer and John Horsman, asking for advice to make it even better!

Clarke died in the late 'seventies, and Martin, through his friendship with son John, a jazz pianist, made it known that he would be interested in buying it. The car wasn't for sale! Martin's interest lay fallow for a couple of years until he received a 'phone call from Leonard Potter, a trustee of Rodney Clarke's estate, saying that they were open to 'substantial' offers. So badly did he want the car that he sold a 7 litre Cobra to get it, and then set about returning it to racing condition, planning a campaign in the Atlantic Computers GT series. He chucked away the concessions for road use — engine cooling fans and so on — and entered it for its first race at Silverstone at the beginning of 1982.

'It was a hell of a handful at first,' says Martin. 'Three of the four Koni shockers quickly seized, and it was so wet that I spent most of my time facing backwards or in the catch-

It looks comfortable, doesn't it? An endurance racer must not be wearing to drive, and the GT40 comes into its own after several hours at the wheel.

fences. We quickly transformed it, though, and since then it has been a very great pleasure to drive.'

Having heard Martin enthusing about his GT40, I was looking forward to comparing my lap times with my best in 1977 — in the 1 min 18 sec bracket. I was able to do only three laps' practice on the day before the race because I was also competing at Silverstone on the Sunday, so when I got into it after Martin's 15 lap stint it was still pretty new to me.

It was terrific to be behind the wheel of a GT40 again, and this one was surprisingly undramatic. In fact, there's no question that it's the best GT40 I've ever driven, a superb car with an incredibly good engine. It was very relaxing to drive because it is set up so well, and the thought occurred to me that a four-hour session behind the wheel at Le Mans really wouldn't have been too difficult in one of these. GT40s are big, heavy cars, and quite unsuited to the 10 lap sprints of today's historic rac-

ing. They only come into their own after several hours.

The car is so stable aerodynamically that its speed is deceptive, and it takes a lot of pressure on the brake pedal to haul it up for a corner. Against that, the clutch is very light, and the gear-change — on the right-hand side — fantastic. The steering is heavy, which doesn't matter too much until you start hanging out the tail. Then the GT40 becomes really tricky! With the weight of that big cast iron engine behind you, the tail will go if you hang it out a little too much. It's all about polar moments of inertia, which means that if you get it wrong you're having an accident . . .

When I took over from Martin I had been hoping to have a go at Jonathan Palmer and James Weaver in Peter Millward's Lola Aston Martin, because I reckoned that I could just about hold them. Unfortunately, they retired with low fuel pressure just as I took over, so I was really only competing against

myself. As I said, my fastest lap in the JCB GT40 — supposedly an identical car — was around 1 min 18 sec, but I found that even on a fairly slippery track most of my 20 or so laps were in the 16s or low 17s, and my best was a 1 min 16.3 sec. That shows how good Martin's car is, and it was nice for me too, because a lot of people say that you're past it when you get to 40. They're wrong!

For the record, we finished third behind the John Foulston/John Brindley McLaren M8D and the Ray Bellm/Mike Wilds Chevron B19. That's not bad, because a CanAm McLaren would have the legs of a GT40 anywhere, and the nimble Chevron was very suited to Donington.

It was good of Martin to arrange this very special track test, and it was super to drive with someone who shares my passion for GT40s. The car has played such a large role in my racing career that I just hope another seven years don't have to go by before I drive one again!

1967
LOLA T70

Heavens, time passes quickly. Looking back, I can barely believe it was 15 years ago that I was racing my Ford GT40, and in those days *the* car to have was a Lola T70. It was hundredweights lighter than the Ford, and the Chevrolet V8 engine that was invariably used was more powerful than the Ford unit in the GT40.

However, I also recall that although T70s would come flying past me in the corners and on the shorter straights, I would reel them in on a long stretch: the GT40 had a good 20 mph on hand in the right circumstances. The T70s may have been lighter and more nimble, but — in spite of that beautiful and apparently streamlined shape — they had relatively poor aerodynamics at the top end. They were also relatively fragile, too, with such assorted problems that they seldom won anything of consequence.

To me the GT40 was like a D-type: it was developed for Le Mans, and was therefore a strong, stable machine. It was also quite heavy, though, with plenty of weight at the back, and if you hung the tail out and lost it, the resulting spin seemed to go on forever!

The T70 was much more of the lightweight, nimble, 'British School of Design' type of car. Mind you,

bear in mind that everything is relative. The Ferrari 512 that came four years later was much lighter again, and more powerful — it made the T70 seem rather lorry-like.

The comparisons with the GT40 don't stop there, for the T70 was born of the same blood. Lola founder Eric Broadley was deeply involved in producing Ford's Le Mans challenger in 1964, and returned to his own sports racing project after 'signing-off' the Ford. Whereas Ford had insisted that its car should have a steel monocoque for easier production manufacture, Broadley decided that his car would have a proper aluminium chassis. This was the T70, a big Group 7 two-seater which was raced in 'sprint' events through 1965 and 1966, and in John Surtees' hands won the first CanAm Challenge.

For 1967 came the T70 GT MkIII, the closed coupé, sweeping-lined endurance racing version launched at the Racing Car Show. Its aluminium monocoque had rearward side extensions supporting Chevrolet's 5.4 litre, 460 bhp V8 engine, mated to a Hewland LG500 four-speed gearbox. Front suspension was by double wishbones acting on Lola's own cast uprights, while at the rear there were wide-angle double wishbones. Many cars would race

with 5.9 litre versions of the V8.

There was also an Aston Martin V8 powered derivative which would capture much more media attention through the first half of 1967. Surtees gave this car an encouraging outing at the Le Mans test weekend in April, setting third best time behind the works Ferrari P4s. This was flattering only to deceive, for the race history of the Lola-Aston was bleak. Surtees and David Hobbs retired early from the Nürburgring 1,000 km with a suspension breakage, and both Le Mans entries (Chris Irwin/Pieter de Klerk drove the second car) retired in the early stages. From here on the Aston Martin V8 was abandoned, and works cars, like the customer cars, ran with Chevy power.

Jackie Epstein bought the first customer T70 GT and gave it its race debut, sharing with Paul Hawkins, at the Spa 1,000 km in 1967. Fourth place showed its potential, but the night-start 12 Hours at Reims that followed Le Mans brought stronger promise. The four cars entered — Surtees/Hobbs now with Chevy power, Epstein/Hawkins, Sid Taylor's new acquisition for Denny Hulme/Frank Gardner and the Mike de Udy/Hugh Dibley customer car — occupied the top four places early in the race, but all

Above *As long as you enter a bend on the power, the Lola T70 will reward you with exhilarating handling — drive through on a trailing throttle and it will try to understeer off.*

Right *Mike Wheatley powering through the rain in a SuperSports race at Spa in 1986; by this stage he had installed a fuel-injected 5.7 litre Chevy V8 producing about 560 bhp.*

Right *The Lola T70 GT MkIIIB often proved fragile in endurance races, but it won many British Group 4 events. This is Sid Taylor's 1969 Brands Hatch World Championship BOAC 500 entry, driven, until its retirement, by Peter Revson and Denny Hulme.*

Above *Wheatley's T70 as I drove it in its 1983 incarnation, in Uni-Petrol colours and with a Mathwall-prepared 5 litre Chevy breathing through four twin-choke Weber carburettors.*

Left *The T70 GT MkIIIB has everything: lovely looks, a beefy engine, predictable handling, excellent roadholding and fine braking. What more could you ask?*

Above right *The Lola was sadly wrecked in an accident in South Africa in March 1988, just as this book was being completed; Mike Wheatley was badly hurt, but as I write this he is thankfully on his way to recovery.*

of them retired. This was to be the pattern of the T70 GT's racing career — occasionally there was a flash of form, but it never really lived up to expectations. Here's an example of what the gorgeous T70 GT *didn't* achieve: apart from the Aston Martin engined works cars, only five customer cars were ever entered for Le Mans between 1967–71, and none finished …

At the end of 1967, the CSI's paranoia about the speeds of the 7 litre Ford Mark 4s, the Chaparral 2F and the T70 led it to impose a new 3 litre limit for Group 6 cars (racing-engined sports-prototypes) and 5 litres for Group 4 (25-off 'production' cars). Lola had produced enough cars for homologation into Group 4, so the T70 GT evolved into Mk IIIB form with 5 litre V8s, suspension and bodywork revisions, and wider wheels and tyres. It was potentially the fastest car of the season, but — in the absence of a works team — no customers ran seriously in major endurance races. Sixth place for Jo Bonnier/Stan Axelsson in the BOAC 500 at Brands Hatch was the T70 GT's best World Sports Car Championship finish of the year. In lesser 'sprint' events, however, the T70 GTs did well, winning every British Group 4 race that year.

Into 1969, the Mk IIIB was the only 5 litre car with the speed necessary to win races against 3 litre 'prototype' opposition (until the Porsche 917 came good by winning the final World Championship round at the Österreichring), but it was invariably too fragile for endurance distances. The highlight of the T70 GT's entire career — and its only World Championship victory — came that year in the opening round at Daytona, where Mark Donohue/Chuck Parsons won in Roger Penske's entry, but even this success was fortuitous as all the leading Porsches retired. Jo Bonnier, the Lola agent in Europe, ran two cars in conjunction with Scuderia Filipinetti (lacking suitable Ferraris to race that season), but frequent suspension and engine breakages meant that the team's best result was a single second place, at the Österreichring.

Against this thin success internationally, the Lolas continued to do well against weaker competition, winning seven of the eight major British Group 4 races in 1969, and four of the five rounds of the Springbok series in South Africa that winter.

By 1970, the Porsche 917 had come good and Ferrari had countered with its new V12 512 —

the Lolas were by now completely outclassed, their 'stock-block' Chevies neither reliable nor powerful enough to compete against pure racing engines. There were no top six finishes in the World Sports Car Championship, although Dickie Attwood, Teddy Pilette (in a VDS car) and Jean-Pierre Beltoise brought a few more second-string victories. The Lola T70 GT MkIIIB faded away through 1971, overwhelmed by Porsche and Ferrari.

Mike Wheatley's car is well-known on the circuits, always looking colourful and beautifully prepared. There have been several changes of sponsorship since I drove it in Uni-Petrol colours in 1983 — after spells carrying the identity of Ashdown Petroleum and Premium Pen it was painted in Agfa's vivid orange livery. Mike had always suspected that his T70 was one of Sid Taylor's cars, and this was confirmed when its original paint scheme was revealed during a strip and respray in 1984. He doesn't know precisely which Taylor car it was, but Mike Hailwood, Brian Redman, Hulme and Attwood all drove it. After that it passed to de Udy's Bahamas Racing and then to one Jack Le-Fort, before Mike acquired it in 1974.

He has raced it continuously since

then, and loves it so much that he says he'll never sell it. In an average year he races it about 14 times, in recent years invariably in the David Piper/Mike Knight SuperSports series, which takes him all over the world. Oddly enough, his first SuperSports win came in Britain, at Donington in 1987. Before the advent of SuperSports, Mike had a good run in the HSCC GT Championship, winning it outright in 1979 and coming second for the following three years.

Mike initially used a Morand-tuned Chevrolet engine, but problems obtaining parts caused him to turn to Mathwall Engineering, who have looked after his engines ever since. David Cottingham's DK Engineering prepared the car when I tested it in 1983, but since then John Sabourin has been responsible for fettling it. The efficiency of the operation is shown by the fact that, with a new engine, the car fired first time, completed several laps of the full Silverstone Grand Prix circuit with both Mike and myself driving in succession and, apart from some blanking tape over the radiators to warm things up a little (the test day was bitterly cold and windy), required no more work on it at all. The car was totally untemperamental.

Compared to the GT40, the T70 is much easier to drive, much more forgiving and yet much more responsive, like a smaller racer. As I've said, if you hung the tail out on the GT40 you were in danger of being carried away by the weight of the engine behind you — the T70 was much more controllable.

I was surprised at the amount of roll on the T70 — later it was confirmed that it was on a very soft setting. This is not necessarily a bad thing, since it makes for more predictability and a more gentle breakaway. It is set up for Mike's tastes, and he has shown how fast it

can be. Were I to drive the car in a race I might well sacrifice some of the chuckability for a stiffer setting and thus perhaps corner that little bit quicker. But who knows?

It is also a power-steerer: if you enter a corner on a trailing throttle the car will want to understeer off, so you have to keep the car balanced with the power, keep it smooth and on a good line. Do so and it rewards you with exhilarating cornering.

The new 5 litre engine that Mike had just had fitted when I drove featured a 'softer' cam, one which perhaps doesn't give quite as much power at the top end — about 480 bhp is the figure — but which has loads of torque lower down the rev range. A load of rubbish is often talked about power: a lot of power is fine, but if it's concentrated in a narrow rev range it's almost pointless. What is needed is usable power, and that is where this engine scores highly. Mike tells me that the 5.7 litre unit which he later installed — 'I needed to be more competitive against the agile stuff' — is even punchier throughout the range, peaking at about 560 bhp. It is also fuel-injected, whereas the 5 litre used four Weber twin-choke carburettors.

The 5 litre will pull cleanly and mightily from quite low revs so you can sling-shot out of a corner without falling into a power hole. This also gives better throttle response, allowing you to steer with the accelerator pedal and not wait for the urge to come in. There is, of course, a third advantage: you don't need to rev the engine to its limit, which would give a longer life. All in all, it's an impressive unit.

The Hewland gearbox has the usual heavy change. It's not particularly pleasant, but if you expect it to be difficult, and treat it as such, then it is no problem. This car, like some others I've driven, has something I hate: a gear-lever that

can rotate about its bottom ball joint — it's not fixed, in other words. You can't 'palm' a change, since your hand would just slip off the knob. You have to hold the lever firmly and feed it into each gear: thus the third to fourth movement, across the gate, requires some concentration and firmness of action.

The driving position is very good, although again with the car set up for Mike, I was perhaps an inch or so too far from the pedals and steering wheel. This was no bother for a few laps, but I would probably have some padding or the seat moved were I to race it. And, like the Aston Martin Nimrod I had driven a little earlier, the windscreen is quite far away from you, so the pillars intrude into your vision. The vision to the rear is very restricted.

To sum up, I thoroughly enjoyed my time behind the wheel of the Lola. More sophisticated than the GT40, less so than the Ferrari 512, it filled a gap in my racing experience. A lovely looking car, a good, beefy, torquey engine, predictable handling and excellent roadholding and braking.

Mike's record has shown that the T70 is a good honest racer which wins races, gives pleasure to driver and spectator alike (in fact, the day I drove was the first time Mike had seen it on a track in someone else's hands, and he was mightily impressed), and sums up an era.

Unfortunately, a sad postscript has to be added to this track test, for Mike Wheatley suffered a horrific crash in his T70 at the time when this book was nearing completion. He was racing with the SuperSports crowd in March 1988 at East London, South Africa, when a suspected suspension breakage sent the car out of control. Poor Mike suffered a broken leg and two broken arms, but is recovering well as I write this — the car was written off.

1970
LOTUS 72

There have been many famous racing cars. There have been many successful racing cars. There have, indeed, been many famous *and* successful racing cars. But the number of truly great racing cars which combined fame, success and pure charisma can be counted on the fingers of the proverbial one hand. And one of those fingers must assuredly point to the Lotus 72.

How else do you describe a car which, simply looking at cold, hard results, won 20 Grands Prix, three Constructors' Cups and two World Drivers' Championships? And the facts, of course, don't even begin to scratch the surface of the magic of the car. When I achieved another personal ambition by driving a 72, I suddenly realized why it was — and is — regarded as one of the greatest racing cars of all time.

The Lotus 72 had a remarkably long life at the top, those 20 victories spanning five seasons. Jochen Rindt won at Zandvoort, Clermont-Ferrand, Brands Hatch and Hockenheim in 1970, but was then tragically killed in practice at Monza. Emerson Fittipaldi's first win, at Watkins Glen, helped to thwart Jacky Ickx's late-season Ferrari challenge for the title and ensure that Rindt became Formula 1's first — and thankfully only — posthumous World Champion.

Oddly enough, the 72 won nothing in 1971, marking something of a grim landmark for Lotus as it was the first season since 1959 in which the team had failed to win a race. But 1972 brought Fittipaldi back to prominence, five wins — at Jarama, Nivelles, Brands Hatch, Österreichring and Monza — giving him, and the 72, the World Championship. The year of the 'superteam' of Fittipaldi and Ronnie Peterson in 1973 brought seven wins and the Constructors' title, but the sharing of spoils between these two drivers allowed Jackie Stewart to sneak through for the Drivers' title. Fittipaldi won three early-season races at Buenos Aires, Interlagos and Montjuich Park, followed by four for Peterson at Paul Ricard, Österreichring, Monza and Watkins Glen. The 72's last three GP victories came in 1974, Peterson winning at Monaco, Dijon and Monza.

The 72 looked a winner the moment it was unveiled. Its striking wedge shape, echoing the profile of Colin Chapman's turbine Type 56 Indianapolis car, was achieved by the novel idea of mounting split water radiators in pods on each side of the cockpit, instead of in the time-honoured position up front. Large front fins and a three-tier rear wing added to the downforce potential. The car displayed smart thinking beneath the skin too, with compound torsion bar rising-rate suspension and inboard brakes all round.

Making the most of Firestone's softer new tyre compounds was the focus of Chapman's and chief designer Maurice Phillippe's thoughts. It was crucial to avoid overheating these tyres, and rising-rate suspension offered progressive springing characteristics which enabled the tyres to work more efficiently. Compound torsion bars, consisting of a solid bar attached to an outer tubular sleeve, gave the most space-efficient and progressive springing medium. As a further aid to tyre life, anti-dive and anti-squat geometry was built into the wishbone suspension. Tyre efficiency was also enhanced by the reduction in unsprung weight allowed by moving the front discs inboard, with the bonus that the tyres were no longer exposed to heat from the brakes.

Although the 72 straight away demonstrated its superb adhesion, not all the theory worked in practice. After its troubled first race at Jarama, apparently, Rindt said that he would never 'drive that bloody car again'. Rindt went back to the

Although the track was damp when I drove John Foulston's Lotus 72, its grip was absolutely staggering. Wet weather roadholding was always one of the 72's many strengths.

The car felt beautifully prepared, apart from the temporary problem of a sticking throttle which slightly masked the Cosworth's progressive power delivery.

This 72 is the first built, chassis 72/1. It was raced by John Miles, Jochen Rindt's team-mate, in 1970 before being rebuilt, renumbered 72/4 and sold to Rob Walker as a private entry for Graham Hill.

Above *Strictly this car should be painted in Rob Walker's midnight blue and white colours and should not carry Rindt's name — it has the more effective 1971 one-piece rear wing instead of the original three-tier structure.*

Right *Unlike many owners of classic Cosworth-engined Grand Prix cars, John Foulston fitted the 72 with a full-house Formula 1 engine (not a detuned sports car unit) which revs to 10,500 rpm and produces around 500 bhp.*

old 49 for Monaco — and promptly won! — while the 72's suspension and braking were re-thought. The anti-dive and anti-squat geometry was discarded in favour of parallel wishbones, and those inboard front discs became ventilated. From here on, the 72 came good.

If the early development of the 72 wasn't quite plain sailing, then the end of its life was positively painful. The spectacular flop of the new 76 early in 1974 forced Lotus to race the 'museum-piece' 72 for a fifth season, but Peterson managed three wins with it. There really should have been a new car for 1975, but still the 72 soldiered on as Lotus simply couldn't afford to replace it, John Player having cut their sponsorship contribution after initially threatening to pull out completely. It was an undignified period of senility for the 72, Ronnie's best GP result that year a mere fourth place at Monaco.

The particular 72 I drove is specially significant because it started life as chassis number 72/1

The great Jochen Rindt at the wheel of 72/2 at Clermont-Ferrand in 1970, on the way to the second of his four Lotus 72 Grand Prix victories that year.

— the first of its ilk. Being the first, it was rather experimental and did not have a notably successful first year. Seventh place in the Dutch GP and eighth in the French, on both occasions in the hands of John Miles, was the best it could achieve.

Mid-way through 1970 it was broken up and rebuilt with a new chassis number, 72/4, before being sold for £5,000 to Rob Walker as a private entry for Graham Hill, who had a rotten time with it. He withdrew at Monza after Rindt's death, finished 23 laps behind at Ste Jovite, retired from seventh place when the clutch exploded at Watkins Glen, and dropped out with an overheating engine after only four laps in Mexico.

Walker sold the car to his former driver, Jo Siffert, who then passed it on to Emerson Fittipaldi. Emerson

kept it more or less as a souvenir along with his other display cars in Brazil until Adrian Hamilton's Bagshot emporium acquired the whole collection in 1985. The late John Foulston bought the 72 and had it completely rebuilt by his Haslemere Sports Cars concern, using an engine from Nicholson-McLaren, for his wife, Mary, to drive in historic races. John had it painted in Gold Leaf colours, although strictly, as 72/4, it should wear Rob Walker's hallowed midnight blue and white.

The first thing to be said about the car is that it is truly immaculate. Just sitting there in its red, white and gold livery, it looks superb, and so right — but so do many cars which have just had a superficial, cosmetic restoration. With this car there is no doubt that its condition matches the looks. As I've said before, there's nothing like *knowing* that a car has been properly prepared to give a boost to the confidence.

The cockpit had been tailored for Mary who is rather smaller than me. To this end the seat had been built up, which simply meant, in my case, that I was sitting a little more upright than would be standard. Otherwise the cockpit held no vices, with all controls decently placed, even if it was a bit cramped.

As I had climbed into the car, John had warned me that the throttle was sticking and that you had to press hard: it would feel solid, then suddenly go overcentre, due to a pedal modification to suit Mary. This had only cropped up when John had tried it earlier, and was to be fixed later in the day. There wasn't time to do it there and then because it was starting to drizzle . . . and I was on slicks. Slicks, in the wet, with an iffy throttle . . .

In fact, the 72 was a total revelation. It was really quite ludicrous what you could do with it — and get away with! This has to be one of the best handling cars I've ever driven. Steering is a fingertip job, and in fact the whole car feels light. Compared with the McLaren M19 which I once drove, the 72 is a whole new ball game. The M19 feels like a lorry after the 72, and the Wolf I used to drive feels a little like a lorry compared with the M19, so that gives you some indication of just how light, how much smaller, the Lotus feels.

If I had to put my finger on the one major characteristic of the car, it would have to be its predictability. Any handling defect in a car is going to show up on slicks in the wet, and yet I could just play with the 72 — it's so well balanced.

You can't really talk about understeer or oversteer under these conditions, because any touch of the former can be turned easily into the latter with a whiff of throttle. As an illustration of the handling balance, I was taking Maggotts absolutely flat, and that manoeuvre is only just on in most machines in the dry! In the conditions of the test day any other car would have flown off.

I was fascinated to read in Doug Nye's book *Theme Lotus*, when he referred to the 1970 International Trophy, that 'Wet Silverstone prac-

tice showed the 72s to be finding grip in conditions which didn't offer any — and that characteristic remained with the type throughout its life'. I can guarantee it . . .

Part of the reason for this astonishing wet-road grip must lie in the rising-rate suspension, and even more in the relatively soft springing provided by those compound torsion bars. If all four wheels are planted more firmly on to the track surface, then the inside wheels in particular will be adding a fair amount to the cornering power. Put it another way: if one (or more!) wheels are waggling about in mid-air, then they obviously aren't doing anything at all.

Another benefit of this set-up is the fact that the ride, due to the supple springing, is much better than you would expect. Silverstone isn't exactly over-endowed with bumps, but even so some cars can throw you around. The Lotus, on the other hand, while not being a magic carpet, is considerably smoother than many similar machines, and, frankly, much better than I expected. The other advantage of this, of course, is that if you hit a bump mid-corner you don't get thrown off line. The suspension actually works . . .

It is also aerodynamically absolutely stable, helped perhaps by the 1971 one-piece rear wing which was introduced when Firestone produced some low-profile tyres, similar to those with which the car is now fitted (original size tyres are unobtainable).

I've driven a fair number of Cosworth-powered cars, but most have been sports car units with which there is no point in exceeding 9,000 rpm. With this device I was given a limit of 10,500 rpm — and I was stunned by the result. You don't really have torque with a DFV, just a glorious steady flow of power. That extra 1,500 rpm is something else again, because it isn't just a case of revs and more revs, it's a case of power and more power as well. I estimate this engine was giving a good 100 bhp more than any sports

car unit, which must put it up in the 500 bhp bracket . . .

I was actually pulling 10,400 rpm down the back straight. Without knowing how it was geared I can't say how fast that is, but take my word for it that I was *flying*! What's more, it's all very progressive once I had overcome that sticking throttle — response can only be described as brilliant. This, of course, helps the sensation of lightness of the car — the engine just seems to pick it up and chuck it down those straights . . .

Braking was also excellent, and, what's more, if the throttle pick-up had been better — the engine snatched, which tended to upset the tail — I could have left my braking to well under 200 yards for Copse, which is very deep indeed considering the surface.

There was another revelation about the car — how well everything worked. All the instruments function, the gearchange is lovely, and so on. It had obviously been sorted by John over a period of time, the one thing it didn't get when it was new, so without doubt it was better when I drove it than it ever was in its day — or, put it another way, the way a *good* 72 should be, which is sensational.

When I originally wrote about the 72, I mentioned that I should have loved to drive it at a proper circuit, such as Oulton Park, since Silverstone Club is not the most taxing in the world. I imagined that it would be fabulous from Knickerbrook up through Druids, and expected it to see off anything likely to race against it. After the track test was published, I was very lucky to be given two races in the car, and it was just as brilliant as I had suspected. From Knickerbrook to Druids was flat: it was very, very impressive.

My thanks to John — who is, sadly, no longer with us — and all those who made, for me, a truly memorable day. Just for a few minutes I was Jochen Rindt, to me one of the greatest drivers ever, in a Lotus 72, one of the greatest cars ever.

1971
LOLA T260

I didn't feel exactly on top of the world when I arrived at Silverstone to take up the late John Foulston's kind invitation to drive his ex-Jackie Stewart CanAm Lola T260. On the drive down from home the radio had been full of the news of America's air attack on Libya, and the sky above Silverstone seemed to be dotted with the eerie silhouettes of circling F111s from nearby Upper Heyford. And it was raining — not just ordinary rain, but as if someone up there was pouring it out of huge buckets. It was real film-set rain.

So here I was, on the grimmest possible day weather-wise, trying to look forward to driving what by in-famous reputation is one of the most fearsome racing cars ever built. Sure, I've driven CanAm cars before, but even Jackie Stewart had said that this Lola is character building. My mind was made up: I was going to wait until the track was dry before I would plonk my backside in this one.

The Foulston equipe's bright yellow transporter, of a size that would look quite at home at a Grand Prix, stood out like a beacon in the paddock. A noise like continuous muffled thunder was coming from near it, and as I approached there was even a tremor in the ground — the T260 was being warmed up!

John, his regular driver, John Brindley, and team manager, Mike Halloes, were all agreed: the car would not go out until it had stopped raining. Well at least it was a chance to talk about the car. In fact, it looked as if we would have all day to talk about the car . . .

Anyone who read *Autosport* in the late 'sixties will remember Peter Lyons' reports of the Canadian-American Challenge Cup races, and how these were invariably dominated by the McLarens of Bruce McLaren and Denny Hulme. Bruce's cars may have had a lean time in Formula 1, but in the big-buck world of the CanAm they were

Its reputation is infamous, but the CanAm Lola T260 surprised me by being very much better than I expected, with enough handling predictability to make it quite chuckable.

Preparing for my drive once the rain had stopped. The theory behind those holes in the front bodywork was that the release of air pressure inside the body would reduce aerodynamic lift.

Bothered about instability which I felt might be caused by turbulence from the tea-tray front wing, I also tried the car with it removed. That caused severe understeer, leading me to appreciate why Jackie Stewart had found the car such a handful.

Carl Haas's L&M team commissioned the T260 from Lola's Eric Broadley for Jackie Stewart to challenge the all-conquering McLarens in the 1971 CanAm; he often led, but poor reliability meant that the Scot won only two races.

invincible. In the four seasons between 1967–70, McLaren failed to win only two races . . .

For 1971, however, Lola's American importer, Carl Haas, persuaded L & M cigarettes to stump up the sponsorship needed to commission Lola's Eric Broadley to design a McLaren-beating car. With his design right-hand man, Bob Marston, Broadley began work on a car which would build upon Lola's CanAm experience with T70, T160–162 and T222. The emphasis would be on straight-line speed, lightness and agility.

Its speed potential was shown when Frank Gardner tested the first chassis at 196 mph down Silverstone's Hangar Straight. At only 1,600 lb the car was certainly light, and small dimensions — its length of 139 in was fully 28 in less than its predecessor T222 — gave it the compactness which Broadley hoped would aid manoeuvrability. But the T260's greatest asset was the driver Haas signed up for 1971 — Jackie Stewart. The wee Scot would spend a busy season commuting between 10 CanAm rounds and the European Grand Prix season, and still end up as that year's Formula 1 World Champion . . .

In the CanAm, though, the T260's promise was ruined by dismal unreliability. As Lyons put it

when describing Stewart's season: 'He did earn fastest starting position twice, managed to scratch into the lead of seven races, and twice went on to win when the McLaren M8Fs failed. Four times Stewart was leading when he had to break off with either car or tyre failure, and one further time he stopped because he *thought* something had broken — he was getting that gun-shy. To be fair about it, none of these troubles was ever repeated; every failure was a new one . . .'

Wins at Ste Jovite second time out and at Mid-Ohio put Stewart in the title hunt at mid-season, but two second places and a sixth were all he could manage in the second half of the year, leaving him trailing third in the final points table behind Peter Revson and runner-up Hulme. It was the end of Lola's brief attempt to return to CanAm glory (John Surtees had won the first championship in 1966 with a T70), and L & M's dollars were transferred to Roger Penske's 1972 team of turbocharged Porsche 917/10s.

The John Foulston car is one of only two T260s built, although Lola had planned to build eight more for other customers. Haas sold the unraced spare chassis to Tom Heyser, and he gave it a few low-key 1972 outings, including one at Watkins Glen where Reine Wisell

drove. Jerry Hansen was allowed a single 1972 appearance in the ex-Stewart T260 at Donnybrooke, but otherwise it remained with Haas as a display car for the best part of 10 years before passing on to the American collector, Don Walker, in 1983 in a newly-restored state. Walker tested it a couple of times, but it hadn't been driven in anger since the rebuild until John Foulston acquired it early in 1985.

The sister car has a fascinating background: it was bought in 1972 and then salted away by a magpie collector of old American racing cars named Chuck Haines. He made his living working for Budweiser as a safety officer checking roller-coasters in their amusement parks, and accumulated his cars shoulder to shoulder in a basement. Since Ian Webb and Michael Cane first located him in 1978, several of the CanAm cars raced in Britain — including Ted Williams' March 707 — have come from this source, and this sister chassis now lives in West Germany, owned by Peter Kaus.

Eventually the rain did stop, and by early afternoon a dry line was beginning to appear on the track. John Brindley did a few laps to check everything over and get some heat into the tyres, and then arrived back in the pits with thumbs up. Just at that moment the sun came out.

Among all the cars he raced, the late John Foulston showed his courage most vividly in the T260, pictured here at Brands Hatch.

There she sat, like a shining white brick with a rounded edge at the front. Only the big tea-tray wing slung in front of the nose, the rear wing (looking peculiarly far forwards) and eight black skew-whiff intake trumpets on top of the engine interrupted the squareness of the profile. The car is really quite small, about the size of a Sports 2000.

Combining high speed with strong downforce was the rationale behind this bluff appearance, with that sharply shelving nose shape harking back to the Porsche 908/3 and Chevron B19. During the 1971 season the Haas team experimented with a less abrupt nose profile and an outslung rear wing, but the T260 today looks just as it first appeared, even down to Jackie Stewart's name painted on the side. One visual oddity of the T260 is the flexible glass-reinforced plastic panel forming the top surface ahead of the cockpit. It is punctured by lots of gauze-covered holes which had been found in the wind tunnel to release air pressure inside the body into the low-pressure area above the curving nose, thereby reducing aerodynamic lift. Whether it worked in practice is hard to say, but the theory sounds good.

By now there was an interesting extra dimension to this track test, for Martin Colvill had let me have a

quick run half an hour earlier in his Lola T222, the T260's immediate predecessor. Whereas that car produces about 485 bhp at around 7,500 rpm from 5 litres, the T260 pushes out an estimated 700 bhp at around 6,300 rpm from 8.1 litres. The comparison would be fascinating.

Once I'd slithered into the T260's cockpit I found it very comfortable, needing only a small chunk of foam rubber at the bottom of my back to make up for the difference in shape between me and John Brindley. Steering wheel and pedals are nicely placed, but I would have liked some padding on the sharp folded edges of the monocoque around my legs, from the safety point of view. In comfort at least the T260 scored over the T222, for the driving position in the latter was adjusted for Martin Colvill's immense height. There are three mirrors on the T260, two on the front wings and one on the right-hand side nearer the driver, but only the nearest seemed to be of much use.

I've driven CanAm cars before — I raced an M8F McLaren for Georg Loos in one Interserie event in the early 'seventies, and track tested Mike Wheatley's BRM P154 — and they're all incredibly quick. The whole ethos of the CanAm was just sheer, outright, no-expense-spared,

balls-out power. But the T260 is in another league again — with the first prod on the throttle I knew that it is staggeringly, unbelievably fast. It doesn't accelerate, it jumps, and it all happens at 4,000 rpm with a breathtaking surge of torque.

When you're on a track, much of the impression of speed comes from comparison with other cars when you're accelerating out of a corner. Everything else just seems to stop when you squirt past in the T260, with a phenomenal kick in the back. Going through Maggotts, the kink after Copse Corner which is a flat-out lean to the left in any racing car, really stands out in my memory. I would judge that the Lola was already doing 150 mph by this point, and suddenly Maggotts becomes a real corner.

Being a very big Chevrolet engine, there's mountains of torque from no revs at all, and the gearbox is almost irrelevant. You don't have to wring every last drop of power from an engine like this, and I was changing up at about 5,800 rpm even though the two Johns said I could happily go another 500 rpm. The T260 was quite under-geared for Silverstone's Grand Prix circuit, and it felt as if it would pull about 12,000 rpm in top as it was set up. The gear-change itself is precise and light, but the knob spins on its lever.

Left *The cockpit was very comfortable once I had put some foam rubber at the bottom of my back; for the sake of safety, I should have liked some padding on the sharp folded edges of the monocoque around my legs.*

Below *The T260, beautifully prepared by John Foulston's mechanics, looks a large machine, but without the huge wings at front and rear it is about the size of a Sports 2000.*

That's my number one pet hate, because you can easily miss a gear as the knob spins across your palm. The T222 had the same problem, as well as a ridiculously heavy throttle, something to do with the linkage having a contorted route.

The power contrast between T222 and T260 is only to be expected, but the difference between the two in terms of handling is considerable. While the older car has nicely balanced handling (sorted by Ray Mallock) with very predictable power-on oversteer which gives plenty of warning when you're near-ing the limit of adhesion, the newer car is altogether more nervous. The combination of less weight, more power and above all a much shorter wheelbase makes it very, very edgy, although its cornering capability is a good bit higher.

But the funny thing is that the

Big intake trumpets sit on top of the 8.1 litre Chevy, an awe-inspiring engine which produces around 700 bhp at 6,300 rpm, and massive torque from 4,000 rpm.

T260 astonished me by being a hundred times better than I had expected. Once I'd got used to the power I could really hang out the tail. It was quite chuckable! Having approached it with trepidation, I was now feeling that I would love to drive it in anger on a tight circuit.

It has huge Girling 12 × 1.1 in brakes, so you can dive good and deep into a corner. There's an interesting aside on the subject of brakes, for the T260 was originally designed with the front discs mounted inboard. Patrick Head, the Williams designer who was then a draughtsman at Lola, tells how Stewart noticed these when he first saw the new car at the factory, and ordered them to be removed before he raced it. The reason? Jochen Rindt's death at Monza in a Lotus 72 was attributed to the failure of an inboard front brake coupling shaft. The trouble with moving the front brakes outboard was that

Broadley's neat suspension arrangement of horizontally mounted inboard front dampers actuating big rocker arms was messed up, and there was no time to develop the new system before the first race.

The car turns in very sharply with all that downforce from the front wing, but once you're powering through it feels distinctly twitchy and not very confidence inspiring. Parts of the track were still wet when I went out, and the T260 felt quite horrible on the slippery bits because it is impossible to feed the power in gently. The car's least pleasant aspect, though, is that it feels very nervous and odd, even in a straight line. I put this down to buffeting from the front wing's effect in a head-wind, and suggested to John when I finally came back to the pits that it would be worth removing the front wing and reducing the angle of the rear to compensate.

There was certainly less tur-

bulence without the tea-tray, but there was now some understeer, the front wheels scrubbing out on medium speed corners. The reduced downforce at the back made the car very edgy on the fastest corners — Abbey and Maggotts were not good for the nerves. I am sure that there is a compromise somewhere with the front wing fitted, but by now I was starting to appreciate why Jackie Stewart had found the car such a handful. You need a hell of a lot of downforce to keep it stuck to the ground.

I'm still not sure whether the T260 or the McLaren M8F is the quickest car — in terms of straight line speed — I've ever driven, but they both leave me full of admiration for the heroes who took part in those long-lost CanAm days. It's good, too, that the people who own them now have the guts to race these big bangers, and bring a taste of CanAm to British shores.

1973

McLAREN M23

Some of the cars I've driven more recently could never have been described as 'historic' when I began track testing for *Classic and Sportscar*. The McLaren M23 is one. Why, it seems only yesterday that James Hunt won his World Championship with an M23, yet there I was, at Brands Hatch in 1987, driving one of these very cars fresh out of a complete restoration.

Although the long-running MP4 series of the 1980s is the most successful Formula 1 McLaren ever, the M23 has to be the most classic. It won 16 Grands Prix, two Drivers' Championships — for Emerson Fittipaldi in 1974 and Hunt in 1976 — and one Constructors' Cup. It must rank as one of the four great 1970s GP cars, alongside the Lotus 72, Ferrari 312T and Lotus 79.

Designed by Gordon Coppuck, the M23 was launched in February 1973 to meet new regulations requiring deformable structures, due to come into force at the Spanish GP. Using an aluminium monocoque formed of two skins of 16 gauge aluminium between which a special foam was injected by aerosol, the M23 had the most rigid F1 chassis of its time. Clothing this was an angular glass-fibre body designed to improve on one of the previous M19's main weaknesses — lack of

straight-line speed. With the bulk of the fuel tankage between engine and cockpit, the driver sat well forward, Denny Hulme saying, 'I could almost lean out and touch the front wheels'.

A wedge-shaped nose with canard fins rose to meet the upper body surface, which continued horizontally back to the engine. Hip-mounted radiators followed Lotus 72 practice, but were mounted within the stressed monocoque instead of being hung in fragile glass-fibre ducts. There was a shapely, high intake above and behind the driver's head to ram air into the induction system. Slung behind the rear wheels was a conventional end-plated rear wing, although it was positioned well forward to meet the new rules. It's not a beautiful car, but its looks have a certain functional appeal.

The rising rate front suspension pioneered on the M19 by designer Ralph Bellamy was retained in concept, even if Coppuck's detailed execution differed. There were wide-based tubular wishbones at the bottom, and those at the top were triangulated in two planes. A top link on each side extended inboard to meet with a pull-rod which actuated a separate rocker, this applying its movement to the top of the spring/damper units.

The geometry of all this gave a small degree of spring compression with initial suspension movement, but further loading produced a relatively greater spring deflection — hence an increasing, or 'rising', spring rate. The effect of this was to instil soft and supple suspension in initial movement, firming up the more the suspension deflected. Rising rate suspension has many theoretical advantages, but essentially it allows lower ground clearance without danger of bottoming under hard braking or cornering, more progressive suspension behaviour near the limit, and a less noticeable change in handling as fuel load lightens.

Since the M23's rear wheels carried a far smaller proportion of the fuel weight, a simpler rising rate arrangement sufficed, the rear springs being of a type which progressively became coil bound from their lower ends. Otherwise, the rear suspension was conventional, with adjustable top links, reversed lower wishbones and a pair of long trailing arms running back from the monocoque.

Mechanically, the M23 was very much Cosworth-DFV 'kit car' state of the art, the 3 litre V8 at the time producing 460 bhp at 10,000 rpm, transmitting this power through a Borg & Beck clutch to a five-speed

Hewland FG400 gearbox. Over the M23's four-year lifespan, John Nicholson wrung another 20 bhp from the Cosworth, and a McLaren-designed six-speed gearbox was fitted.

Denny Hulme did the initial development driving at Goodwood before the new car was flown to Kyalami for more testing prior to its GP debut in Yardley colours. He loved the M23 straight away, as he wrote in his *Autosport* column: 'Our F1 cars in the past have never been super efficient when it came to penetrating the air, but we hope the fantastic new shape with the sexy streamlined tail and air box to round off the aerodynamics will provide all the answers to aerodynamics ...' Of the handling, he wrote, 'I could set it oversteering and control it to a far greater degree than ever I had been able to with the M19. When the M23 did oversteer the back stayed out and did not go back to neutral and oversteer, back to neutral and oversteer again as the M19 tended to do on occasions. The new car oversteers and stays out there in a nice comfortable slide, and this may be one of the reasons why it was so fast around Goodwood.'

The M23 lived up to expectations at that first race in South Africa, Hulme qualifying on pole for the first time in his long career. A puncture cost him his early lead, but he salvaged fifth place. A good season followed, with one win for Hulme at Anderstorp and two for team-mate Peter Revson at Silverstone and Mosport. That British GP was the famous one when a wild young Jody Scheckter, in a third M23, careered across the track coming through Woodcote on the first lap, taking out nine cars in the multiple accident which this triggered ...

Major changes were made to the M23s for 1974 after a long winter of testing by the team's new recruit, Emerson Fittipaldi. Weight distribution was improved by fitting a bell housing spacer between engine and gearbox to lengthen the wheelbase by 3 in, rear suspension geometry was altered and the track widened

by 2 in to improve traction out of slow corners, and the rear wing was brought forward by 10 in relative to the rear wheels to meet new regulations. Three different wheelbase lengths would be used through the season, and there was a high-downforce 'winklepicker' nose for slower circuits. There was a new sponsor too, Marlboro's mega-bucks squeezing the Yardley money to a separate, but still works-run, operation fielding one car for Mike Hailwood.

Two wins at Buenos Aires (Hulme, after taking the lead on the penultimate lap) and Interlagos (Fittipaldi, in front when heavy rain caused the race to be flagged to a halt) made a super start to the new Texaco-Marlboro McLaren team's season. This was such a fiercely competitive year — Ferrari, Brabham and Lotus each gathered three wins, and Tyrrell two — that another couple of victories for Fittipaldi, at Nivelles and Mosport, were enough to give him his second World Championship and McLaren its first Constructors' Cup. There was one dark day for McLaren that year, however, when Hailwood crashed heavily at the Nürburgring. At first it was thought that his broken ankle, shin and knee would put him out of racing for three months, but sadly this was the end of his career.

With Ferrari's new 312T proving to be superbly competitive in 1975, McLaren had a quieter year. Fittipaldi seemed to go off the boil a little, some people speculating that he was thinking of retirement (actually, he's still racing successfully nowadays, in Indycar events), but the team still took three wins. The M23 was substantially unaltered, apart from front suspension revisions to improve adhesion and turn-in. Two of those wins, if truth be told, were somewhat fortunate, coming in depleted races stopped before the distance. Jochen Mass won the 'half-points' GP at Barcelona (stopped after a terrible spectator accident), and Fittipaldi was in front at Silverstone after

almost half the field went off the track during a cloudburst.

Fittipaldi did indeed leave McLaren at the end of the year, to join his brother's new Copersucar team. The decision was sudden, but coincided with Lord Hesketh's announcement that his 'playboy' team would not be racing in 1976 owing to lack of sponsorship. James Hunt, on the ascendancy after his debut win for Hesketh in 1975, was on the market, although not in a position to bargain. He signed a deal within 36 hours, Marlboro's John Hogan later remarking that James must have been the cheapest World Champion in recent racing history ...

By this stage, Coppuck's new M26 was on the stocks, but it would be raced only twice (by Mass) in 1976 as the M23s steamed onto their best season of all. The main innovation was a six-speed transaxle developed with Hewland by Alastair Caldwell to make best use of the Nicholson-developed Cosworth's torque curve. About 30 lb was trimmed off the M23's weight, part of the saving coming from another Caldwell idea, that of a compressed air starter. Operated by a rechargeable on-board compressed air reservoir, the system eliminated the need to carry a heavy battery.

That 1976 season was absolutely magnificent ... and traumatic. For more than half the season James really had little chance of the World Championship, but then came Niki Lauda's Nürburgring crash. James won there, and took three more victories in the next five races to give himself a shot at the title. For the final race of the year, in Japan, James needed to finish third and Niki nowhere.

What happened at Fuji must be one of the most famous episodes of motor racing history. Lauda withdrew after two laps because of the appallingly wet conditions, and James settled down to lead, with a clear view of the road ahead. Then came a slow puncture, but James — mistakenly as it turned out — struggled on. With only five laps to go, the tyre burst. Fortunately it happened close to the pits, and the McLaren limped in for new rubber. James rejoined in fifth place, needing to make up two places with only four laps to go. He tigered hard, and within two laps he had secured the third place he needed for the title. After a couple of hours on tenterhooks, the McLaren team was jubilant. James, on the other hand, was livid when he stepped from the car, needing considerable persuasion to convince him that he had indeed finished third, and was actually the World Champion ...

For me, James will always have a tally of seven wins in this World Championship year, but officially the total is only six. His victories in France, Germany, Holland, Canada and the USA weren't disputed, but those at Jarama and Brands Hatch were controversial, to say the least. In Spain his M23 was disqualified because its rear wing was found to be $\frac{5}{8}$ in too wide, but after an appeal the result was allowed to stand. That rankled with arch-rivals Ferrari throughout the season, and they were the first to protest when James won at Brands Hatch in an allegedly ineligible spare car.

It has always struck me as extremely ironic that Ferrari protested this win when its drivers were actually the cause of the fracas. James

Compared with other 'seventies Formula 1 cars I have driven, the McLaren M23 does not seem to be on such a knife-edge, its rising rate front suspension endowing notable stability under braking.

needed his spare chassis in this re-started race only because his regular car was put out in a first-lap accident triggered when the two Maranello entries tangled at Paddock Hill Bend. Fair and square though this victory was, it was later — and wrongly — taken away from him by the CSI, because he wasn't running when the race was stopped. Without this, he would have equalled Jim Clark's record of seven wins in a season.

Intensive development testing of the M26 followed that winter, but for the early races of 1977 McLaren played safe with its venerable M23s. Hunt used an M23 for the first four GPs and Mass for the first nine, but in all those outings the best results were only two second places, for James at Interlagos and Jochen at

Above *As I drove it, 'straight out of the box', the M23 was noticeably tail-happy, but a little suspension tuning would have cured the tendency of the rear wheels to dart out of line.*

Right *It was incredible how fast the M23 felt around Brands Hatch's Indy circuit: going round and round, hard into the dips, was like being cork-screwed into the ground.*

Right *The cockpit is comfortable even though it is set up for James Hunt's height, with an extended pedal box and monocoque cut-outs around the knee area.*

Anderstorp. By now, more than four years since the M23's debut, the M26 was badly needed.

Chatting with Gordon Coppuck, I asked him how he viewed the M23 and its drivers in retrospect: 'I think it was the best F1 car for three seasons. Yes, it was a good design, but it also benefitted from a lot of good development. The chassis changed very little, but we did a great deal of suspension work to keep it competitive. The chassis was much stiffer than those of our rival cars, but it was still pretty flexible by modern standards.

'Of all our drivers, Emerson was the hardest worker. He did fantastic testing mileages, and always enjoyed this side of his job more than the races. He was crucial in our development of the car. James was clearly the quickest — he enjoyed his racing much more, but never liked testing. Denny was somewhere between the two.'

A total of 13 M23s were built, and

With Ernst Schuster (left) and Kerry Adams before my first run: compressed air equipment is needed to start the car, saving the weight of a battery.

the one I drove, M23/11, didn't even see light of day until the 1977 South African GP, exactly four years after the type's debut. As such, it has a relatively poor provenance as M23s go, but all the same it is a proper works car, built to tide the team over until the M26 was ready.

James qualified it on pole at Kyalami, but lost the lead to Lauda's Ferrari on lap 7, slipping back to finish fourth. At Long Beach, the M23s were at last showing their age, James qualifying M23/11 only eighth for a race best remembered for his spectacular first-corner vault over the rear wheels of John Watson's Brabham-Alfa. Despite the jarring, the car survived to finish seventh. Hunt had his first race with the M26 at

Jarama, but returned to M23/11 for Monaco with a specially-tweaked Cosworth developed in response to the Ferrari flat-12's clear power advantage. The engine failed in this race, the last works outing for M23/11, and the M23 run as a whole.

M23/11 then passed to the Chesterfield-sponsored BS Fabrications team and its journeyman driver, Brett Lunger, as a spare car alongside its regular M23/14, the last of the run (the number 13 was omitted from the sequence). It had one more outing in 1977, finishing tenth at Watkins Glen.

Still M23/11 soldiered on into 1978, taking Lunger to fourth place in the non-championship International Trophy at Silverstone, but failing to qualify at Long Beach. When Lunger got his hands on an M26, M23/11 was entered in three GPs for a young Nelson Piquet, fresh out of F3. The Brazilian crashed at the Österreichring, retired with

The final race of the 1976 season, the Japanese Grand Prix, gave James Hunt his World Championship title, but this pit-stop to change a punctured tyre caused McLaren hearts to flutter in the closing stages.

transmission failure at Zandvoort and finished ninth at Monza. So, I've driven the car which put a three-times World Champion on the map ...

Into 1979, M23/11 enjoyed a sort of active retirement in Aurora AFX British F1 races, first with Ricardo Zunino and later Dennis Leech, who sold the car at auction to a German-born Swiss businessman and car collector, Ernst Schuster. He then had the car totally rebuilt, and the day he — and I, for that matter — first drove it was at Brands Hatch in the summer of 1987. It now resides in the Nürburgring Museum, and as I write this hasn't been driven since. Ernst did plan to let Alain Prost give it a run at an *Anciens Pilotes* gathering in Switzerland that autumn, but was unable to get hold of the compressed air equipment needed to start it!

No one is better equipped to have carried out M23/11's rebuild than Kerry Adams, who used to be a

mechanic with McLaren during the M23 era but now operates a restoration shop close to Tiga Cars in High Wycombe. Kerry says that the car was a ground-up job, although it was thankfully complete. The monocoque had deteriorated badly and needed patching up, but otherwise the work was largely a case of refurbishing existing components, and sending the Cosworth to Nicholson-McLaren for a complete overhaul. Kerry has also restored a second M23, since Albert Obrist hired him to fettle his M23/8, Hunt's championship-winning car.

So it was that M23/11 had come 'straight out of the box' when I tried it at Brands Hatch. It was a difficult day, with millions of Formula Fords

out on the circuit, but Brands Hatch's officials kindly allowed Ernst and I to run in a quieter saloon car session. This track test was one of those moments of sheer opportunism: Ernst told me a couple of days before that he would be giving his new machine its first run, and would I like to assess it for him after its rebuild?

I wondered whether I was going to be comfortable in M23/11's cockpit, as it was tailored for James Hunt's gangly frame. It still has the pedal box extended a few inches through the bulkhead, and cut-outs in the monocoque in the knee area. With some seat padding, however, I was soon very comfortable, and surveying the minimal instrumentation. The main dial bang in the centre is a tachometer positioned so that its needle points vertically at the 10,000 rpm limit. Lower down on either side are two other gauges for oil pressure/oil temperature and fuel pressure/water temperature.

The ignition cut-off switch is in the traditional position on the little leather-rimmed steering wheel (detachable in emergencies), there is another switch to over-ride the rev limiter (but only when going for a place on the last lap!) and the gearshift is a stumpy lever on the right-hand side.

With the compressed air starter engaged (you can't push or tow start this car), the Cosworth DFV screamed into life with its characteristic raucous bark. A quick check of the gauges, build the revs to 5,000 rpm or so, release the sharp clutch and we're away down the pitlane to play, like a pike among minnows, on the Brands Hatch Indy circuit.

I've driven several 1970s F1 machines at Brands, but the M23 is easily the best. Obviously I wasn't trying particularly hard in someone else's car, but it was incredible how quickly the car went round this tiny circuit. Going round and round, and hard down into the dips, was like being corkscrewed into the ground! You sit so low that the top straight seemed incredibly fast. The top F1 drivers now clock 180 mph past the pits, and I should estimate that the M23 was doing a good 150 mph.

You might expect a higher speed on the top straight with a faster run-in from the GP circuit, but in fact the M23 accelerated so quickly that I don't think the Indy circuit made any difference to my speed into Paddock. Ernst told me to use all 10,000 rpm just to check the engine, and I came close to that in sixth gear. The acceleration, the bumpiness along the top straight and the speed with which I approached the sharp dip into Paddock added up to a *very* thrilling experience. It made me

realize just how brilliant the current drivers must be. Good aerodynamics were also one of the M23's strong suits, and the lack of buffeting in the cockpit at high speed bore this out.

Although the Cosworth is basically very flexible, the six-speed 'box allows you to keep the engine right in the power band. This DFV naturally is to F1, not sports car, camshaft specification, so it's fairly peaky. Compared with the sports car spec, the top of its power curve is 1,000 rpm higher, and you have probably 30 bhp extra at around 10,000 rpm. There's not a lot of urge low down, but by 7,000 rpm it's really starting to fly. Changing up at 10,000 rpm drops you down only to around 8,500 rpm in every gear, since the six-speed 'box has slightly closer ratios than a five-speed.

The handling is noticeably tail-happy, the back end having a tendency to dart out suddenly, but then a little suspension tuning would, I'm sure, make the oversteer less instant. It is very controllable, and with a bit of adjustment you could revel in long, glorious power slides, not that this is the quickest method in a recent F1 car. Adhesion at the front is absolutely incredible, and the car turns in more smartly than other F1 cars of the period that I've driven.

But the most distinctive feature about the car's handling is the way its rising rate suspension makes it so comfortable to drive, even at Brands. Since it's comfortable, it's also much easier to drive, and much more controllable at the limit. Unlike, say, a Lotus 72, the M23 doesn't slam down on its bump stops when you stand on the brakes, and you get much tidier behaviour

as a result. The nose dips with braking, and can scrape the road because rising rate suspension allows a lower ride height, but the change of attitude isn't so dramatic, as if there's strong anti-dive geometry built in.

The brakes are absolutely amazing, and again I think that the rising rate makes them work that little bit more reassuringly. The firm pedal pressure is just right, as is the weight of all the other controls. The steering is a joy, and razor-sharp, while the gearchange needs just a gentle flick of the wrist. To select first or second you have to push firmly against the springing on the central plane — I unwittingly went out of the pits on one occasion in third. The pattern of the six ratios is like a conventional H with an extra plane over to the right for fifth and sixth.

I thought the M23 was absolutely wonderful in every respect, but it's terribly difficult to measure F1 cars from this period against each other as they were all so similar. The Cosworth and Hewland packages were the building blocks from which everyone, except Ferrari, started, and as a result any differences are hard to identify. But where the McLaren M23 stands clear of other 1970s F1 cars I've driven is in how comfortably you can drive it quickly. It doesn't seem to be on such a knife-edge when you start to push it, behaving progressively and controllably in its handling and braking.

I loved the M23, and was tremendously impressed with how 'together' it felt on this first post-rebuild run — that's a fine testimonial to the quality of Kerry Adams's work. My thanks to Ernst Schuster for letting me have a go on such a rare outing.

1977

LOTUS 78

Quite a few milestone racing cars have been subjects for my track tests, but this one, the Lotus 78, has to be one of the most significant of the lot. It took people's breath away when it was launched, introducing as it did the concept of the 'wing car', which every other team in Formula 1 was bound to imitate. It was the fastest car of 1977, and in the following year, with unreliability conquered, it and its successor, the 79, gave Mario Andretti a runaway win in the World Championship.

The Lotus 78 spawned the brief, but dramatic, generation of awesomely fast 'ground effect' cars, ultimately banned by FISA because their prodigious cornering powers were fast overtaking the safety standards of the circuits on which they raced. On top of that, the cars with skirts were always unpopular with drivers, requiring more guts than skill to wring the best from them. It was a unique era of F1, but no one's sorry it's gone.

The 78 was born from the radical thinking imposed on Colin Chapman by Lotus's bleak period in motor racing in 1974–75. The new 76 had proved to be a complete failure in 1974, and the faithful old 72 design was wheeled out again to do battle for another two years. The 77 'adjustacar', which raced

through 1976, was the product of one line of thought, while the 78 resulted from another . . .

Chapman presented his partially-formed ideas for a wing car in a 27-page document during August 1975 to his Research & Development man, Tony Rudd, who set to work on the concept with designer Ralph Bellamy and aerodynamicist Peter Wright. In essence, the idea was that the downforce conventionally produced by wings at the nose and tail could be dramatically increased if the entire car could act as a wing. A year later, after a staggering amount of theoretical and practical work (including 400 hours of wind tunnel time), the first prototype 78 began testing in Andretti's hands. Although the aerodynamic benefits were only 75 per cent of the figures which had been calculated, the car worked.

The secret of its effectiveness lay within the pannier sections slung either side of the cockpit. The undersides of these curved upwards towards the rear to create inverted wing sections with tapering tunnels beneath, so that as air passed through its pressure decreased, thereby sucking the car down to the road. The system could work only if air was prevented from spilling away between the pannier sides and the

road, so rudimentary bristle skirts were fitted to contain the low-pressure area. Skirts were the key to the whole thing working, and it was only after much more development that the definitive solid sliding skirt was devised. Adding to the aerodynamic effectiveness of the layout, the water radiators were housed on the leading edge of these side wing sections, in the style of the Mosquito aircraft.

The 78 was advanced in other ways too, its aluminium honeycomb monocoque being especially strong. Front suspension comprised raked-back rocker arms operating coil spring/damper units neatly recessed in the monocoque sides, with the wide-based wishbones providing the lower hub location. Parallel top links and large lower wishbones formed the rear suspension. All four disc brakes carried the twin calipers seen on the 77. A clever design feature was the positioning of the oil tank as a collar around the bellhousing between engine and gearbox.

Much of the 78's success must be attributed to Andretti's superb testing sensitivity, and the rapport he developed with Chapman as a result. Very quickly the Italian-American arrived, for example, at a 1 in wider front track to give sharper turn-in, all his work refining the 78

into a race-winning car. He used Indycar techniques like 'stagger' (the use of slightly unequal circumference tyres) and 'cross-weighting' (setting springs to give diagonal stiffness). Andretti also proposed a cockpit-adjustable rear anti-roll bar and a tap to control flow from the three fuel tanks. By trimming the car's decreasing fuel load through a race, a weight bias towards the 'inside' of the car could be achieved — on clockwise circuits, with more right-handers than left-handers, the left-hand tank would be emptied first. It was a clever arrangement,

but beautifully simple.

But for severe engine reliability and other minor problems, the new 78 would have won the 1977 World Championship and Constructors' Cup. Andretti won at Long Beach, Jarama, Dijon and Monza, while Gunnar Nilsson took a fifth victory in the wet in Belgium. Although Andretti finished only third in the title race, his four wins were more than the three of Niki Lauda and Jody Scheckter who finished ahead of him, and he led more laps than any other driver that season. The Lotus 78 was undoubtedly the best car of

the season, and if it had any weakness it was in straight–line speed, although the team always suspected that higher speeds could have been achieved if Andretti and Nilsson had been happy to dial out some of the immense cornering downforce which gave the 78 such superb adhesion and traction.

While the 78 'wing car' was being developed into the full-blown 'ground effect' 79, the older car raced on into 1978, with Ronnie Peterson joining Mario in the team. Andretti won at Buenos Aires and Ronnie at Kyalami before the 79

Above *Even though Bill Friend's Lotus 78 was running without the flexible skirts which Neil Twyman has since developed for it, I found the car a revelation, with explosive performance and superb handling.*

Left *This is 78/1, the first chassis of a design which triggered the 'ground effect' revolution in 1977. Bill Friend bought the car after it had served a spell with several drivers in the Aurora AFX British Formula 1 series.*

made its GP debut in Belgium, winning first time out. Lotus wound up with eight wins that season, six of them achieved by the stunningly gorgeous 79. The works team retained a 78 as a spare car, and it was in this that Ronnie started the tragic Italian GP after damaging his 79 in the race morning warm-up. Going away from a botched start, James Hunt's McLaren and Ronnie's 78 touched, sending the Lotus into a horrific, fiery crash. Both of Ronnie's legs were broken, and sadly he died in a Milan hospital that night. This was the last time a 78 would

Above *The Cosworth-DFV can be revved safely to over 10,000 rpm, and power arrives strongly at 7,000 rpm. Since my test, a more powerful engine tuned by Alan Smith Racing has been fitted.*

Right *Skirts were missing when I drove the Lotus 78 in 1982 because the only tyres available required a higher ride height, which broke the contact of the original Lotus-type cantilever-operating skirts.*

start a race in works hands.

The car I drove was the original 'long chassis' prototype, 78/1 (or JPS15 in sponsor's jargon), one of only four 78s built. It has a pretty slender racing record — 78/2 and 78/3 took all seven GP victories — amounting to only two fifth places, for Andretti in Argentina and Nilsson in Brazil. After one more outing in South Africa, where Nilsson finished twelfth, 78/1 was retained as a training car before passing on to Hector Rebaque. The Brazilian went to Argentina and Brazil with it, failing to qualify at

Buenos Aires and retiring at Rio, before acquiring 78/4 for his lacklustre effort.

The original 78/1 then spent a successful spell in the Aurora AFX British F1 Championship, first with Emilio de Villota and then with Colin Bennett Racing, for whom Norman Dickson, Gianfranco Brancatelli and Desiré Wilson drove it. Bill Friend then bought it to join his collection of Lotus 'firsts', and returned it to John Player Special colours. It shares garage space with Bill's other significant Lotus machines, such as the Mk3 (Chap-

Those huge side panniers conceal the underbody tunnels which produce 'ground effect' by creating a low pressure area under the car — skirts are essential to prevent external air spilling into these channels.

But for poor engine reliability, Mario Andretti would have won the 1977 World Championship with his Lotus 78. Here he is at Monza on the way to his fourth Grand Prix win of the year.

man's third Austin Seven based special) and Graham Hill's 12 (the first F1 Lotus). Bill's nephew, Roger, has since driven it occasionally in British F1 races, although he admits that he's achieved 'nothing terribly exciting'.

When I track tested this car in late 1982 it was a mere five years old, so I felt it necessary to justify its inclusion in *Classic and Sportscar*, which in the normal run of things rarely publishes stories about cars unless they are at least a decade old. In my

view, the Lotus 78 qualified as a classic from the beginning, for it was the car which brought the phrase 'ground effect' into the motor racing history books. I am sure there were plenty of readers who regarded with disdain any GP machine made since the 3 litre formula began in 1966 — and who looked with horror at the mobile advertising hoardings of the 1970s and 1980s. In my opinion they are wrong.

The scene of the test was Goodwood, a track that rarely sees modern GP machinery these days. It remains, however, my favourite circuit. It has some really fast corners and others with tricky apexes and so on, and it is set in the most fabulous countryside — I just wish it wasn't so far from my Derby home. It also proved to be a superb place to try this type of car.

I had driven — indeed raced — one of Bill Friend's cars before, his Lotus 47, so I knew that the 78 would not only be beautifully-prepared, but also that it would be a perfect fit, as Roger is about the same size as me. As soon as I stepped into the cockpit, I knew that I was going to enjoy it.

The first proviso I must make is that these were early days in Bill Friend's ownership, and Neil Twyman, who prepares the car, had yet to develop a modified skirt system for it. The problem stemmed from the fact that the correct front tyres had long been unobtainable, so taller profile tyres meant an increase in ride height, which broke the ground contact of the Lotus-type cantilever-operating skirts. A previous owner had tried to circumvent the problem by lowering the car until its front shock absorbers were running on their bump stops, which, as Neil says, 'was quite dangerous'. So it was that I drove the car with a slightly high ride height, imperfect suspension geometry and without skirts — eventually Neil was able to improvise a rudimentary skirt system by using $\frac{1}{4}$ in flexible rubber matting.

Apart from making 'wear and tear' improvements, like replacing a cracked front disc, Neil's main task since my test has been to fit a new latest specification 500 bhp Alan Smith Racing Cosworth-DFV in 1985, as the old engine (producing about 470 bhp) dropped a valve in a race at Brands Hatch. With this

engine and rubber skirts, the car has run very well, recording a best finish in Roger's hands of third place behind John Foulston's McLaren M19 and Richard Peacock's Tyrrell at Brands Hatch in 1987.

The cockpit fits like a glove, and in front of you is a very thick-rimmed, three-spoke steering wheel carrying the ignition cut-out switch right in its centre. There's a large tachometer in the middle of the 'dashboard' plate mounted on to the front roll-over hoop, with smaller dials on either side for oil pressure/oil temperature and water temperature/fuel pressure. The gear-lever is on the right, by a little bulge in the cockpit side to allow room for hand movement. The fuel tank tap is still in position, although it's now redundant since only the central fuel tank is piped up for today's 'sprint' races. The lever to alter the five settings of the rear anti-roll bar is on the left, like a little gear-lever, but I figured I would be too busy driving the car to fiddle with that!

I spent the first couple of laps acclimatizing myself to the circuit and warming up the tyres before I started to have a bit of a go. My first impression was how much shorter the straights seem in something like this. The car is shattering! It simply explodes out of a corner. Even though the gear ratios were not ideally suited to the circuit (these have since been lowered), it was still evident that the acceleration is staggering, just like all the other Cosworth–DFV cars I've driven. I've written about the Cosworth's characteristics elsewhere, but suffice to say that it can be revved safely to a whisker over 10,000 rpm, and really comes on cam at around 7,000 rpm.

With such acceleration it is vitally important that driver and machine get along together, and in this case such harmony was instantaneous. The gear-lever — which at Goodwood was in use virtually all the time — has a switch-like action with very short positive travel. All foot controls are perfectly positioned. The

deceleration has to be experienced to be believed — I wish it was a two-seater as I can think of a great many people I would love to frighten . . .

The handling is completely predictable. To use that old cliché, it simply goes round corners. I felt that I could do almost what I liked with the car. The steering is so good and quick that you can flick the car sideways and catch it very easily, although with the extra suction afforded by the skirts, it might have been a different story. Certainly watching the 78 — and more particularly the 79 — being driven when new, it was apparent the neater the driver, the quicker he was. Not as much fun, but quicker. The only thing I have to add is that if you do throw it sideways your reactions have to be like lightning, if you are to catch it . . .

Treated with respect, though, the car is very safe indeed. With that superb, predictable handling and those incredible brakes you would have to be very clumsy to make a mess of things. In fact I believe the Lotus is as faithful and safe as the Cooper I raced in 1982 in the Lloyds & Scottish series is unnerving, the Cooper having a veritable mind of its own.

Unfortunately, I can't comment on the 'ground effect' aspects of the 78's handling, but Roger — who has known it with and without skirts — says that the difference is remarkable. There isn't so much grip that you can throw caution to the winds through corners, but apparently the gains are very obvious. You can feel the car pulled lower with speed, and the advantage you have in a race situation — where you can measure your car directly against others — is clearly in cornering power, with superbly sharp response to the steering, amazing grip and equally effective traction.

I am very envious of Roger, and grateful to Bill for trusting me to drive such an exciting — and significant — machine. On second thoughts, though, damn him! The Lotus 78 spoiled me for almost everything else...

1978
FERRARI 312T3

Over nigh on four decades of World Championship Grand Prix racing, Ferrari has had its ups and downs. In between the occasional lean times for Maranello the good times have been magnificent. Perhaps the most sustained period of success was that of the *trasversale* series of cars introduced in 1975, Ferrari winning 27 Grands Prix in five seasons.

The chance to drive any Formula 1 Ferrari is rare as few cars have been released by the factory over the

Its fabulous flat-12 engine is my most enduring impression of the Ferrari 312T3. It is just like a turbine, beautifully smooth, with progressive power delivery and none of the vibration typical of a Cosworth-DFV.

years, so the opportunity to test Nick Mason's 1978 312T3, part of his Ten Tenths collection, had to be grasped with both hands. This was going to be one of the highlights of all my years of track testing for *Classic and Sportscar* ...

This isn't just any old flat-12 Formula 1 Ferrari, for it is the very car which rocketed Gilles Villeneuve,

one of my all-time motor racing heroes, to prominence. Villeneuve was the brightest 'comingman' for many a year when he started his first season with Ferrari in 1978, but by the end of the season he was being heralded as a future World Champion.

To put the *trasversale* cars into perspective, consider these facts. Ferrari won the FIA Constructors' Cup four times in five years, in 1975, '76, '77 and '79. Ferrari had World Champion drivers with Niki Lauda in 1975 and '77, and Jody Scheckter in '79. It's fair to speculate that Lauda also would have won the 1976 title but for the Nürburgring accident which almost killed him. The one year absent from this string of successes is 1978, the season when Colin Chapman mastered ground-effect with the Lotus 79, giving the World Championship to Mario Andretti. But Ferrari still managed five GP victories that year with the flat-bottomed T3, the car which I tested.

The term *trasversale* refers to the gearbox lay-out introduced with the 312T in 1975. Ferrari designer Mauro Forghieri's aim was to concentrate mass towards the centre of

the car to minimize the polar moment, and mounting the five-speed gearbox transversely put the whole unit ahead of the rear axle line. Bevel gears transmitted power at the input side of the 'box, and a system of spur gears formed the final drive. 'Revolutionary' is too strong a word to describe this innovation, but it produced a dramatic improvement in comparison tests with the old B3 at Fiorano. Lauda said that the car's finest quality was remarkably neutral handling which enabled him to drive that bit closer to the limit.

Victories that year for Lauda in the Monaco, Belgian, Swedish, French and United States GPs, and for Clay Regazzoni in the Italian GP, proved conclusively that the 312T was the new F1 benchmark. Further wins came in 1976 for Lauda in Brazil and South Africa, and for Regazzoni at Long Beach, before an updated T2 appeared for the Spanish GP at Jarama. The

Although the handling displayed some twitchiness which more suspension work could eliminate, I loved the way the Ferrari could be driven on the throttle.

most significant difference was that the tall air box was removed to meet new regulations, and replaced by ducting along the cockpit sides to feed air to the engine. Around 20 lb was pared from the weight, and the chassis was lengthened by 2.2 in. Lauda tested a de Dion rear end, but couldn't produce better times with it.

Through 1976 Ferrari and McLaren dominated, with six wins apiece. On top of the three already achieved with the 312T, Lauda added three more in the T2 at Zolder, Monaco and Brands Hatch. He was well on the way to his second World Championship, but then came that Nürburgring accident. Remarkably, Niki missed only one GP, returning to the cockpit at Monza six weeks after receiving the last rites from a Roman Catholic priest. His courage brought fourth place in Italy, but courage of a different sort saw him withdraw in appallingly wet conditions from the end-of-season Japanese GP, leaving James Hunt with the world title.

Lauda took three more wins (in South Africa, Germany and Holland) in the T2 to give him his

second World Championship in 1977, and Carlos Reutemann backed up with one win in Brazil. The T2 began the year in virtually the same form as it finished in 1976 apart from a 12 bhp increase achieved by the engine department, but during the season small modifications — like revised bodywork and rear suspension pick-up points, and a new rear wing — kept the T2 reasonably competitive in the face of stiff opposition from Mario Andretti's Lotus 78.

Although the T3 brought five GP victories in 1978, this was the only season which didn't produce a Constructors' or Drivers' title for Ferrari's *trasversale*. Many of the changes introduced with the T3 were dictated by the new arrangement to run Michelin radial tyres, forced upon Ferrari by an increasingly strained relationship with Goodyear in 1977. The huge downforce generated by the Lotus 78 had prompted Goodyear to develop tyres with stiffer sidewalls, and several other teams — Ferrari included — found their cars unable to generate sufficiently high tyre temperatures.

The T3, therefore, was very different. It featured a new monocoque design which gave a very flat profile to the upper bodywork, allowing clean air-flow to the single-post rear wing. The suspension was totally changed at the front: whereas the T2 had used long fabricated rocker arms operating tiny inboard coil springs, Forghieri gave the T3 shorter tubular rocker arms operating larger coil spring/damper units mounted outside the monocoque. Rear suspension comprised a transverse top link, a pair of radius arms and outboard coil spring/damper units.

I'll come back to the T3 shortly, but let's briefly fill in the final chapters of the *trasversale* cars, for yet another spectacularly successful season followed for the T4 in 1979. This was the first ground-effect Ferrari, developed in Pininfarina's wind tunnel around the under-body limitations imposed by the wide flat-12 engine. The car was 6 in longer in the wheelbase to allow one central fuel cell between cockpit and engine, and nearly 10 in longer overall. Many of the changes were made to make those under-body air channels as large as possible, so the footwell was narrowed and the rear coil spring/damper units moved inboard. The T4 was visually distinctive too, with a flat top surface stretching back from a sharp lip just ahead of the front wheels.

The old T3s were used for the first two races of 1979 in Argentina and Brazil, but in South Africa the T4 made the most sensational debut, with Villeneuve first and Scheckter second. There were two more one-two victories that year, Villeneuve heading the order at Long Beach and Scheckter at Monza. By the end of the season, each driver had notched up three wins, and Scheckter had taken the world title by a mere four points from Villeneuve. It was pretty convincing stuff, but Alan Jones and his Williams were looming on the horizon that year.

Ferrari answered for 1980 with a revised version of the T4, designated T5. Although it was a better car, ground-effect technology was developing so quickly that Ferrari were left behind with the T5, and not a single race was won in a year plagued by mechanical unreliability and tyre problems. The *trasversale* era — and the flat-12's glorious decade — ended sadly with a whimper, cast aside to make way for the turbos.

But back to the T3. Nick Mason's car, chassis number 034, was raced in 1978 by Gilles Villeneuve. Villeneuve's first race with it was the United States GP West at Long Beach, and what a debut! He lined up alongside team-mate Carlos Reutemann's pole position T3, and snatched the lead out of the first corner, a hairpin, after John Watson put his Brabham-Alfa into a do-or-die outbraking manoeuvre which all but removed Reutemann's Ferrari and Lauda's Brabham. Gilles held off all challenges, including an unexpected charge from Alan Jones's Saudia-Williams FW06, for 39 laps until a minor error cost him his first Grand Prix win. He clipped a wheel against Regazzoni's Shadow DN8 as he lapped it, and hit a tyre barrier, leaving victory on a plate for Reutemann.

Monaco saw Villeneuve run fourth in 034 until an accident in the tunnel caused by the left front tyre suddenly deflating, the car emerging into the daylight on three wheels. There was another valiant drive in the Belgian GP at Zolder, Gilles chasing Andretti's Lotus 79 hard in second place until a tyre blow-out at the left-hander after the pits forced him to stop for fresh rubber, and dropped him to fourth place.

Designed as it was for Michelin's new radials, the T3's effectiveness depended upon tyres. Already two of Villeneuve's three races had been spoiled by tyre failures, and poor rubber put him right out of the picture in the Spanish, Swedish and French GPs. At Jarama his tyres went off so badly that he made two stops for fresh rubber and finished tenth. Anderstorp (the race of the notorious Brabham 'fan car') resulted in ninth place after one tyre change, and Paul Ricard brought even worse problems as Villeneuve came home twelfth (in 035) after two tyre stops. Reutemann went through five sets, but a set of supersoft qualifiers fitted near the end of the race at least gave him the consolation of fastest lap!

Things looked up at Brands Hatch for the British GP, but only for Reutemann, who won the race. Villeneuve was in for new tyres after only 10 laps, and retired when a driveshaft broke nine laps later. Yet more tyre troubles and fuel vaporization caused by stifling humidity kept Gilles down in eighth place (in 035 again) in the German GP at Hockenheim, but he achieved an excellent third place in a wet Austrian GP at the Österreichring. His tyres went off again during the Dutch GP at Zandvoort, but the French-Canadian decided to stay out this time and clung on to sixth place.

From here on Villeneuve's season

improved dramatically. The tragic Italian GP, the one in which Ronnie Peterson died, saw Gilles lead Andretti's Lotus for all bar the last six laps, but second place on the road became seventh when a 1 min penalty was imposed because he — and Andretti — had supposedly jumped the start. Reutemann won again at Watkins Glen in the United States GP, but Gilles was right with him in second place for 22 laps until his engine let go.

If you were a fan of Gilles Villeneuve — and who wasn't? — Montreal was the place to be at the end of that season. The Canadian GP was his first GP win, and on home ground too. He drove beautifully, hauling 034 steadily up from fourth to second place, and was ready to pounce when Jean-Pierre Jarier's Lotus retired from the lead 20 laps from home. 'I didn't know it could be so easy,' said Gilles after the race.

The old T3s were used for the first two GPs of 1979 in Argentina and Brazil (where Villeneuve finished fifth in 034), but then superseded by the ground-effect T4. The Race of Champions at Brands Hatch brought a T3 swansong with Villeneuve's victory in 035, but that was the end of the car's run.

Chassis 312T3/034 was then bought by Michael Vernon, from whom it passed to Dallas entrepreneur Don Walker. With Walker's spectacular bankruptcy in 1984 the car came into the hands of Adrian Hamilton, from whom Nick Mason acquired it. Nick had one drive before lending the car to the Villeneuve Foundation for exhibition in Canada. It eventually returned by sea to this country in 1986, but somehow the ship carrying it was holed at Rotterdam and partially sank. The car had been ravaged by salt water by the time Ten Tenths finally extricated it from the Dutch authorities.

A complete rebuild was necessary, and this was entrusted to the highly-respected Ferrari specialist Bob Houghton. The car was stripped to the last nut and bolt, and

carefully restored and reassembled to race-worthy condition by Pete North.

'You can't mess about when you're working on a car as sophisticated as this,' says Pete. 'Everything has to be right. We crack-tested the uprights, checked all the suspension, all the brake calipers were overhauled, everything. Parts of the car were in a very poor state. For example, the two big magnesium castings which hold the engine to the tub, and which carry oil and water piping, were so badly corroded that we had to make new ones. That was the most difficult job. We haven't needed the factory's help, but at the moment we are chasing Speedline for some original aluminium split-rim rear wheels.

'Another problem is that Michelin radial tyres can't be obtained now, so we've had to set up the car to run on Avon crossplies. This is no real problem as everything in the suspension is adjustable, but it needs time to get it right. Otherwise the car is really quite straightforward to work on. Clutch adjustment is the easiest thing in the world — just a nut poking through the top of the casing.'

My track test was the third outing for the T3 since this rebuild. The first was a brief shakedown at Silverstone with Ten Tenths' John Dabbs driving, but that ended when one of the old rear tyres blew, fortunately when John was going very slowly. The wheel rim was smashed, but otherwise damage was limited to the front and rear wings. As the car was due to go to Imola just a few days later to take part in Ferrari's fortieth anniversary celebrations, a new front wing was fabricated, the rear wing was repaired and two rear wheels were loaned by Adrian Hamilton. Jacky Ickx and Neil Corner drove it at Imola, and soon after it returned it was my turn.

It was a bitterly cold November day at Silverstone when I met the Ten Tenths crew of John Dabbs, Mike Hallows and Paula Webb, together with Bob Houghton's Pete

North. The T3 looked absolutely sensational, authentic in every detail right down to Gilles Villeneuve's name on the side of the cockpit. He was small, the great French-Canadian — would I fit into the car?

It looked tight as I slithered into the cockpit, but actually I found it very comfortable. There's no seat as such, just a carefully shaped monocoque floor which rises up under one's thighs and knees to give an ideal driving position. I needed a piece of folded-up blanket to give the small of my back a little support, but otherwise I felt quite at home. The three-spoke leather-rimmed Momo steering wheel, with ignition cut-out switch mounted close to the centre boss, is nicely placed, the reach to it giving just a slight bend at the elbows. The positioning of the pedals is excellent, and there's even a decent rest for your left foot. All in all, the driving position is perfect.

Three instruments mounted on to the front roll-over bar dominate the cockpit. In the centre is a large dial calibrated in white on black to 14,000 rpm, positioned so that the needle points straight up at the 12,400 rpm maximum. Two smaller gauges flank this, the one on the left registering oil and water temperature, that on the right fuel and oil pressure. Down by your left hand is the starter button and a spring loaded momentary fuel pump switch used only for starting. Set back from this on the side of the monocoque is a small lever for adjusting the rear anti-roll bar, but this I thought I would leave alone!

After strapping me into the Arexons four-point harness, John Dabbs and Pete North lifted the large top section of bodywork into place. This is one piece stretching from ahead of the windscreen, forming the cockpit sides and upper bodywork surface as well as the engine cover. Suddenly I was sitting in a proper F1 Ferrari, instead of a monocoque with four wheels sticking out at the corners.

There's a simple routine for starting the engine. Press the button to turn over the engine, then flick the ignition on. It fires straight away,

Left *As the last flat-bottomed Ferrari before the 'ground effect' 312T4, the T3 was overshadowed in 1978 by the Lotus 79, but still managed five Grand Prix victories that year.*

Below *Nick Mason's car had to be given a complete rebuild in 1987 after being damaged by salt water; the boat carrying it back from an exhibition in Canada, in honour of Gilles Villeneuve, was holed in Rotterdam.*

and as long as you keep the revs up enough to maintain fuel pressure you can trickle away from rest. You don't need to be cruel to it at all.

Once I was out on the track and warming the car through, my first impression was of the incredible smoothness of the flat-12 engine. I've driven quite a few Cosworth-DFV powered cars from the same era, and always noticed the high frequency vibrations they transmit. This engine, however, is just like a turbine, and beautifully smooth. Power swells up evenly, and it goes faster and faster and faster. Nowhere does the engine feel that it's coming on cam — it just builds and builds. By 7,500 rpm it's really

John Dabbs helps me to settle into the 312T3. The entire top surface of the body lifts clear, and the seat is just an area of contoured aluminium.

pulling strongly, so there's a very wide usable power band. The engine is nowhere near as fussy as a Cosworth, and it is so tractable that you could almost put it in a road car. It's comfortable too, with no buffeting at high speed. On this cold morning the temperatures were on the low side, water reading about 80° and oil 75°.

I kept to around 10,500 rpm out of deference to Nick's pocket, and at that speed this lovely engine is really beginning to wail. Through ear plugs, balaclava and helmet I was assailed by its glorious crisp note, which is quite unmistakably that of a flat-12 Ferrari — there's nothing else like it. Power output

was reckoned to be 510 bhp at 12,200 rpm, which is around 25 bhp more than Cosworths were delivering at the time. For the statistically-minded, capacity is 2,992 cc from 80 mm bore and 49.6 mm stroke.

The five-speed gearbox has a conventional pattern: first is towards you and back, second and third are in the central plane, fourth and fifth over to the right. Reverse is opposite first, with a locking catch to prevent getting it wrong on the grid! Since this is a Ferrari, there is that typical slotted gate at the base of the gearlever, which is a mere 2 in long. With a delightfully short throw, changing gear is just a case of flexing your wrist. There's a bit of stiff-

Pete North tends the glorious 3 litre flat-12 engine. One of the best engines I have ever experienced, it develops more than 500 bhp and revs to 12,400 rpm.

ness from cold, but once the oil has warmed up the change is light and precise, just like a switch.

Using this 10,500 rpm limit, when the car really starts to fly, the T3 is rather undergeared around the Silverstone Club Circuit. I was lifting off in top about a third of the way down the straight, so I reckon it could probably pull at least another 20 mph. I took Copse in fourth, and Becketts and Woodcote in third. But the car is so tractable that you could probably get all the way round in fourth without too much effect on lap times.

The only quirk with the gearbox is something I've noticed on other monocoque Ferraris, and that's if you change gear in the middle of a corner you can get second instead of fourth, or third instead of fifth. The gate is so tight that the slightest flex of the monocoque, or a bit of wear in the linkage, can give you the wrong gear — a little more lateral movement in the gate might help. You have the lever slotted into fifth, but that little bit of movement tells the gearbox you want third. The answer is *not* to change gear in the middle of a corner!

At first the brakes — ventilated Lockheed discs all-round, inboard at the back and outboard at the front — weren't as good as I expected, but that was probably because the car hasn't been used much since the rebuild. The cold weather can't have helped, although

half of the ducts feeding air on to the brakes were taped over. They improved as I did more laps and as the tyres became scrubbed, and by the end of my session they were working very well. You can brake very late and deep into corners, and the pedal — firm to use, but not strenuous — gives a very reassuring, instant bite. Not many cars I've driven allow you to leave your braking until the 150 yard board before Woodcote.

It's terribly difficult to evaluate the handling characteristics of such a recent Formula 1 car because the traits show up so close to the limit. I wasn't about to start chucking Nick's T3 around to find out what it does at ten-tenths (oh look, a pun!), but it certainly felt rather tail happy. It suddenly flicks sideways in the middle of a corner, but it's very easy to catch with such light and responsive steering. None of this is criticism, for there could be all sorts of reasons.

Having so little temperature in the tyres must have encouraged the twitchiness, and the new Avon crossplies which the T3 now wears make quite a difference compared with the Michelin radials for which it was designed. Pete North agreed that the T3 could do with a good setting-up session in warmer weather to tune the chassis to crossply rubber. Why does *Classic and Sportscar* always put me in the most powerful cars in the middle of winter?

Reading about the T3 before I

drove it, I was interested to learn that Carlos Reutemann felt it an inferior car to the T2. Some of his outspoken comments, which speeded the deterioration of his relationship with Ferrari, are recorded in Alan Henry's excellent *Ferrari: The Grand Prix Cars*, and I quote: 'It didn't seem to me that any adjustments to the chassis made any difference. The car just understeered, and that's all there was to it: and when we fitted it with skirts it just understeered all the more.'

It could be that the Avon crossplies have removed that inherent understeer. What I can say categorically, though, is that you can drive the T3 on the throttle, and this is really why I fell in love with it so much. It is the last Ferrari of the flat-bottom era, and everyone remembers how drivers used to complain that cars with skirts were unpleasant to drive. The cars either stuck to the road or they didn't — there was very little in between. And you drove as fast as your neck muscles could stand.

The T3 may not be the biggest landmark in F1 history, but it's a significant car nonetheless. It's difficult to explain what an enjoyable car it is — you almost put it on and wear it. Its incredible engine, combined with the highly responsive chassis, creates a very rewarding character which a confident driver can enjoy, but which *might* be too challenging for a journeyman driver. I loved it.

INDEX